A PARTNER *in* HOLINESS

VOLUME 2

A

PARTNER

in

HOLINESS

VOLUME 2

Leviticus • Numbers • Deuteronomy

Deepening Mindfulness,

Practicing Compassion and

Enriching Our Lives through the Wisdom of

R. Levi Yitzhak of Berdichev's *Kedushat Levi*

RABBI JONATHAN P. SLATER, DMin

Foreword by **Arthur Green**
coauthor, *Speaking Torah: Spiritual Teachings
from around the Maggid's Table*

Preface by **Rabbi Nancy Flam**
codirector of programs, Institute for Jewish Spirituality

For People of All Faiths, All Backgrounds

JEWISH LIGHTS Publishing

Nashville, Tennessee

A Partner in Holiness:
Deepening Mindfulness, Practicing Compassion and Enriching Our Lives through
the Wisdom of R. Levi Yitzhak of Berdichev's Kedushat Levi—*Volume 2*

Library of Congress Cataloging-in-Publication Data
Slater, Jonathan P., 1952– author.
  A partner in holiness : deepening mindfulness, practicing compassion and enriching our lives through the wisdom of R. Levi Yitzhak of Berdichev's Kedushat Levi / Rabbi Jonathan P. Slater, DMin.
    volumes cm
  Includes bibliographical references.
   ISBN 978-1-58023-795-6 (hardcover) — ISBN 978-1-58023-810-6 (ebook)
1. Spiritual life—Judaism. 2. Bible. Pentateuch—Commentaries. 3. Hasidism. 4. Levi Isaac ben Meir, of Berdichev, 1740-1809—Teachings. I. Levi Isaac ben Meir, of Berdichev, 1740-1809. Kedushat Levi (Avot) II. Title.
  BM723.S6125 2014
  296.7—dc23
                                        2014019128
10 9 8 7 6 5 4 3 2

Manufactured in the United States of America
Cover Design: Michael Myers
Interior Design: Michael Myers

For People of All Faiths, All Backgrounds
Published by Jewish Lights Publishing
An Imprint of Turner Publishing Company
4507 Charlotte Avenue, Suite 100
Nashville, TN 37209
Tel: (615) 255-2665
www.jewishlights.com

To rabbis Nancy Flam, Sheila Peltz Weinberg, Rachel Cowan,
and Lisa Goldstein
With gratitude for faith, support, and love

To Arthur Green
Because you sent me out to find my path,
I have been able to trace it back to you

Contents: Volume 2

The Book of Leviticus

Vayikra	3	Acharei Mot	41
Tzav	11	Kedoshim	49
Shemini	16	Emor	57
Tazria	24	Behar	67
Metsora	32	Bechukkotai	72

The Book of Numbers

Bemidbar	81	Chukkat	127
Naso	85	Balak	139
Beha'alotekha	92	Pinchas	155
Shelach Lekha	100	Mattot	167
Korach	116	Mase'ei	172

The Book of Deuteronomy

Devarim	179	Ki Tavo	229
Va'etchanan	190	Nitzavim	235
Eikev	200	Vayeilekh	244
Re'eih	209	Ha'azinu	248
Shofetim	215	Vezot Haberakhah	254
Ki Teitzei	222		

Acknowledgments	257
Suggestions for Further Reading	263

Here Is What You'll Find in Voume 1:

Foreword   ix

Preface   xi

Introduction   xiii

The Book of Genesis

Bereishit	3	Vayeitzei	61
Noach	12	Vayishlach	75
Lekh Lekha	24	Vayeishev	85
Vayeira	33	Mikkeitz	97
Hayyey Sarah	43	Vayiggash	109
Toledot	52	Vayechi	120

The Book of Exodus

Shemot	137	Terumah	220
Va'eira	149	Tetzavveh	235
Bo	161	Ki Tissa	249
Beshallach	177	Vayakheil	266
Yitro	190	Pekudei	270
Mishpatim	208		

Notes   277

The Book of
Leviticus

Vayikra

"[He] called to Moses [and *YHVH* spoke to
him from the Tent of Meeting, saying]"
(Lev. 1:1).

The final letter, *aleph*, of the opening word "**He called**" (*vayikra*) is
written in the Torah such that it is smaller than the other letters.

We can make sense of this in light of the verse "Then He said to
Moses, 'Come up to *YHVH*'" (Exod. 24:1). When we perform a mitzvah,
this mitzvah makes an impression above, which arouses and inspires us
always to fulfill the will of the Creator through this mitzvah. Now, this
was Moses's desire, to constantly ascend toward God, as we learn from
the Zohar on the verse "Moses went up to God" (Exod. 19:3). From this
we learn that it was his constant desire to ascend toward God, and this,
in turn, would arouse him constantly to ascend toward God! So, this is
how we should understand these verses: "Then he said to Moses, 'Come
up to *YHVH*'"—Moses's own desire to ascend to God was that voice that
said to him, "Come up to *YHVH*."

This, too, is hinted at in the small *aleph*. Moses's quality was that
he was more humble than any other person on earth (cf. Num. 12:3).
Therefore the *aleph* is small, to indicate his particular quality.

FOR FURTHER THOUGHT

In this lesson, Levi Yitzhak seems uncharacteristically terse. His
ultimate point is that Moses's humility, which surpasses all others, was such that he never thought that he had "made it." He
always sensed that there was more he could learn, that there
was another level of awareness he might attain, a more profound
capacity to serve God to uncover. It was this humility, signified by
the small *aleph*, that generated the energy that constantly moved
him upward toward God. We know about Moses's deep desire to
move constantly toward God from the two verses from Exodus.

First, "Moses went up to God." He set out to serve God and experienced delight in that movement. In turn, it registered above, and his original devotion continued to come back to inspire him. "He said to Moses"—that is, Moses repeated and reiterated his desire to himself—"ascend up to God."

What we do registers in us. It makes an impression through patterns in our body, in our nervous system, in our brains, and in our hearts. Particularly when we do a mitzvah (perhaps best understood in its broadest, colloquial sense of "good deed"), we feel pleasure at what we have accomplished. In the brain, hormones are released by which we sense that pleasure. In turn, the body seeks to feel that pleasure again. We look for ways to "do a mitzvah"—either that same one (isn't that how we form habits?) or another, just so that we can feel that pleasure again. The impression above calls to us, reminds us to do again what was so satisfying and good before. Our own bodies—and our own awareness of God—energize us to continue on this path, to "go up to God."

Here is the passage from the Zohar (II 79b) that Levi Yitzhak cites:

> "Moses went up to God." How pleasant is Moses's portion, that he merited this great honor: that the Torah testifies to his quality. R. Yehudah taught: See the difference between Moses and all other people. Everyone else, when they go up, they go up in wealth, they go up in honor, they go up in power. But, when Moses went up, what does the Torah say? "Moses went up to God." Happy is his portion. R. Yose said: On this basis the *chaverim* say, "One who comes to purify himself, is helped" (Yoma 38b). It says, "Moses went up to God." What is written afterward? "*YHVH* called to him." Anyone who wishes to come near is brought near.

Note that the Zohar cites Exod. 19:3 correctly—the phrases do follow one after the other—and that Moses moves toward God (*elohim*), after which *YHVH* calls to him directly. In our original verse in Leviticus, it is not clear who is speaking to Moses at first. It simply says, "He called to Moses," and only afterward does it say that "*YHVH* spoke to him." So, Levi Yitzhak is reading very carefully and creatively in bringing these verses into conversation with our verse. On the basis of his reading of the Zohar and the verses from Exodus, he hears into our verse even more deeply. He suggests that it is Moses who calls to Moses at first. It is out of his inner process, his constant devotion to moving toward God, that God then responds, speaking to him from the Tent of Meeting. And, it will be Moses's voice—our own inner voice—that will call to him continually to draw nearer to God.

Questions for Reflection

1. In the commentary above there is a very concrete biological explanation for how doing a "good deed" can generate the energy that moves us to do another. But Levi Yitzhak is precise in his language: the act "makes an impression [*reshimah*] above." How do you understand this? What is the permanent effect of our actions? What changes in the world in response to our actions? How does that affect us in turn?

2. What experience have you had in which you sensed that you were being called to do something? Where did the "voice" that called you come from?

3. In your experience, what is the difference between doing something again out of habit and doing something again out of a renewed interest, desire, or commitment? Which is more pleasurable? Which is easier? Which brings about more commitment and determination? How do you distinguish between the two?

Taking It into Your Life

This lesson resonates with the practice of spiritual direction. In that practice, we investigate our inner awareness, our sense of how God is moving in us, what God wants of us. We conduct this inquiry in the company of another whose role is to mirror back to us what is going on in our inner life; to accompany us as we look even more deeply into our hearts and souls; and to midwife the emergence of a new understanding of our spiritual path. The goal is discovery, and we are the ones who discover our own soul's path.

One of the difficulties of this practice is in discerning what God is calling us—individually, specifically—to do. It is hard to know how to hear God's voice. Our lesson offers some help. Initially, what we may hear is, indeed, our own voice. We will want to listen for that voice that is most persistent, that is clearest in calling us to serve God through the mitzvot, the good deeds, that we do. Eventually, if we follow that voice, paying very close attention, we may hear God's voice echoing deeply in ours. We may learn how to do the mitzvah more fully, how to go up in our service, how to perfect our devotion.

Each of us knows for ourselves what we consider to be "our mitzvah" or our particular set of mitzvot. We sense what is most necessary, most compelling, and most important in our lives. Yet we do not always follow through. Sometimes we even forget. But the movement of our hearts does not stop. When we slow down to pay attention, we may sense it once again. We may struggle against what we hear (if it is hard to change our course). We may despair of ever living up to our ambition and commitment. But recognizing that there is a voice that calls to us—our voice, God's voice—can be a source of inspiration, solace, and strength. Listen.

A general rule regarding sacrifice.

As **a general rule, sacrifice** (*korban*, signifying "drawing near") takes the form of the blessing (*shefa*) that the blessed Holy One pours out due to His great love, without any influence from below. For this reason, *korban* needs to be alive, since life is from the blessed Holy One. But, in libations (*nesakhim*) the *shefa* is more constricted, since they come about by means of work in the lower realms: people have to do something to make them—planting or sowing. Libations, then, signify the *shefa* that pours forth from the blessed Creator in response to the work of the lower realms. Due to our good deeds, we merit that the blessed Creator pours blessings out on us.

Now, when Israel were in the desert, their state was such that the blessed Holy One poured out blessing to them due to His great love, and the outpouring came to them in that manner. Neither the manna nor the well required any sort of human endeavor. But in the Land of Israel, the blessing poured out on them due to their work in the lower realms. Through their actions the blessings poured out on them—they ate from that which they sowed and planted, in the manner of the blessings that come from the deeds of the lower realms, as above.

This is the meaning of the verses, "When you enter the land that I am giving you to settle in and you would present an offering by fire to *YHVH* [from the herd or from the flock, be it burnt offering or sacrifice, in fulfillment of a vow explicitly uttered, or as a freewill offering, or at your fixed occasions, producing an odor pleasing to *YHVH*: The person who presents the offering to *YHVH* shall bring as a meal offering: a tenth of a measure of choice flour with a quarter of a *hin* of oil mixed in. You shall also offer, with the burnt offering or the sacrifice, a quarter of a *hin* of wine as a libation for each sheep]" (Num. 15:2–10): the libations are tied to being in the "Land," similar to the above, since the libations signify the outpouring of blessings in the Land. This connects with what Rashi says relative to the quotation in Arakhin (11a): "Song is only sung over wine." The outpouring of blessing that comes to us by means of our work in the lower realms brings us joy.

FOR FURTHER THOUGHT

Before we turn to address the subject matter of this section, it would help to place it—and the whole of Levi Yitzhak's commentary on the book of Leviticus—in a larger context. In my edition, the whole of the commentary covering the book of Leviticus totals twenty-five pages. The commentary on *parashat Beshallach* is equally as long, and his combined commentary on Passover and Song of Songs is nearly as long. Indeed, the commentary on this book is the shortest in the whole of *Kedushat Levi*. So apparently the subject matter of Leviticus in general did not spur his imagination or demand deeper investigation. (He does use various verses for study in other sections of the book, but not here in the commentary on the Torah, and in any event to a much lesser degree than the other books of the Torah.)

Still, we should not say that sacrifices had no meaning in a spiritually awakened Jewish life. Surely Levi Yitzhak has shown us his capacity to lift words, phrases, and whole passages out of context to interpret them according to his needs, program, and interests. So we might suggest that the paucity of teaching early in Leviticus is due to the absence of narrative. This would jibe with the general Hasidic use of stories as a means of communicating spiritual teachings. Where there is no story in the Torah, there is less movement, and so less opportunity to insert Hasidic spiritual teaching. Nonetheless, we should not exclude the possibility that Levi Yitzhak felt able to communicate, in a focused and powerful manner, his deepest and most important teachings on Leviticus. So we would do well to pay close attention to this lesson.

Levi Yitzhak distinguishes here between animal offerings (*korban*) and libations (*nesakhim*). For those who are not expert in the system of sacrifices—which may be most contemporary Jews—such a distinction may seem odd. After all, both constitute elements of the sacrificial cult. Both make up the elements of many of the recurring sacrifices that we read about regularly—for example, the daily offerings and the additional offerings on Shabbat and festivals (cf. Numbers 28). That Levi Yitzhak introduces this distinction here, at the opening of the book of Leviticus, is also curious. The connection of libations to the sacrifices does not appear in Leviticus until chapter 23, and its full role in the sacrificial cult is only spelled out in the book of Numbers.

So we are left to ask: what was bothering Levi Yitzhak, and what is the point he feels compelled to make here? Sacrifices are no longer practiced by the Jewish people. It is true that there is virtue in their recitation (cf. Ta'anit 27b: "God replied: I have already long ago provided for them in the Torah the order of sacrifices, and whenever they read it I will deem it as if they had offered them before me and I will grant them pardon for all their iniquities"). Yet that practice lends itself to rote repetition, and Levi Yitzhak wants to wake up his followers and to break that habit. Moreover, he wants to raise their spiritual ambitions. So he constantly encourages them to move beyond serving God for the sake of receiving some boon or another. Instead, all devotion should be for the sake of bringing delight to the Holy One. Arousal from below generates more—and more focused—outpouring of blessing from God, and that is what Levi Yitzhak seeks.

So here, at the start of Leviticus, he inserts his concern, raising up what may seem insignificant and diminishing what seems central. The animals we offer exist independently of us. They come into life through the miraculous and hidden process of procreation. God's power is evident there, as if the original Creation were repeated over and over with each birth cycle. When we offer a live animal, we declare our recognition of God's love, offered freely, sustaining us and all life *gratis*. Wine, however, can only come about through the application of human energy and ingenuity. It symbolizes our role in transforming creation for the good—for our own benefit and sustenance, and for the sake of all existence. Our offering of wine epitomizes the process of arousal from below, bringing delight to God and blessing to the world. While life itself may be God's "grace," the outpouring that is God's freewill gift to us, still our lives are made fuller in the fact that the work of our hands can bring God joy, and so we rejoice.

And let's not ignore the significance of inebriants and song in the Hasidic tradition. The former are a "disinhibitor," opening hearts and souls to God, and to fellow Hasidim. Song is a practice that helps focus and deepen spiritual experience. Together, they help create, sustain and deepen the awareness Levi Yitzhak hopes to develop among his followers.

Questions for Reflection

1. Hidden behind this lesson is Levi Yitzhak's teaching that the blessing that results from our endeavors is greater still than that which flows spontaneously from God. For which are you more grateful: the very fact of your life (God's gift) or what you are able to do because you are alive (your use of your life)?

2. One emphasis of spirituality is gratitude: the awareness of our dependent role, our participation in the unfolding of the life of the universe as opposed to celebrating our control over nature and our self-sufficiency. Which offering—*korban* or *nesakhim*—reflects the awareness and expression of dependence? Is the focus of your gratitude on what comes to you *gratis*, as grace? What would be the consequence of our adopting a practice of *korban* as opposed to *nesakhim* or vice versa?

3. If the lower realms are the locus of superior service, does this change your sense of what a balanced spirituality might be regarding matters of the body?

Taking It into Your Life

Levi Yitzhak cites Rashi to explain that the song that arises from the offering of *nesakhim* shows the joy we experience from the blessings that flow to us from our devotions.

Here is the passage from Arakhin 11a, followed by Rashi's comment:

R. Samuel ben Nahmani said in the name of R. Yonatan: Whence do we know that the song is not sung [in the Sanctuary] except over wine?—Belvati, in the name of R. Yohanan inferred it from here: "To do the work of service [*la'avod avodat avodah*]" (Num. 4:47). Which work needs [depends on] service? That is the song.

Song: [The song] required the service of the sacrifice, for it was sung only over the libations of the sacrifices, which were accompanied by the trumpets (Num. 10:10).

The importance of the libations for Levi Yitzhak did not negate or do away with the sacrificial offerings. Rather, the sacrifices were required, but they only reflected God's vital force in us, given graciously, lovingly. Beyond the sacrifices were the libations that reflect our devotion to God, our offering of our own efforts. And those efforts are represented most clearly by our song.

Our daily liturgical prayers may be seen as the sacrifices. They are incumbent upon us. They are not our words; they do not automatically express our personal, direct appreciation of God's blessings. In that they are inherited from generations past, we may sense them to be like God's gift of life: undeniable, necessary, requiring gratitude—expressed through their recitation and performance. But we know—like Levi Yitzhak—that the product of our efforts, the work of our hearts and heads and hands, is more meaningful for us—and we hope to God.

This lesson suggests that we investigate how the application of music to our prayers can affect the transformation that Levi Yitzhak suggests. When reciting the liturgy, we are offering our lives, that which was given to us. When we sing the liturgy, we express our personal sentiments, we apply our unique and human efforts. As you engage in liturgical prayer, pay attention to the shift in your own energy when you are singing versus when you are simply reciting. Notice when a spontaneous melody arises to accompany a passage. This may occur during prayers or at some other time. When you notice it, allow the melody to rise in your consciousness, bring it to voice (or hum it, even if in your head). Sense the energy generated by the melody, by singing; add energy to it in turn. Notice as well the quality of your heart. How does the presence of song affect your emotional state of being? Does song help bring you joy? Reflect.

Tzav

"Regarding the sin offering and the burnt offering."

Regarding the sin offering (*chatat*) **and the burnt offering** (*olah*): the sin offering takes precedence to the burnt offering. The sin offering has the quality of direct light from the upper world to the lower world, while the burnt offering is reflected light from the lower world to the upper. This is why the burnt offering is completely burned.

This is the significance of the verse, "He brought forward the burnt offering and sacrificed it according to regulation" (Lev. 9:16). This is similar to the start of the month of Tishrei, the letters that spell this month appearing in reverse order (in the *aleph-bet*), which shares in the mystery of reflected light.... (The conclusion is missing.)

FOR FURTHER THOUGHT

In the collection of teachings that compose *Kedushat Levi*, there is only this lesson for *parashat Tzav*. This reflects something of the development of this text: it was redacted by Levi Yitzhak's son, based on an earlier version, and contains not only Levi Yitzhak's own writing but also notes recollecting his teachings on Shabbat recorded by others after the fact. There are therefore, occasionally, lacunae. This is one of those occasions, and we are, indeed, left wanting.

The text as we have it seems to function as a bridge between the first and third weekly readings from *Vayikra*. The verses that are referenced in the text are from the weekly readings preceding and following *Tzav*, rather than from this parashah itself. The reference to *Vayikra* is in the opening line. "The sin offering [*chatat*] takes precedence to the burnt offering [*olah*]" is a quotation from Rashi on Lev. 5:8, referring to the offering of two doves brought by a poor person as a "guilt" offering. That is, having discovered an otherwise unknown inadvertent transgression, one is obligated to bring a "guilt offering" (*chatat*). In this case, the Torah designates one of the two doves as a sin offering (*chatat*) for the guilt, and the other as a burnt offering (*olah*), in this order. Thus, the sin offering takes precedence (cf. Zevachim 89b–90b).

Further, the Zohar identifies the *olah*, completely burnt on the altar, as the response of the lower realms to the upper. ˙

> As has been said, the upper world is world of the male. Once anything ascends above Assembly of Israel, all is male. How do we know? From *olah*, an ascent offering. Why is it called *olah*? Because it "ascends" above the female. Therefore, *an ascent offering an unblemished male (zakhar tamim)* (Lev. 1:10)....
>
> Now, you might say, "Look at what is written: *an unblemished female (neqevah temimah)*" (Lev. 4:32). Certainly so! Just as Righteous One [*tzaddik*] is called *tamim*, so Righteousness [*tzedek*; the *Shekhinah*] is called *temimah*, for She absorbs everything from Him. Therefore *olah*, ascending from female to male; from this place upward all is male, and from female downward all is female, as we have established. (Zohar I 246a; Daniel C. Matt, trans., *The Zohar*, Pritzker ed., vol. 3 [Stanford, CA: Stanford University Press, 2007], p. 507ff.)

The movement from the female—the Assembly of Israel (*Knesset Yisrael*, the *Shekhinah*, but also Israel)—to male is the movement of the *olah*. This is like the "arousal from below," our actions instigating God to pour out blessings on the lower world out of delight in our wholehearted and selfless service. This dynamic is characterized, as well, in the concept of direct and reflected light. The *olah*, moving from below to above, is the "returning light," carrying back that which has been received from above, offering all in response.

This is curious, in light of Levi Yitzhak's teaching in *Vayikra*. There he suggests that *olah*, the sacrifice of a live animal, symbolized God's spontaneous, gracious blessing. In that instance, Levi Yitzhak focused on the fact that we cannot create life, and therefore offering life to God is to acknowledge God's grace and love in giving us life. Here, however, Levi Yitzhak seems to focus on the movement of the smoke—all that remains of the burnt sacrifice—as representing our intention to raise up the physical, the mundane, the worldly to God. It is our offering given in response to God's gracious blessings. It is the offering of the female, the receiver, to the male; reciprocation that is itself initiation, generating delight in the giver/receiver, prompting even more blessing.

This, in turn, connects to the issue of words written in direct or reverse order. The month in which Rosh Hashanah and Yom Kippur fall is one of judgment. The name of the month is Tishrei, and the letters spelling the name are actually the reverse of the last three letters of the Hebrew *aleph-bet* (*TiShRei*). These letters, inverting the alphabet, signify rising up, moving from this lower world to the upper realms.

The inversion of the letters, moreover, reflects a more complex nexus of issues. The Zohar (II 186a) relates that the month of Tishrei is particularly God's, as opposed to Aviv, which God gave to the Jews. God—and God's blessings—remains concealed in the former month, while God's blessing of Israel is revealed in the latter. Therefore the letters that spell *Aviv* (*AbiB*) are in alphabetical order. But that is not the case in *Tishrei*. "Why is this so? Because your movement is from below above, and Mine is from above below." In the month of Tishrei, we have to do the work of repentance. We have to activate the connection between us and God, our effort clearing out and straightening the channels by which God's blessing comes into this world. In that sense, our work "from below above" (*itaruta deletata*) takes place in the context of God's judgment, and the movement up the alphabet is to reverse that flow, to return to the proper order. In the spring, at the time of the Exodus, God takes the initiative and redeems us with love and grace, "from above below" (*itaruta dele'eila*).

Further, the lowest level of creation is that of the letter *tav*, the last letter of the *aleph-bet*. It is the place in which the fullest expression of God's rigor, limitation, and judgment are manifest. If we can move that letter up a level or more, we redeem that which is flawed. We come closer to the realm in which what we perceive as "judgment" is actually not so, in which "judgment is sweetened." What is more, moving up the ladder of the alphabet, we move from the realm in which God is most hidden, in which the divine light is most constricted, toward that in which God is most present, most expansive. Offering the *olah* and the month of Tishrei share the quality of being reflected light: they point in the direction of redemption, turning judgment into love.

It is this association with judgment that draws Levi Yitzhak to a verse in *Shemini* (Lev. 9:16). The *olah* is to be performed according to regulations, *kamishpat*, according to the law. But *mishpat* also has the mystical meaning of the blessed Holy One who provides for all out of love. The sin offering, *chatat*, is offered first, to establish the quality of God's love, in the manner of direct light. But, the *olah* is to be offered like it, *kamishpat*, arousing God above through our actions, to bring delight to God and blessing to all existence, in the manner of reflected light.

Questions for Reflection

1. What associations do you have with the image of direct light and reflected light? Do the valences in the Jewish mystical system resonate with you (direct light being love, reflected light being constricted, and so an aspect of judgment)? When do you sense that the opposite might be true?

2. The letters of the *aleph-bet* serve as the mechanism, the formula by which Creation comes into being. How does that help you understand how in reading the letters in reverse we reveal what had been concealed in the lowest level of *tav*? What does this suggest about how we "read" Creation, how we discover God in all things?

3. Does this passage help you better understand or make sense of the idea of the sacrifices as a means for drawing closer to God? How?

Taking It into Your Life

Here is an opportunity to play with the image of "direct light / reflected light." In the mystical system, the source of the direct light is God. In our lives, we might want to reimagine this. We are all both the source of direct light—the blessings that we offer to others spontaneously, our goodwill and generosity—as well as the recipients of such light, responding with our reflected gratitude. You might imagine that this system is constantly renewing itself. That is, as we receive the light from others, we reflect gratitude back, but we are also energized to generate our own projected direct light of blessing. Others, receiving our gratitude, are energized to bless others, and those whom we bless are activated in a similar manner.

There are clearly two elements to making this process work, both of which reside first in our consciousness and intention. We need to nurture both the heart that wishes blessing for all others and the heart that is receptive and grateful for the blessings of others. One will lead to the other, and each will reinforce the other. Pay attention to the quality of your heart. Can you notice the source of gratitude? Can you look at other people, as you pass in the street, as they come to mind, as you engage with them at work, and sense the gratitude you feel for their existence (even if in the moment your interaction is not the easiest)?

Alternatively, can you sense the source of blessing in your heart? As you look at other people, passing them in the street, as they come to mind, as you engage with them at work, can you then offer your own heartfelt blessings (even if in the moment your interaction is not the easiest)?

What blocks your gratitude? What holds back your blessing? Reflect.

Shemini

*"YHVH spoke to Moses and Aaron, saying to
them: [Speak to the Israelite people thus:]
These are the creatures [that you may eat
from among all the land animals]"* (Lev. 11:1–2).

We should pay attention to the phrase "**saying to them**" (lit., to say to
them). Consider: Rashi commented regarding Exod. 2:7, "Shall I go
and get you a Hebrew nurse to suckle the child for you?": "She had
taken him around to many Egyptian women to nurse, but he did not,
since he was in the future to speak with the *Shekhinah*." Moses did
not wish to nurse from someone impure because in the future he was
to prophesy to Israel, speaking the words of the *Shekhinah* (from the
mouth of the *Shekhinah*).

Further, Ramban wrote (perhaps on Lev. 11:13, and Levi Yitzhak
paraphrases and generalizes) that the Torah prohibited the impure
animals because eating them induces a brutal quality in the human
body. But Israel, a holy people, are supposed to have the quality
of love (*chesed*; loving-kindness, as opposed to brutality) since, in
the future, the blessed Holy One will speak directly with each
individual Jew, as it says, "Your sons and daughters will prophesy"
(Joel 3:1).

So, if in the future the blessed Holy One will speak to each of us,
how should the *Shekhinah* speak to that mouth that has eaten impure
things? This, then, is what our verse means to say: "**YHVH spoke** [to
Moses and Aaron], **saying to them**"—that is, in the future I am going
"to speak to them" (*leimor aleihem*), to each and every one. Therefore,
they are not to eat anything impure.

FOR FURTHER THOUGHT

This lesson is built on the Hasidic practice of reading carefully, almost
literally. Our verse begins with God speaking to Moses and Aaron:
vayedabbeir YHVH. We would have expected the common continu-

ation, which we find in verse 2: "speak to the Children of Israel—
dabbeir el benei yisrael." Instead, there is an unusual phrase stuck in
between, concluding verse 1: "saying to them" (*leimor aleihem*). We
know already that God is speaking to Moses and Aaron, so what
does this phrase add? What is it that God says in addition? Or how
shall we understand what does God intend "to say to them" (or,
"regarding them"; *leimor aleihem*)?

Levi Yitzhak interprets this seeming redundancy, shifting the
word "to them" (*aleihem*) to mean the Israelites. That is, God speaks
to Moses and Aaron now, giving instructions regarding the proper
food to eat, because at some future time God will "speak to them"
(*leimor aleihem*). This will induce a response of prophecy, of the
people speaking with the voice of the *Shekhinah* (just as the *Shekhinah* spoke from Moses's mouth). And, they must be worthy of the
direct address of the *Shekhinah*. To be worthy—and prepared—for
this elevated experience, the people have to remain pure.

The question of following the traditional Jewish dietary
restrictions is, apparently, not only a modern one. Virtually all
Hasidic teachers spend time explaining the meaning of the dietary
laws, justifying their purpose, and encouraging their observance.
The Baal Shem Tov cites the Rambam to justify the practice: eating
proper foods helps purify and clarify the blood, so that one's brain
(and so reasoning) can perceive the truth more clearly (cf. *Degel
Machaneh Efraim, Eikev, umaltem*). But, Levi Yitzhak seems to
have a different take. The purity of one's vision and imagination
is not rooted in the physical purification of the blood. It is the
consequence of clarity of awareness and application of that clarity
in moment-to-moment decision making. Consider our teaching in
light of this other passage (*Kedushat Levi*, Avot):

> "Yalta said to R. Nahman: For every food that the Merciful One has
> forbidden us, the Merciful One has also permitted us something in
> its place" (Chullin 109b).
>
> The blessed Holy One created all of the fowl, the cattle, and
> other pure animals so that the sparks in them might be raised up
> when we eat them. But how can the sparks in the impure fowl,
> cattle, and animals be raised up if no Jews will eat them? Rather,
> God commanded that they not be eaten, and it is in this manner
> (observing the prohibition) that their impure sparks are raised.

But no Jew has ever eaten these impure creatures, and therefore they do not know what they taste like. From this we can be certain that they do not eat these animals in deference to God's commandment not to eat them. We might otherwise have thought that they are not eating them because they don't taste good. But if that were the case, the sparks of the impure animals would not be raised up. This is what Yalta meant to teach when she said, "For every food that the Merciful One has forbidden us, the Merciful One has also permitted us something in its place." Because they have the opportunity to eat things that taste like the impure foods, they learn that they taste good. Therefore, when a Jew refrains from eating them despite their good flavor, it is because God has commanded them, and this is how their sparks are raised up.

We raise sparks through affirmatively fulfilling the commandments, both the positive and the negative. We can generalize from this to suggest that Levi Yitzhak teaches it is not that physical-spiritual contamination comes from eating something "impure" (*tamei*), but from allowing our consciousness to be sullied by inattention. When the infant Moses refused to suckle at the breast of an Egyptian woman, it was not that she—in her body, in her created being—was "impure." Rather, her allegiance to the Egyptian ruler, her acquiescence to the brutality of the regime, and her willful ignorance of the consequences of the genocidal program (after all, Pharaoh's daughter could identify the child as a Hebrew) made her unfit, and so "impure."

When we blur distinctions—ignoring what is kosher but tastes like the non-kosher instead to eat the latter, acceding to ease, ignoring the suffering of others, hiding from the consequences of our acts—we cloud our minds. We lose the capacity to raise up sparks. We, in speech, deed, and even thought can become impure and unworthy of uttering words of God or speaking to God. This is not (only) a matter of keeping kosher; it is also about awareness, being awake in the moment to what we—as Jews, as human beings—are called to do in response to the divine command: be holy!

 ## Questions for Reflection

1. How aware are you of your own bodily cycles—of hunger, of satisfaction, of physical need for this or that food? Can you sense when

you are feeling down because your blood sugar level is low? Can you tell when a food makes you feel sluggish, somnolent, or self-satisfied? What difference, if any, does your awareness make in how you behave at those times?

2. What are the circumstances that you find when you eat beyond your physical needs? What provokes this overeating?

3. There are other Hasidic teachings regarding eating food that quote the Talmud (Yebamot 20a): "Sanctify yourself through that which is permitted to you." Even that which is permitted—without being prohibited or obligated—can be employed to help us attain a sense of holiness. Most of our lives fall into that dimension of time and activity. How can we make those dimensions holy? Perhaps that means staying awake and making decisions on the basis of awareness, not habit or inner urges. When are you able to make such decisions? When do you feel that you are living a life of holiness? Is there ever a time when you can "take a break" from holiness? When, how, why?

Taking It into Your Life

Levi Yitzhak makes a connection between our embodying the quality of loving-kindness (*chesed*) and our being fit to have God speak directly to us (and for us to merit speaking in God's voice). What we eat and how we eat affect the manifestation of that quality in us.

Bring mindfulness practice into your eating. When you sit to eat, pause before taking the first bite. Take in the full experience of the food you are about to eat. Notice its colors, its smells, its textures, its variety. Consider how it came to be before you: who produced it—from the start—and who made it now? What is your relation to those people and all those in between? Can you experience your gratitude for their labors and your wishes for their well-being in response to having food in front of you? When you are about to start eating, notice the inner movement of preference and avoidance, how you select one bite over another. Do not judge—notice; become aware. When you lift the fork/spoon to your mouth, feel its weight; notice how you balance it in your hand. Smell the food as it approaches your mouth. Allow all the flavors to manifest in your mouth. Continue to chew consciously, noticing the habitual arising of the desire to swallow and move on. Taste the food again. Notice the sensation of it moving down your gullet. Feel it enter your stomach. Witness the sensation of aroused desire, wanting more. Pay attention as you eat, trying to discern when you are no longer hungry but may still wish to eat. Notice the feelings that lead you to continue eating.

Again, do not judge—notice. It can be quite disconcerting to eat in this manner. Chewing can become awkward, swallowing weird. In paying attention in this manner, you will also notice how much loving-kindness you may need to bring to your own body, your own habits of mind and stomach and heart. You may also come to recognize your true inner desire to extend loving-kindness to the people who produce the food, transport the food, market the food, and prepare the food. You would not have sustenance without them.

Even when you cannot eat in this manner, offer yourself loving-kindness. Notice what is true in this moment. Do not allow yourself to eat unconsciously. Remain connected to your experience, even when in a rush. Breathe.

Make your consumption of food a means to prepare to receive God's word: "Not by food alone do we live, but by all that issues from the mouth of *YHVH* do we live" (Deut. 8:3).

Regarding the verse "And speak to the Israelites, saying: 'Take a he-goat for a sin offering; [a calf and a lamb, yearlings without blemish, for a burnt offering']" (Lev. 9:3).

Essential to the high priest who brought atonement for all Israel was that he had to be of a higher spiritual degree than the rest of Israel. That is why he could bring atonement for them all. At the same time, *Shekhinah* essentially comes to dwell on a person when he leads the people and engages with each and every one, seeking to bring him or her closer to service of the blessed Creator; each and every one according to his or her level. Then, through the merit of the whole community with which he engages, in the hope that they will thereby do *teshuvah*, the Holy One causes His *Shekhinah* to dwell with us. But there is a tzaddik who does not draw so close to engaging with each person, to bring him or her closer to the Creator, who only strives to strengthen himself. The *Shekhinah* does not dwell with this tzaddik so much, since he lacks the merit of the community.

This is then how we should understand the verses at the end of chapter 9. "Aaron lifted his hands" (Lev. 9:22), that is, at first he lifted himself to be separated off and set apart from the people, to be by himself and not engage with them. "Toward all the people" (*el kol ha'am*): up to this point he had been "toward (with) the people," engaging with them, yet he now lifted himself away from them. That is why "he stepped down from the offering of the sin offering": he came down from his personal experience of the *Shekhinah*. Up to this point, he had not been able to complete the sin offering, the burnt offering, or the offering of well-being (of the people), for just as we have written, in order for a high priest to offer a sacrifice for the people, he must be at a very high spiritual level. But now, having separated himself from the people, and therefore not bearing the merit of the whole with him, he is not at a sufficiently high level to offer a sacrifice for all Israel.

But after that, "Moses and Aaron went inside the Tent of Meeting and came out" (*vayeitzu*) (Lev. 9:23). That is, they came out of the level they had attained before, separated and set apart from the people, only now to engage with them as earlier such that "they blessed the people, and the Presence of *YHVH* appeared to all the people." The *Shekhinah* now also spread over them (Moses and Aaron) as earlier, because they now were engaged with the community. The merit of the community brought about the indwelling of the *Shekhinah* with them even more than when they had been separated off and distinguished from the community.

FOR FURTHER THOUGHT

This commentary comes at the end of a long essay that attempts to deal with a number of difficult issues in the opening section of *Shemini*. It is interesting that Levi Yitzhak does not deal with the incident of Nadab and Abihu (who brought "strange fire and died"; Lev. 10:2), except very indirectly in his discussion of what makes for a proper sacrifice. And in that sense, his final discussion leads us to consider what sort of models we wish to be and what kind of tzaddikim Nadab and Abihu were.

In his interpretation here, Levi Yitzhak presents two sorts of tzaddikim. One separates himself off from the people to develop himself, to seek his own ascent on the holy mountain toward God. This is not a bad practice. It does produce formidable spiritual results. But the level that this tzaddik can attain is still not as elevated, not as powerful, as that of the tzaddik who engages with the people. By working with them, teaching them, encouraging them, he can turn their hearts to *teshuvah*. In this manner, he raises them up and also gains merit through their inner transformation.

Aaron, returning from his separate experience to reengage with the people, gains merit through this. It is this concern for the people that attracts the presence of the *Shekhinah* among the people. It is also what makes him a proper servant, one who is qualified to offer sacrifices on behalf of the people.

In working with this text it will be helpful (as always) to have the full text of the Torah at hand, to see how Levi Yitzhak parses the verse, how he plays with the movements ascribed to Aaron and Moses (and when the Torah focuses on one, the other, or both) and uses them to create a much larger narrative.

 ## Questions for Reflection

1. This lesson once again suggests that the higher role of a tzaddik is to engage with the people. Yet there are other models of tzaddikim, some that might appear to be closer to the role of the high priest. Still, Levi Yitzhak shows his bias. Which is more important—bringing atonement for the people or engaging with them to help them do *teshuvah*? In which case will the *Shekhinah* dwell among the people?

2. Could Aaron perform his function as the one who brought atonement for Israel if he didn't set himself apart? What is the cost of doing so? What would be the cost of not separating himself, in order to connect with the people?

3. Levi Yitzhak writes, "Then, through the merit of the whole community with which he engages, in the hope that they will thereby do *teshuvah*, the Holy One causes His *Shekhinah* to dwell with us." This sounds like a fact statement: this act brings this consequence. Is it a fact for you—that is, does your work in the community, on behalf of or with other people, cause the *Shekhinah* to dwell in you? Does it bring the *Shekhinah* into the community? Or is this more like a statement of faith for you? Is it somewhere in between—faith that is sometimes proved and so sustained? What is the basis of faith—experience or intention?

 ## Taking It into Your Life

Pay attention to the verbs in the verse that Levi Yitzhak quotes: "he lifted," "he stepped down," "they went inside," and "they came out." Lifting oneself to separate off, to find solitude and room for self-improvement, may succeed. We may indeed grow spiritually and develop greater aware-ness. This is good but also comes with its own baggage: the higher we go, the more likely it is that we will come down again. This is not a bad thing. Indeed, it may be necessary, both to generate greater energy to strive to go even higher and also to allow us to reconnect with others.

There is another process in the second set of verbs: going in and coming out. Rather than seeing spiritual practice as one of separation and ascent, we might consider it a process of going in (into our own hearts, minds, and bodies) for the sake of coming out (more honest, more transparent, more able to act freely, to connect with others). What is more, the process of moving inward brings with it the necessary and equal movement out toward other people. When we connect with honesty and compassion to our own inner lives—seeing ourselves truly, without judgment but with clear discernment—we naturally find that our hearts are able to perceive the lives of other people clearly, to recognize their suffering, and to respond with the same compassion.

Martin Buber reports this story regarding R. Moshe Leib of Sasov:

> How to love people is something I learned from a peasant. He was sitting in an inn along with the other peasants, drinking. For a long time he was as silent as all the rest, but when he was moved by the wine, he asked one of the men seated beside him: "Tell me, do you love me or don't you love me?" The other replied: "I love you very much." But the first peasant replied: "You say that you love me, but you do not know what I need. If you really loved me, you would know." The other had not a word to say to this, and the peasant who had put the question fell silent again.
>
> But I understood. To know the needs of others and to bear the burden of their sorrow—that is the true love of others. (Martin Buber, *Tales of the Hasidim: Later Masters* [New York: Schocken Books, 1948], p. 86)

Spiritual practice means going inside for the sake of coming out again, to learn to know and bear—and offer solace for—the suffering of others. Practice. Reflect.

Tazria

An alternative interpretation of "[Speak to
the Israelite people thus:] When a woman
brings forth seed and bears a male, [she
shall be unclean seven days; she shall be
unclean as at the time of her menstrual
infirmity]" (Lev. 12:2).

"**When a woman brings forth seed** first, she **bears a male**; when a man
brings forth seed first, she bears a female" (cf. Berakhot 60a). In light
of this teaching we can understand the disagreement between the one
who says that the Jews were redeemed in Nisan and will be redeemed
in Nisan and the one who says the Jews were redeemed in Tishrei and
will be redeemed in Tishrei (Rosh Hashanah 11a).

This is what we hold. There are times that the blessed Holy One
spontaneously, with great mercy, has compassion on the people Israel,
without any arousal from below. There are times that the blessed
Holy One experiences self-compassion due to acts in this lower world
of His people Israel; their pleasant deeds, doing mitzvot. The second
way is preferred by Israel. The reason is that when God pours out life
and vitality each and every moment on all of the worlds, God has the
quality of "male"; the worlds that receive life and vitality from God in
each and every moment have the quality of "female."

So, "when a woman brings forth seed first"—that is, when the
outpouring of blessing comes in response to the deeds of the lower
worlds—"she bears a male." When the flow of blessing arises
in response to the lower worlds, no criticism is possible, and no
accusations can be brought against them. That is the significance of
"she bears a male": "strength comes with manhood" (*kha'ish gevurato*,
Judg. 8:21—i.e., when Israel stimulates God, God is "like a man"
and overcomes the negative forces). "When a man brings forth seed
first"—when the blessed Holy One arouses the flow of blessing for
the sake of Israel, then "she bears a female": "He [i.e., God] has grown

weak like a woman" (Berakhot 32a), for in this instance there is room for accusations against them.

So back to our original dispute in the Talmud: there really is no disagreement between the two parties. For when (God willing) the final redemption comes about by virtue of arousal from below (may it be soon, in our days), then redemption will come about in Tishrei. And even though this month is one of judgment, when redemption comes about due to arousal from below, that factor will not apply. But when the redemption comes about due to God's own compassion, then it will come about specifically in Nisan, at a time that no judgment applies. That is why Nisan is called "the month of Aviv [Abib]"—where the letters appear in their order in the alphabet. But the letters of the month Tishrei run backwards. Nisan has the quality of direct light, which is love, and Tishrei is reflected light, which suggests judgment.

FOR FURTHER THOUGHT

Levi Yitzhak once again inserts his preference for "arousal from below" into the Torah reading. In this instance, however, he did not have to reach too far. The Talmud reads the opening verse of our portion in such a manner—with its gendered biases—that inverts what would seem to be the "natural" order. When we act from below, when we as "female" initiate divine service, we bring delight to God and generate the flow of blessing as if we were "male." Arousal from below—serving God without expectation of reward, serving God out of love and devotion—is pure and leaves no opening for criticism, accusation, or judgment. When we wait for God to act on our behalf, we rely on God's own compassion and leave ourselves open to accusation and judgment. It takes more effort on God's part—God must be "male"—to provide for us and all the lower worlds waiting to receive God's life-giving flow, in the position of "female."

Levi Yitzhak adds an element to this familiar discussion. He ties it to the month of Nisan, the month of Passover. Over the course of the years, this parashah falls both before and after Passover, but always close to or in Nisan. The season of redemption is shaped by its teachings and concerns. In a year in which this parashah follows Passover, when the final redemption has not come to pass on the holiday, Levi Yitzhak finds the opportunity to encourage his students to redouble their engagement in the seven-week process of redemption that culminates in Shavuot. Clearly, God has chosen not to have redeemed Israel from His side and requires our efforts. By redoubling our dedication, striving to serve God for God's own sake and not for our own, we may stimulate that final redemption. Having received the blessings of the holiday, we can turn them into energy that returns to God, arousing the possibility of redemption in Tishrei, six months from now.

The images of the direct light and reflected light, of letters in order and reversed, appear elsewhere in this book. Levi Yitzhak introduces them here to plant seeds that will be harvested in the fall, at the High Holy Days. Now, in spring, everyone feels relieved to have survived the winter, excited by the change in weather and the potential of the new season. Levi Yitzhak builds on that sentiment. That, he says, is a gift from God, but it is not free of consequence. We have to work to be worthy of that grace. If we use the joy and energy of the Passover season to help us devote ourselves to serving God through the rest of the year, then we may find that our devotions serve to nullify the negative forces and quality of judgment of the High Holy Day season. To experience those holidays as a time of grace, free of danger and unburdened by accusations of fault or failure, would truly be to experience redemption.

 ## Questions for Reflection

1. We might address the problematic gendering of "providing" and "receiving" by investigating our own experience of these acts. How do you experience the power dynamics of "giving and receiving": When do you feel "one-up" and what leads you to feel "one-down" relative to other people? When is receiving a way of gaining power, and when is giving a sign of subservience? How does this affect your understanding of this passage?

2. Play with the image of direct light / reflected light. Direct light may be subject to accusation and judgment because it must be contracted to be perceived below, while reflected light moves from greater restriction to less, and so less rigor or judgment. Alternatively, reflected light is not self-generated; it cannot add anything new and may not contain all that

was in the direct light. How do you understand these images in general and our passage in particular?

3. What is your experience of the relationship between Passover and the holidays of Tishrei? Do they speak to one another? Do you carry a sense of one into the other? How? When?

Taking It into Your Life

Contemplative practice has the potential to be quietistic. It demands close attention to what is, deepening awareness of the ultimate source of all things in the Divine. In a sense, it is always attending to the arousal from above.

What would be the contemplative expression of arousal from below? To truly experience that "there is nothing but God" requires first letting go of all those aspects of experience that affirm our separateness from God. Letting go of each aspect of these qualities—our self-image, the perception of the "natural" course of a life and the habits of mind and heart that flow from it, a sense of independent power and personal initiative—thins the membrane separating us from God. It is an offering to God. Letting go in this manner diminishes the potential for competition with God, instead affirming God as sole sovereign ruler. As our sense of self founded in our ego recedes, God's presence in our lives and in the world expands. Actively seeking to diminish the ego, to "let go and let God," is a contemplative form of arousal from below.

The response to this arousal, as Levi Yitzhak describes it, is renewed and more precisely directed flow of energy, vitality, life, and blessing. Those qualities do not flow indiscriminately; they are directed to and through the one who serves God selflessly. As that energy returns, it fills us. We find our place in the world, we act and do, performing deeds of loving-kindness and devotion to God through the mitzvot. The ultimate consequence of contemplative arousal from below is our fuller capacity to act wisely, energetically, and wholeheartedly in the world.

When you sit in meditation, or do yoga, or chant (or whatever your contemplative practice), consider how it serves to thin the membrane between you and God, to make God more present and your "self" less so. Explore how your practice of being—and of being quiet—can also serve as arousal from below. Reflect.

> Yet another interpretation of "[Speak to the Israelite people thus: When] a woman brings forth seed and bears a male, [she shall be unclean seven days; she shall be unclean as at the time of her menstrual infirmity]" (Lev. 12:2).

Consider the Zohar III 42b (end): "From the moment that a woman conceives, all she talks about is whether she will bear a boy or a girl."

Our service of the blessed Creator is to be constant. Our thoughts, reflecting the movement of our soul, constantly worry, "Let my service not be for the sake of reward, but only that the blessed Creator will have delight from His creatures," that is, from His people Israel. If we can accomplish this, we will then be the ones who affect the Creator.

Read our parashah in this light. The soul is called "woman," since the soul emanates from the blessed Creator. And so, in the Zohar: "from the moment that a woman conceives," that is, as soon as the soul serves the blessed Creator, she only worries, "Will I give birth to a girl?"—that is, will my service be for the sake of reward, which has the quality of female/receptive? Or "Will I give birth to a boy?"—that is, will my service not be for the sake of reward, but only so that the blessed Creator will have delight? In this latter manner will we be the one who affects God.

FOR FURTHER THOUGHT

What can we give God? We are so much in need, and we may work hard to develop a properly grateful heart. Yet, always taking, always expecting to receive can be debilitating. Here Levi Yitzhak suggests that we do have something to give God: God needs, even delights, in being a recipient, and so also, by the way, being female.

This teaching is both challenging and complex. The image from the Zohar is certainly skewed—doesn't this sort of text imply that everyone would want a boy instead of a girl? Isn't that what all the worry was about in a pre-feminist, patriarchal society? Is to read this text only to reinforce and accept this attitude?

Let us investigate what Levi Yitzhak may have been trying to get at. Yes, this teaching valorizes boys (or the male gender) again, by making the male side of the practice/intention the better one. That is, "male" is to serve without expectation of reward, the preferred attitude. But, doesn't this generate a conflict with the male reader's own desire for male children, for his "personal reward"? Might engaging in this teaching be a way, perhaps, even to deal with his own female children with love and acceptance and interest? That is, the male reader may come to recognize how much delight he receives from his daughters and so be inspired further to serve God for God's delight. This may be too much, I acknowledge, but it does lead into the other part of the teaching.

Levi Yitzhak says that the expression "Will I give birth to a boy?" means acting "not for the sake of reward, but only so that the blessed Creator will have delight." The soul seeks to be in relationship to God of male-to-female, provider-to-recipient. In this manner, we who act, we who engage in *avodah*, become the ones who "affect (God)." In essence we are trying to behave in such a manner that God is female/recipient relative to us, the worshipper (again, a highly gendered attitude, but challenging). How does that play out in our reading/critique? Does it only reinforce the gendered roles and assumptions of the patriarchy, or does it require us to rework those roles—that is, if men (the worshippers Levi Yitzhak had in mind, no doubt) really have a chance to sense that God relates to them as a female, will they have to change their own attitudes about gender and gender roles? And, what might the effect be on these men to intentionally act in such a manner that God would be "female"? And, even if the men who heard this teaching couldn't change, could this be a way for us to open up the matter of the gender experience, to bring both aspects of male and female into all of us?

 ## Questions for Reflection

1. The song from the hit parade: "Heart and Soul." But here it is "Thought and Soul." Does this association surprise you? Does it work for you? If we have no thoughts, if we do not connect with the supernal realm of thought, do we have no soul? If we can't feel, if we have no empathy, have we no soul? Or is our soul cut off, unaware even of itself? How do you nurture you soul's awareness?

2. Is Levi Yitzhak's interpretation of the passage from the Zohar sufficiently creative to redeem what otherwise is a "non-feminist" perspective? In

our struggles to find texts that speak to contemporary egalitarian values, can we get past his assigned gendered roles? How can we bring both genders into conversation in our own beings?

3. Can this discussion suggest—with its gendered assumptions and inversions—a new way of thinking about devotional worship, of relating to the Beloved?

Taking It into Your Life

The image of the pregnant mother always expressing her desire, always muttering her deepest wish, is quite moving (even if biased). It suggests that even when she is carrying on other conversations, even when engaged in other activities, this fundamental concern remains a constant undercurrent in her heart, mind, and soul.

Let us take Levi Yitzhak's lesson as instruction for our own prayer lives. What do we most deeply desire? What do we wish to see unfold in the world? Is what we yearn for to bring us pleasure or ease, or is it ultimately for God's sake, for God's delight? What is the relationship between our deepest desires, God's delight, and peace and well-being in the whole of creation?

Spend some time with these questions. Watch your own inner conversation. Notice the most prominent movements of your heart and soul. When you can discern your true desire, try to put it into a few brief words: "May there be peace" or just "Peace"; "May all people be free of suffering" or just "Ease their suffering"; "May I see God in all people" or just "In God's image"; "May we be worthy of Your light" or just "Delight in us"; "God have mercy."

Whatever it is that you find expresses your deepest yearning, that which you would place before God as your devotion, that which undergirds and energizes your action in the world, make it your constant prayer. When you are not in conversation or otherwise speaking, say it to yourself and to God. When you are washing the dishes, walking to the train, making a sandwich, taking a moment to rest, recite this prayer to yourself and to God. When you are engaged with other people, come back to this prayer in the "in between" moments, when there is a lull in the conversation, when you are not needed "front and center." Make this prayer your constant companion, until it arises naturally, unbidden, always in your heart and mind.

Notice how you respond to your prayer. When is it troubling to sense this prayer; when is it boring; when is it difficult to recite? When does it illuminate your present activity in a new manner? When do you experience delight at its arising in your heart and mind, coming to consciousness? How does this help you feel connected to God? How do you sense this helps God feel connected to you and the world? What do you learn about your own investment in this prayer, in bringing it to fulfillment, in manifesting it in your own life? How does this prayer change you?

Metsora

"[When you enter the land of Canaan that
I give you as a possession,] and I inflict an
eruptive plague upon a house in the land
you possess" (Lev. 14:34).

See Rashi on this verse. He explains that this is meant to be good tiding
to the Israelites, because of the treasures that the Amorites hid in their
houses.

The primary source of joy is when we raise up sparks to serve the
Creator. When we raise up a spark, we raise up its innerness, leaving
aside its externality. The outside that we throw away is the source of
the **eruptive plagues** in the house: it is the leftover husk disconnected
from the spark that rots.

In that vein, with regard to the seven Canaanite nations in the Land
of Israel, God commanded, "You shall not let a soul remain alive"
(Deut. 20:16): leave only the sparks in the houses. So, when Rashi says
that the **eruptive plague** in the houses is meant as good tidings because
of the treasures that they hid, he is referring to these sparks. This is the
good tiding, which suggests joy, the chief joy of raising sparks.

FOR FURTHER THOUGHT

Here is Rashi's comment in full:

> This is good tiding for them, that the "eruptive plague" will afflict
> them. That is because the Amorites hid their treasures of gold in the
> walls of their houses for the forty years that Israel was in the wilder-
> ness. But when the plague erupts in the house, they will have to
> break the walls open and thereby find them.

Here is one of the sources of this teaching (cf. Lev. R. 17:6):

> R. Hiyya taught: Was it then a piece of good news for them that
> plagues were to come upon them? R. Shimon bar Yohai taught:

When the Canaanites heard that the Israelites were approaching they set to hiding their valuables in the houses and in the fields. Said the Holy One: "I promised the Israelites' ancestors that I would bring their children into a land full of all that is good, as it is said, 'And houses full of all good things' (Deut. 6:11)" [but it will all be hidden]! What did the Holy One, do? He brought plagues upon their houses so that when they would pull it down, they would find a treasure.

Rashi and R. Shimon bar Yohai seem merely interested in the treasure to be exposed in tearing apart the afflicted house, unlike Levi Yitzhak. Yet Levi Yitzhak transforms these rather mundane and materialistic lessons into something quite profound.

First, Levi Yitzhak recognizes the immense incongruity in the slaughter of the seven nations. Of all aspects of creation, it would seem that the holiest sparks, and the greatest concentration of them, are in human beings. It is through our moral and loving attention to other people that we raise up these holy sparks. How can that be accomplished through violence and death? The text of the Torah that he cites—"you shall not let a soul remain alive" (*lo techayeh kol neshamah*; Deut. 20:16)—makes this even more stark. In slaying the nations, we are undoing God's own gift: God enlivens (*mechayeh*) all things. Yet, in a radical manner, Levi Yitzhak rereads this verse, in light of its Rabbinic understanding. That is, this rule means that Israel was not to sue for peace with these nations, but if they approached seeking peace and accommodation with Israel, they were to be received in peace. It is as if, then, Levi Yitzhak reads this phrase, "No, you shall enliven those souls." Through engaging with them in peace, in finding the holy sparks even in these Canaanite nations, we can bring them to full life. And so also with their homes: Israel was to find in them the holy sparks, which, once removed, would leave only putrefaction and plague. This may be a stretch, but it is making an attempt to redeem this difficult text.

Second, Levi Yitzhak shifts the emphasis from treasures of gold to holy sparks. When we seek our truest joy, we are not to think in materialistic terms. We will not be made happy by things—even valuable things. We will be happy only when we seek God, seeing the possibility of connecting to the Divine in everything.

Third, Levi Yitzhak reminds us that we make a mistake when we turn up our noses at what "stinks." That is, the eruption in the houses seems to be a negative event. The midrash surely tries to make this something positive. Levi Yitzhak goes a step further. Everything is made up of a mixture of good and bad, of internal and external, of spiritual and material. The two interact and are interdependent. Without the spark (spiritual), the physical dies, becomes waste, and rots. But without the form (physical), the spark cannot be present in the world, filling it with divine presence. When we divide up the world into what we like (what is pleasant) and what do not like (what is unpleasant, rotten, and stinky), we miss out on seeing God's presence in all things. We might be tempted to think that there is nothing spiritual in houses and the like. We will be even more tempted to think so when there erupts some sort of rot or plague. We would be wrong. Indeed, the eruption itself is the sign that there is a spark present that needs to be redeemed. It is in reconnecting with the rot, opening it up to reveal the spark, that we can encounter true joy.

Questions for Reflection

1. How do you experience "raising sparks"? How do you conceive of the divine sparks in all existence? What does it mean to you to identify that spark, and how can you devote it to God?

2. The classical texts suggest that one way that we raise sparks in inanimate things is through use, particularly when that use is devoted to or supports spiritual practice or awareness. Does that make sense to you? How do you understand that we raise sparks from inanimate things?

3. Is it your habit to look away or look at things that are ugly, revolting, or hard to see? Why? When? How does Levi Yitzhak's teaching affect your sense of what these sights might hide for you to discover?

Taking It into Your Life

Alan Lew in his book *Be Still and Get Going* identifies the moment that Israel stood at the shore of the Sea as a model for mindfulness meditation and practice. It is applicable here as well.

The Israelites found themselves sandwiched between the approaching Egyptian chariots and the Sea. They turned to Moses in complaint, prepared to return to Egypt rather than die in the wilderness.

> But Moses said to the people, "Have no fear! Stand still, and witness the deliverance which *YHVH* will work for you today; for the Egyptians whom you see today you will never see again. *YHVH* will battle for you; you be silent!" (Exod. 14:13–14)

The Israelites were to look at the Egyptians carefully, to see who they were in this moment, so that they will know in the future that these Egyptians never reappear. This sort of observation required a clear head, steady attention, and a degree of composure. In the face of their deepest fears, the people were told to stand still and watch. What was more, they were to watch and be silent. It was only in this manner that the people truly could be saved.

And in a sense, it is what Levi Yitzhak is telling us as well. To be saved in our lives, to truly see God's salvation, we have to pay attention even in the moments of our greatest fear, even in the face of the most horrifying occurrence. Our capacity to maintain contact with the terrifying and horrific allows us to know what is true and witness to it. When we do not turn away, we are able to testify that "this, too" is part of God's world. This is reflected in the *berakhot* of sight and awareness:

> When hearing bad news: "Blessed is the judge of Truth" (*barukh dayan ha'emet*).
>
> When hearing thunder: "Blessed is God whose power and might fill the whole world" (*shekocho ugevurato malei olam*).
>
> When seeing the ocean: "Blessed is God who made the great sea" (*she'asah et hayam hagadol*).
>
> When seeing exceptionally beautiful people, trees, or fields: "Blessed is God who has such in His world" (*shekakha lo be'olamo*).
>
> When seeing exceptionally strange-looking people or animals: "Blessed is God who makes creatures different" (*meshaneh haberiyot*).

Nothing is beneath God's notice, and nothing should be beyond our attention.

Bring awareness to what you allow your gaze to rest on and what you turn away from. In both cases, bring full awareness to what is before you. In the former, notice what attracted you. Notice when you are drawn to look at what is attractive, what is appealing to you. Notice when and if your gaze is one of appropriation or of appreciation. Let go of what you desire, and allow the beautiful to exist in itself for God's glory.

When you notice that you have turned away, bring your gaze back to the object. Pay attention to the thoughts, feelings, and judgments that arise in your mind and heart. Do not judge yourself in turn, but acknowledge them so that you can let go of them. Then pay close attention to what had at first repulsed you. Can you allow it just to be? Can you find in it the potential of God's presence? Could it exist if it were not for God's vital force in it? How can you draw out the spark in this instance and once again fill the world with God's glory?

> "If a man has carnal relations with a woman,
> they shall bathe in water and remain
> unclean until evening" (Lev. 15:18).

How shall we understand the teaching in Avot (2:1): "Know what is above you: an eye that sees and an ear that hears and all of your deeds are inscribed in a book." It does not make sense to say "Know what is above you" (*mimkha*). Is not God above all possible worlds, beyond the seraphim and the holy beings? Why does this mishnah then say "above you" (*mimkha*)? To answer, we must consider the verse in Psalms (34:16): "*YHVH*'s eyes are on the righteous, God's ears attentive to their cry." This is too fanciful an image even to imagine. Should we not believe that God has no physical being? But King David actually meant something quite profound with his words.

We find in the midrash a comment on the verse "*YHVH* is your shadow" (*tzilkha*) (Ps. 121:5): whatever we do, our shadow mimics our actions. Whatever we do, our shadow does exactly the same thing, as we move and as we behave. So, too, when we serve God, Creator of all universes: whatever a righteous person does here below, each and every one of her movements is done above as well, crowning the Creator as sovereign with her holy words. This is the sense of the Zohar: every night when the soul of the righteous ascends above, all the angels cry out, "Give honor to the image of the King."

Think of it this way: a child may do something smart according to his understanding, and his parent takes delight and pride in the wisdom of the child, even though relative to the parent's understanding it is really nothing. Still, for a five-year-old child, this act shows wisdom. So it is with us. We are called "children of the Omnipresent" (Avot 3:18), and when we serve God, we display great wisdom, as it says, "The beginning of wisdom is fear of God" (Ps. 111:10). Therefore God takes great delight and pride in our childlike wisdom and says to the heavenly retinue, "See my children whom I have raised, how they strive to do my will and desire, so that I will take delight in them—and this is their whole intention!"

So we find that whatever good we do with our eyes, this eye is engraved above to bring ease to the Holy One. So, also, when we hear Torah with our ears (taking care not to do anything against the Holy One with them, nor to listen to any sort of frivolity or foul-mouthed speech, heaven forbid!), then this ear is engraved above. This is what the Sages meant when they said that the image of Jacob was engraved under the Throne of Glory (Gen. R. 82:2). He served the Creator, and so his image was engraved above.

So our verse says "*YHVH*'s eyes are on the righteous" (Ps. 34:16): where does God get eyes? Scripture explains that it is "from the righteous" who do good with their eyes, making eyes above as well. The verse continues, "And God's ears" (ibid.)—and where does God get ears? The verse says, "God is attentive to their cry" (ibid.), that is, to those who cry out to God in prayer and who serve Him. They thereby do good with their ears, since when we pray we must make our ears hear what our mouth expresses, and in this manner the ear is engraved above.

This means that if the eye sees something negative (heaven forbid), then the eye that is engraved above will be shut. And if we do some good with our eyes, then the eye engraved above will be open. This is implied in the verse, "Incline Your ear, O my God, and hear; open Your eyes and see" (Dan. 9:18). This verse means: we have, to this point, done evil things with our eyes, and as a result the eye above is closed, and we therefore plead that God open the eye that is shut.

This is the intent of the teaching "Know what is above you" (*da mah lema'alah mimkha*) (Avot 2:1). That is, all that is above is "from you" (*mimkha*): what you do below is then engraved above. Know then that there is "an eye that sees and an ear that hears" (ibid.)—a supernal eye that sees and a supernal ear that hears. What is the source of this ear and eye above? They are from the deeds that you do.

FOR FURTHER THOUGHT

This is a portion of a longer teaching about the importance of intention. The bodily fluids of sexual intercourse do not, in and of themselves, cause impurity (this is a concern of this parashah; cf. Lev. 15:18). Rather, impurity arises from the intrusion of personal desire and impure thoughts during intercourse; were our thoughts of God alone, there would be no impurity. Our passage is one of the ways that Levi Yitzhak explains the significance and power of our intention.

We open this passage with a familiar trope, the teaching of the Baal Shem Tov that our deeds have significance in the heavenly realms. This is not meant in an egotistical way; nor is this magic, compelling God to act according to our will. Rather, it is a reminder that our behavior in this plane has implications for how the world will work on a cosmic scale. When we do good, then we generate good for all; when we are selfish, we limit the capacity of the world to provide for all.

Levi Yitzhak expands this image. While God may not have eyes or ears, there are eyes and ears in the divine realm, engraved on the Throne of Glory. Those organs are animate, and they respond to our behavior. When we employ our eyes and ears in worthy ways, when we devote them to God's service, we enliven eyes and ears of blessing above; if not, we stop them up. All of this is to make more dramatic the teaching from Avot: "Know: what happens above is from you." Your behavior makes possible the eye that sees and the ear that hears. And, know as well that your endeavor to keep the eye open and the ear attentive is not for your sake alone, but for the good of all creation.

I am partial to the midrash on Psalm 121—"Me and My Shadow," God and me doing an intimate, synchronized dance. Who is Fred Astaire and who is Ginger Rogers? Who leads and who follows? Remember Ginger's comment: Fred may have looked great, but she had to do everything he did, backwards in high heels.

Questions for Reflection

1. Think of the various superstitions we have about shadows, such as not stepping on another person's shadow or crossing shadows. Think of Wendy sewing Peter Pan's shadow back onto him. Are you aware of your shadow as you go through your day? Would you miss it if it weren't there? Is there a part of you that follows you around, that "mimics" you? When that shadow does exactly what you do, even those things that you might wish were not visible to others, how do you feel? Could it be that having a shadow might help "keep you honest"? Are you concerned about protecting, preserving, or hiding your "shadow," from yourself or from others? Or do you welcome the sun so that you can happily sing "Me and My Shadow"?

2. "Know what is above"—whatever it is, however it is, the nature of God's being and manifestation in the world—"is from you." Is this a threat, a warning, an invitation, or a blessing? How do you experience it?

3. What does this teaching imply about prayer? Can we still pray, "My God, stop my tongue from evil ..."? Can we honestly quote the psalm "Turn my eyes from seeing vain things" (119:37)? Does our intention have any implications for how this teaching might actually work in the world?

Taking It into Your Life

The Talmud reports a popular saying or proverb: "From the very forest itself comes the handle of the axe that fells it" (Sanhedrin 39b). This is a way of talking about our psychological shadow. It is part of us, the record of our suffering, stifling, stuffing, and sloughing off of pieces of our true hearts, minds, and souls. Those parts remain in us, seeking expression, causing pain at their silence, generating anger and aggression toward those who manifest what we wished we could or who are similarly stopped up.

A significant component of spiritual practice is learning to identify and uncover what resides in our shadow. We learn over and over that the story we tell of how it is someone else's fault, how someone else is unbecoming, unhappy, too aggressive, too greedy is frequently a projection of our own inner struggles. We know these traits of our own behavior, yet we are unable to acknowledge them directly or are too pained to accept this truth. It is easier—if even more complicated and painful—to attribute these negative qualities to others. Yet when we sit quietly and pay attention, when we allow ourselves to tell the truth without judgment, we are able to bring that truth out into the open. We are able to recognize that we are indeed the person we are pointing to, the person we are criticizing. And knowing that, we can let go of the self-judgment and find greater ease—with ourselves and with others.

To say, then, that God is our shadow is to recognize how often we project onto God our own frustrations and failures. We accuse God of not seeing; we resent God for not hearing. We come to see, however, how that is our projection, our anger and resentment that we are not able to see and hear clearly, for the good.

Spiritual practice can be liberating when it helps us see clearly in the moment, without judgment, making it possible to own up, to be accountable for our actions. We will be freer in responding to our misdeeds, we will be more able to say, "I'm sorry." And we will be less likely to hold grudges or begrudge others who seek our pardon. As we live more freely, we will want others to do so as well, as we will recognize how this contributes to the free flow of love, life, and well-being in all creation.

Watch your inner conversation. Pay attention to moments of conflict, when you are inclined to blame others for your situation. Notice when you insist that someone else is wrong; that they made you do something; that you are not normally this way, so it must be something they did. These are clues that the shadow is at work. Step back and loosen your grip on the story. Ask over and over: What is going on? What really happened? How do I truly feel? How can I bring more loving-kindness to this situation—to myself and to all others? This is not to let others off the hook for their behavior, nor is it to blame ourselves as the victim. It is to invite them in, with us, to the truth of interconnection and interdependence. We all do everything all the time; and we all need each other, all the time.

Acharei Mot

"[YHVH spoke to Moses] after the death of the
two sons of Aaron who died when they drew
too close to YHVH's presence" (Lev. 16:1).

Two *Tannaim*, R. Eliezer and R. Yehoshua, disputed as to the reason
Nadab and Abihu died. R. Eliezer argued that they had offered
halakhic instruction in the presence of their teacher. R. Yehoshua
argued that they had been drunk when they entered the *Mishkan* (cf.
Lev. R. 20:6, 9). Each view can be challenged. For the one who argues
that they had given halakhic instruction before their teacher, what is
the connection to the phrase "[they] **died when they drew too close to
YHVH**"? If this was because they did not ask permission of Moses,
then this essential element is missing from the text. And this question
also stands for the other *Tanna*.

To connect the first view with the phrase "**when they drew too close
to YHVH's presence**," we need to understand why one who gives
instruction before his teacher merits death, even if what he taught was
correct. The answer is that the Holy One created separate divisions
(between each world and realm), and any angel who goes above its
division is burned up. The emanation of the worlds from the world
of the seraphim—which is the Throne of Glory—to the world of
the *chayyot*, and from the world of the *chayyot* to that of the *ophanim,*
takes place by way of contraction. So if an angel ascends above its stage
of contraction (to the next higher one), it would be nullified in that
greater reality.

This is true for us as well. The Holy One contracted His *Shekhinah*
in Moses, and from Moses to Aaron, and from Aaron to his sons, and
from his sons to the elders, and from them to the prophets, and from
them to all of Israel—just as the Sages taught the order of instruction
(Eruvin 54b). But Aaron's sons wanted to ascend above their level of
contraction, yet did not ask permission of Moses their master. "They
brought themselves before God"—they wanted to receive instruction

directly from the Holy One, and not through the transmission of Moses, Moses to Aaron, Aaron to them. As such, they were nullified in reality and were burned up.

This is the case for us in every generation: the Holy One contracts His *Shekhinah* in the *Gadol Hador* (leading scholar of the generation), and from him to his students, and from them to all Israel. One who teaches, then, before his teacher, who desires to ascend from his level and from his degree of contraction, to learn on his own and draw near to the Holy One outside of the process of the conduits descending from his teacher, this one merits death.

This, then, is the meaning of the phrase "[they] **died when they drew too close to YHVH**"—that is, they drew themselves up to the Holy One outside of the conduit of instruction that flows to Moses, from Moses to Aaron, from Aaron to themselves. That is why this happened to them. Scripture then says, "Do not come at any time (into the Sanctuary)" (Lev. 16:2)—"at any time" is above the realm of contraction. Each and every day has its own process of contraction. This explains how the phrase "at any time" fits with the argument of the one who argues that they had given halakhic instruction before their teacher.

FOR FURTHER THOUGHT

We have not included the sequel, dealing with the second opinion, for two reasons. One is that the text itself, in *Kedushat Levi*, is incomplete. The other is that while Levi Yitzhak begins his explication of the position of the second *Tanna*, he does not provide us with enough information to understand his intent.

This passage takes the form of a Talmudic argument. There, different rabbis use the same verse to teach a particular law or practice. The assumption is that each verse, each phrase, each word is connected in a deep and intimate manner with the law that can be derived from it. Each rabbi argues how his position accounts for all the words in the proof-text. What happens when two rabbis use one verse to teach different lessons, to derive seemingly opposite laws? Their later interpreters (or their colleagues in the yeshiva) will pick at their arguments to find inconsistencies, to identify ways in which the application of this verse for this or that teaching is insufficient, unsupported by the verse to which it is attached.

Levi Yitzhak creates a dispute between R. Eliezer and R. Yehoshua, one that does not actually appear in Rabbinic literature as he presents it (an interesting issue in itself). Each of the two teachers reads this verse to teach something about why Aaron's two sons merited death before God. R. Eliezer claims that they had taught their own lessons, presented their own halakhic decision before their teachers (something that the Talmud otherwise identifies as a horrendous, unforgivable, even capital offense). Levi Yitzhak proceeds to explain how R. Eliezer's position is tenable, even though there is nothing in the Torah to support it.

It is in the context of this legalistic argument that Levi Yitzhak inserts his spiritual teaching. He describes the nature of the world, how spiritual forces are organized, and what happens when we interfere with that order. God's divine blessing flows downward, from its purest, unbounded state through greater and greater contractions, from world to world, until it reaches us in our human, physical plane. Movement from below to above moves from greater contraction and concealment of divine light to greater light, more direct divine power. That is why one who ascends above his plane is "burned," or nullified. The tzaddik (Moshe, Levi Yitzhak) is the primary conduit by which this blessing flows to us. If we reject his teaching or authority, if we present ourselves as his equal or superior without permission or acknowledgment, we risk the world, and our own lives.

It is not that independent action is unacceptable. It is not that initiative is prohibited or that it is impossible for a student to supersede a teacher. Rather, it has to do with process. How one couches one's teaching—with deference to a teacher, with acknowledgment of possible inaccuracy—conditions its acceptability. And in seeking the approval of one's teacher, in acknowledging the teacher's contribution to one's capacity to teach, one participates in the flow of awareness. Humility does not allow self-promotion. It seeks connection, acknowledges the contributions of others, and resists claiming even legitimate status. Nadab and Abihu did not behave in that manner.

 ## Questions for Reflection

1. Early on, Hasidic leaders challenged the authority and legitimacy of the establishment communal leaders. How does this teaching fit? Is this a warning that not everyone can "set up shop" as a tzaddik? Do you

have a sense that some sorts of religious initiatives or interpretations are "out of bounds"? Have you ever felt threatened by a student/partner/ questioner's interpretation? When? How did you respond?

2. Do we have a responsibility to ground our teachings in what came before us? Do we have a responsibility to seek guidance, instruction, and approval from our teachers to innovate? If conditions change "at any time," are you confident that you can discern what is called for, without instruction from a teacher?

3. Why is "drawing on the conduits" so important? Where are and who make up the conduits that feed and nurture us? Do you feel that you can reach the source of inspiration and teaching, the source of all divine truth, on your own? How do you sense that you are part of a chain of tradition?

Taking It into Your Life

Levi Yitzhak reminds us that we are not self-generated, that we are affected by multiple and often unknown forces. His metaphor is that of "conduits" (*tzinorot*), the special channels by which the divine flow is brought down into our world. In the Hasidic tradition, it is the tzaddik who serves as the conduit for Torah instruction as well as for the blessings of life and well-being. It is the tzaddik, as well, who helps raise our prayers and deeds to God. But, there must surely be other means by which we are affected in our lives and by which we influence the world.

All of us are the products of innumerable interactions with other people, all of which have an effect on our lives. What is more, we benefit from (and also are adversely affected by) the actions of people we do not know and have never met—indeed, who may live on the other side of the world. We, in turn, have an impact on other people, both those we meet and those far from us. While we can see that our acts have effect, mindful awareness reveals to us that we are neither the sole authors of our fates nor in full control of our lives. Believing and behaving otherwise may create greater suffering for ourselves and for others.

This awareness invites two practices. The first is when we find that our plans succeed, that our lives unfold in ways we perceive to be positive, as we would like them to be. In response, offer a prayer of gratitude, recognizing the contributions of untold others to your success. You should include in this prayer both your acknowledgment that others may have suffered in the process and your wish that your pleasure in your success may return blessings to them.

The second practice is when we find our plans obstructed—and our lives frustrated. In response, acknowledge how you have done your best, that perhaps you could have done better, yet that you are not solely responsible for this unpleasant pass. Recognize that there are untold others whose lives are also tied to yours. Pray that those who suffer find solace. Pray that those who have benefited in your distress share their blessings for the good of others.

Seek the well-being of others in all others. Acknowledge the hand of others in the unfolding of your life. Find gratitude for each moment.

> "You shall follow My rules, and keep My laws [to go in their ways; I *YHVH* am your God]" (Lev. 18:4).

Chukkot (laws) are commandments that have no apparent reason. *Mishpatim* (rules) are commandments for which there is a reason. When we perform commandments that have no apparent reason, we become purer and are more able thereby to understand the commandments for which there is a reason. But (heaven forbid) if we do not do those commandments that are *chukkim* (laws), we will have no awareness at all by which to understand those commandments that have a reason in order to do them.

This is the significance of the language of Scripture here: "**keep My laws.**" When you do those commandments that are *chukkim*, without any apparent reason, you will purify your intellect, so that you will better understand those commandments that have a reason and do them (*la'asot*). That conclusion is implied in the opening phrase: "follow [*ta'asu*] My rules." Indeed, this is reinforced in the next verse: "[You shall keep My laws and My rules,] by doing which [*asher ya'aseh*] man shall live: [I am *YHVH*]" (Lev. 18:5). You will come to understand that the commandments are the life force in you.

FOR FURTHER THOUGHT

Levi Yitzhak emphasizes the verb "to do" (*la'asot*). Commandments are important not as ideas, but as directions for action. It is only in doing them—and in doing them with awareness—that we benefit from them. We might think that it is easy to do those command-ments for which we are given reasons, but Levi Yitzhak suggests otherwise. Even knowing why we are supposed to do something may not be sufficient for us to feel motivated to do it and surely is not enough for us to do the commandment with full awareness. That requires purification of the intellect, which is accomplished by fulfilling the *chukkim*, those commandments for which there is no apparent reason.

The emphasis on "doing" flows from these verses in the Torah. In Lev. 18:3, the verb appears four times; we are warned "not to do" (*lo ta'asu*) according to the "ways of doing" (*kema'aseih*) of the Egyptians and the Canaanites. Nor are we to "go in the ways of their laws" (*chukkoteihem*). Levi Yitzhak sees in our verse the instruction to do the opposite: to go in the ways of God's laws, which will, in turn, lead to doing according to God's rules. The commentator *Or Hachayyim* points out that verses 2 and 4 conclude, "I am *YHVH* your God" (*ani YHVH eloheikhem*). He suggests that in this manner the Torah points to both of God's qualities: compassion (*rachamim*, signified by *YHVH*) and judgment (*din*, signified by *elohim*). This, in turn, suggests that one might serve God out of fear (connected to *din*), but also out of love (connected to *rachamim*).

This leads Levi Yitzhak to read Lev. 18:5 quite closely. That is, he notices that it concludes differently: "I am *YHVH*." Here, then, we are pointed to God's love alone, suggesting that we are to keep the laws and rules beyond fear of God, but only out of love. When we serve God out of love, no longer fearing God's punishment, we realize with great wonder, without any self-concern, that the force that enlivens us derives from the commandments: "You shall keep My laws and My rules; it is by doing them that a person connects with the life force that is in them, for I am a loving God."

Another aspect of Levi Yitzhak's teaching: He claims that by performing the *chukkim* we purify our intellect such that we are able to understand—and so perform—the *mishpatim* more completely. His notion seems to be based on the commentary of the *Or Hachayyim* (Lev. 18:4). R. Hayyim ben Attar focuses specifically on the laws of prohibited sexual relations that make up this chapter. He sees in the strong emotional and physical energies of sexuality that which will cause coarseness and distance from God. Levi Yitzhak seems to accept his framework but expands it and softens it, making it easier to apply to our lives. Levi Yitzhak understands that doing the *chuk-*

kim purifies the mind and body so that we can perform the other mitzvot with full awareness, but he does not seem concerned to emphasize the negative, as does the *Or Hachayyim*.

Questions for Reflection

1. How do you understand the process by which one's intellect becomes purer through performing the *chukkim*? What happens to our heart/mind when we do something simply "because that is what the Creator has decreed"? How might this transform our acts when there are grounds for rational motivation?

2. Levi Yitzhak emphasizes the outcome of this process: to do the commandments. Do you share that goal? What do you see as the outcome of purifying your heart/soul? What does it mean to you to say in our prayers, "Purify our hearts to serve you in truth"? What is your experience of the connection between doing the mitzvot and serving God?

3. The classical gloss on the verse "You shall keep My laws and My rules, by the pursuit of which man shall live" (Lev. 18:5) is "so that you might live by them and not die by them" (*Sifra, Acharei Mot*, 13). Levi Yitzhak says that by doing the commandments we learn that our very life force is in them. How is his teaching different, and how is it the same?

Taking It into Your Life

Levi Yitzhak seems to read the end of Lev. 18:5, "Life is in them [the *chukkim* and *mishpatim*]—I, YHVH, am that life." Spiritual practice is how we come to perceive God in every moment, in every act.

A young teacher in an inner-city school recently discovered Thich Naht Hanh and has been transformed (for the moment). She told a story: Getting out of the car one morning, she dropped all of her papers on the ground and spilled her coffee. Previously she would have been in tears, berating herself for being so clumsy, despairing of ever being a good teacher, a decent, acceptable person. But this time she was able to say, "I've dropped my papers and spilled my coffee. Let me pick them up and go on to class." She was not stuck in despair—"Nothing ever works out right" or "Today is going to be a disaster"—and did not beat up on herself—"I'm such a jerk" or "You're kidding yourself if you think you can really do this job." She reported that she felt great relief at just being able to say what was true and energized to move on to the next thing.

This might be what it means to find our vital force in doing the commandments, of finding God in the moment. Our practice is to pay attention and not get distracted from moment to moment. That means letting go of stories—how we characterize what we experience, how we fit it into categories of previous experience, how we judge ourselves or others. It means seeing clearly: this is just what is, just like this. When we see clearly, we are more able to act with wisdom. We have energy to respond. And we can act with compassion, for ourselves and for others.

Start with small things. Pay attention to how you hold a cup of tea or coffee. Notice: This is a cup of coffee. I feel the handle. I feel heat. I feel weight. I smell the coffee. I sense my mouth watering. I lift the cup; it is heavy. I bring it close to my mouth and sense the heat. I notice a sense of fear that I might burn my lips. I blow on the coffee....

Pay attention to walking up the stairs: I feel my feet. I place my hand on the railing. I lift my right foot. I feel the lightness under the sole of my right foot. I feel the weight of my body on my left foot. I place my right foot on the next step. I move my weight forward and lift my left foot. I feel pressure on my right foot. I swing my left foot up to the next step, as I slide my hand up the railing....

There is nothing significant about these acts, except that they are what make up our lives. There is no "reason" for doing them, except to eat or to go upstairs. But in noting them, in sensing the energy in our bodies, the sensations of awareness, we come alive in these "nothing" moments. That aliveness can spill over into the rest of our lives, particularly when we are involved in doing the "important" things in life. Pay attention. Reflect.

Kedoshim

"[Speak to the whole Israelite community and say to them:] You shall be holy, [for I, *YHVH* your God, am holy]" (Lev. 19:2).

Consider the midrash (Lev. R. 24:9): Scripture says, "**You shall be holy for**": You might think that your holiness is equal to Mine. "**I, YHVH your God, am holy**" : my holiness is above (*lema'alah*) yours.

The question that appears to me (and my predecessors have expounded as well) is how can we actually undertake divine service, which is prayer, the service of the heart? When we first begin, we behold the greatness of the blessed Creator and respond, "Who am I to cry out and plead the great King, the King above all kings, the blessed Holy One? Am I not so lowly, dust, a maggot, a worm, full of sins and transgressions?" Yet despite that, we might then think, "From today onward I take on myself the yoke of God's sovereignty in truth, with a full heart." If we do this, from day to day we will grow in spiritual capacity and awareness. "The wise person, hearing this, will take a lesson" (Prov. 1:5).

We read in the Talmud (Shabbat 21b): "The House of Shammai maintain: 'On the first day (of Hanukkah) eight lights are lit and thereafter they are gradually reduced'; but the House of Hillel say: 'On the first day one is lit and thereafter we add and increase.'" The rationale of the latter is that on each day of the eight days of Hanukkah we fulfill the mitzvah, and as we know "one mitzvah brings another in its wake" (Avot 4:2), so that we connect more deeply in devotion to the Creator. Each day that we do another mitzvah we connect more deeply to the Creator, yet we also become more aware of our lowliness. The closer we draw to the King, the more we sense our own humbleness. In this manner, we can approach the state of *ayin* (nothingness) and the deepest state of humility. That is the way of the House of Hillel: they were more modest, yet they framed their response as "we add and increase."

That is the point of the midrash: "You shall be holy. You might think that your holiness is equal to Mine. But Scripture says, 'For I, YHVH, am holy'—My holiness is above yours." That is, due to your efforts to become holy, My name is made even more holy. That is the sense of "My holiness is above yours"—My name is sanctified through your efforts. How good and how pleasant it would be if we each were to cleave to the quality of humility, as it says, "The outcome of humility is fear of YHVH" (Prov. 22:4), then God's great name will be made holy even by important people who do mitzvot and good deeds, yet see themselves as nothing before the Creator, and thereby they sanctify God's name in public.

So, may God give us humility and bless us with all the upright qualities. Amen.

FOR FURTHER THOUGHT

The midrash that Levi Yitzhak quotes is a classic (Lev. R. 24:9):

> R. Shimon ben Lakish said: There are two sections in the Torah that Moses wrote whose meaning we can learn from the words of the wicked Pharaoh. One verse says, "[YHVH will make you the head, not the tail;] you will always [rak] be at the top [and never at the bottom—if only you obey and faithfully observe the commandments of YHVH your God that I enjoin upon you this day]" (Deut. 28:13). This might be taken to imply that you will be like Me, and so Scripture purposely states "only [rak]," a limiting term, signifying: "My greatness is higher than yours." We can infer this from the wicked Pharaoh. He said to Joseph, "You shall be in charge of my court, [and by your command shall all my people be directed]." This might be taken to imply: you shall be like me; and so Scripture plainly states, "only [rak] with respect to the throne shall I be superior to you" (Gen. 41:40), as much as to say, My rank shall be greater than yours.
>
> This is similar to our passage as well: "You shall be holy." You might think that your holiness is equal to Mine; and so Scripture plainly states, "For I, YHVH your God, am holy." That is to say, My holiness is above yours. And this also we can learn from the wicked Pharaoh; for it says, "Pharaoh said to Joseph, 'I am Pharaoh; [yet without you, no one shall lift up hand or foot in all the land

of Egypt']" (Gen. 41:44). Lest you think that you will be like me, Scripture plainly states, "I am Pharaoh," as much as to say, My rank shall be higher than yours.

The midrash uses the speech of a human king—and a "wicked" one at that—to understand the speech of God. When God promises that we will be "on the top" (*lema'alah*) and when God declares, "You shall be holy," we might think that means we will be God's equals— above all others, holy like God. Yet we are taught by analogy to Pharaoh's language that God will always be superior, God's qualities always above ours.

This is a classical Rabbinic lesson. It reinforces the separation between divine and human realms. By implication, it also negates Pharaoh's claims to power. Pharaoh may have claimed superiority to Joseph, reminding him that "only" he "is Pharaoh"—yet when God speaks to Israel, it is to make clear that "only" God is the source of power and authority in the world; humans may share in God's holiness, but we will never be God's equal.

Levi Yitzhak accepts this lesson and then upends it. He receives this reminder that we humans are nothing before the awesome, transcendent majesty of God's creating power, and that our truest, most authentic attitude can only be humility. Yet, that is not all. Our honest awareness of our position before God carries with it a consolation. When we see clearly and act with wisdom—that is, with humility—when we strive for holiness despite our lowly station, we add to God's holiness. Levi Yitzhak rereads the midrash: God is not merely saying, "My holiness is superior to yours." Rather, God, with appreciation, with love, and with deep desire, encourages us to be holy because "My holiness is raised up, made great through yours." Again, holy endeavors in the lower realms have effect: uplifting, transforming the upper.

 ## Questions for Reflection

1. How do you respond to Levi Yitzhak's use of the classical trope that we are "lowly, dust, a maggot, a worm, full of sins and transgressions"? When, in your experience, can this approach produce meaningful spiritual awareness? How might it impede that awareness? How would you work with it in a positive manner?

2. What awareness prompts you to change, to try to be better? How is "doing better" a form of accepting the yoke of divine sovereignty? When you choose to do other than what your inclination and proclivity lead you to do, who or what is sovereign?

3. What do you feel when God says, "You shall be holy for I am holy"? Is it a revelation to you that it is possible for humans to be holy? Is it an honor to be compared to God? Are you amazed that you might be holy in some manner like God? Would you have thought that your holiness would be the same as God's? How do you feel hearing that "My holiness is superior to yours"? Alternatively, how do you feel when you learn that God's holiness is increased, raised up, by your striving for holiness?

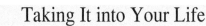

Taking It into Your Life

Levi Yitzhak describes a process that has two elements: awareness of unworthiness approaching a sense of nothingness, and increasing holiness. The more we recognize our nothingness before God, the more humble we become. The more humble, the less we account ourselves and our initiative independent of God's will to be of value. Yet, paradoxically, it is just the emptying of self-interest that makes it possible for us to move closer to God, adding to and increasing God's holiness. The closer we get to God, the less we see of ourselves; the less we are present as independent selves, the more we increase God's holiness through our increased holiness.

Another way of saying this is: the less there is of "me," the more there is of God. Again, this is paradoxical. Diminishing the scope of my ego requires effort on my part—always a dangerous undertaking, since it risks self-aggrandizement ("See how well I'm making myself smaller?"). My effort, however, is not to show how "I" am nothing, but to expand my awareness of God, allowing that awareness to fill my consciousness and motivate my actions. Whatever I do, then, is not my accomplishment.

Yet God recognizes our efforts. God knows our devotion. God reflects back to us the greatness we attain through our efforts: the glorification and sanctification of the divine name. We do, in the end, expand the realm of God's sovereignty and holiness. By our "not doing" we "do"; by our diminishing ourselves, we increase God's holiness.

Reflect on your experience of this paradox. Notice when you disappear and when you fill the space in your heart and mind. Notice how you invite God in and how God fills you up.

"You shall rise before the aged and show
deference to the old [you shall fear your
God: I am *YHVH*]" (Lev. 19:32).

I have written elsewhere that the essential spiritual fear (*yirah*) is before
God's transcendence, that is, that God is Master and Ruler, the essence
and root of all universes, none of which adds up to anything before
God. When we can attain that level of *yirah*, then we merit the title
"beloved child of the Omnipresent" (*Hamakom*).

Children whose parents love them with great and eternal love will
fear greatly trespassing their parents' will (heaven forbid), to prevent
suffering to the parents who love them so much. Understanding this,
all of our efforts should be to bring ease and pleasure to our Heavenly
Parent. This is the sense of the teaching "Israel sustain their Heavenly
Parent" with Torah, divine service (*avodah*), acts of loving-kindness
(*gemilut chasadim*), and doing mitzvot. And if we do the opposite
(heaven forbid), the Sages said, "What does the *Shekhinah* say? 'My
head is too heavy for me …'" (Chagigah 15b). It will be as if the blessed
Creator suffers thereby. A tzaddik is always careful not to bring
suffering to the Heavenly Parent (heaven forbid), trying always only to
bring ease and pleasure.

Here the quality of *yirah* is that we fear for the aspect (*middah*) of
compassion. There are those who fear the *middah* of judgment (heaven
forbid). But this capacity of which we speak is when a tzaddik fears for
the quality of compassion, that there be no suffering (heaven forbid) in
the *middah* of compassion. The primary purpose of Creation is so that
God might do good for His creatures, and "more than the calf desires
to suck, the cow desires to suckle" (Pesachim 112a). God's very intention
is to pour out love and every good thing for Israel, but when (heaven
forbid) they do not do God's will, "what does it [the *Shekhinah*] say? 'My
head is too heavy for me (My arm is too heavy for me).'" This is why,
then, the key fear of a tzaddik is that any grief should come to the *middah*
of compassion; that it might continue to pour out love and compassion,
life and peace for Israel. This is the blessed Creator's true delight.

It is known that "**aged**" (*seivah*) and "**old**" (*zakein*) are terms for the
middah of compassion. The Sages said, "At Sinai God appeared to Israel
as an old man [*zakein*] full of compassion" (*Mekhilta, Yitro, Anokhi* 5).

This, then, is how we can understand our verse: "**You shall rise before the aged**"—that is, the key quality of *yirah* is to fear for the "**aged**," that is the *middah* of compassion; "**show deference [*vehadarta*] to the old**"—that it should not say, "My head is too heavy for me" (heaven forbid). For if "majesty and glory [*hadar*] are before Him, then strength and joy are in His place" (1 Chron. 16:27). This is how we fulfill "**show deference to the old**."

FOR FURTHER THOUGHT

Levi Yitzhak transforms this very human, interpersonal commandment into spiritual instructions. Perhaps he intended that we transpose the qualities of God ("the compassionate elder") onto the very present, human elder before us. Just as likely, he invites us to take our feeling for our elders—grandparents, teachers, sages, friends— and extend them toward God. He does this by reading the term in the Torah—"elder," *seivah*—in kabbalistic terms. That is, "elder" is another name for *Tiferet*. The *sephirah* of *Tiferet* is the blessed Holy One, and this *middah* is the "heart" of God, compassion.

The *Shekhinah* is the partner of the Holy One, the object of God's love. When the blessed Holy One is angry, or alienated, or distant— due to our actions—He is also distant from the *Shekhinah*, and She suffers. What Levi Yitzhak teaches is that our fear of angering or hurting the blessed Holy One (*Tiferet*, compassion) helps support and maintain a favorable relationship between God and the *Shekhinah*. In many other Hasidic texts, prayer is said to be for the sake of the *Shekhinah*, for Her suffering. Here, our concern is not to harm *Tiferet*, not to insult or cause embarrassment to the Holy One, so that the *Shekhinah* will not be even further distanced, further alienated, from Her Partner.

"You shall rise before the aged" (*mipnei seivah takum*): you shall fear causing harm to your Heavenly Parent. But, also remember: "one shall fear one's mother and father" (*ish imo ve'aviv tira'u*; Lev. 19:3) as well.

 ## Questions for Reflection

1. Perhaps our prayers should be for the suffering of the *Shekhinah*, but our *yirah*, our awareness of our every act, our comportment in this world and

the work that we do, should be directed toward *Tiferet*. How might you differentiate the meaning of "divine service" (*avodah*), given this division of efforts, in your practice? Do you easily distinguish between a form of *avodah* that is grounded in *yirah* (in this case, concern not to injure the *middah* of compassion) and *avodah* that is prayer (for the sake of the *Shekhinah* and Her exile) in your daily life and spiritual practice? What, when, how?

2. Could this lesson help us deepen our understanding of the two commandments regarding parents, that is the balance of "honor" (*kavod*) and "fear" (*yirah*), between what is owed to one's father and what is owed to one's mother (cf. Exod. 19:13 and Lev. 19:3)? And now, having come to sense the interplay of *kavod* and *yirah*, we might investigate how this plays out in how we treat others. That is, do you show them *kavod* or respond out of *yirah*? How does this play out in how you wish to be treated? Which *middah* do you as a leader find is more effective in "getting things done"—*kavod* or *yirah*?

3. On the other hand, could it be that the blessed Holy One (the *middah* of compassion) and *Shekhinah* are not really being played off each other in the text? That is, could the image of the *Shekhinah* crying out simply be a way to give God a voice here? How else can God express pain, disappointment, and loss? How else can we be moved not only to obey God's commandments (*yirah* of judgment?) but also to care for God's inner emotional life?

 ## Taking It into Your Life

Levi Yitzhak warns us about the danger of causing constriction or limitation to the quality of compassion. Our capacity to feel compassion—for ourselves and for others—in all circumstances is a goal of spiritual practice. But it is not easy. Surely there are times that we recognize our fault, our having made a mistake and caused others pain—and we beat ourselves up. We are able to feel compassion for others, but not for ourselves. In that moment, we limit the extent of compassion in the world. There are times that we fall into old habits, doing what is harmful to ourselves and possibly to others. Withholding compassion for ourselves would again constrict its flow in the world.

In just those moments, there is no one who is more deserving of our compassion than ourselves—even as there may be others who are no less deserving. Our capacity to offer ourselves compassion makes more likely that we will feel free to express regret at our mistakes and fully extend ourselves in compassion for others.

Surely, there are times that others cause us harm or hurt others. We may spontaneously seek to protect the harmed, to stand up for the defenseless. We see that compassion is due them. But what about the one causing harm? Would extending compassion to that person, to those people, undermine our righteousness? Would feeling compassion for evildoers keep us from resisting their actions, from preventing further harm? It need not. Compassion may actually prevent us from acting unwisely, aiding us to do only what is necessary to stop the harm, without compounding that harm with further violence.

Watch when you notice compassion arising spontaneously in your heart. Watch when you withhold compassion. Who is in your circle of compassion and who is outside? To whom do you respond easily, and where does it take work? What holds you back, and what allows compassion to flow? What might you do to raise up the quality of compassion, to bring wholeness to your heart, to the heart of the world?

Emor

"When the daughter of a priest defiles herself through harlotry, it is her father whom she defiles; she shall be put to the fire" (Lev. 21:9).

We know that when we sin (heaven forbid), we cause harm above and add power to the husks (*kelippot*). The cure for this is to burn off externalities by becoming enflamed with the Creator, may God and God's name be blessed. This burning in us actually comes from the sin, from having sinned and having dark thoughts.

So, let's interpret the verse in this way: "**When the daughter of a priest**"—that is, when the soul (identified in the Zohar as "daughter of a priest")—"**defiles herself ... it is her father whom she defiles**"—this causes harm above and gives power to externality. The healing comes through "**putting to the fire**": by means of a burning enthusiasm that enflames us afterward to serve the blessed Creator due to the sin that we sinned we burn up all of the *kelippot*. Amen.

FOR FURTHER THOUGHT

You may be familiar with the prayer that appears early on in the morning service, "My God, the soul that You have given me is pure" (*Elohai neshamah shenatata bi tehorah hi*). We start out clean, pure, unblemished, open, and available to God. But our hearts are not fixed, and our actions and reactions are not determined. In response to the events of our lives, we constantly choose (consciously, and often unconsciously) to remain open or to close off in anger, in fear, in jealousy, in avarice, etc. We reject the truth of the moment to instead create or perpetuate a story—justifying our behavior, blaming others, etc. In Levi Yitzhak's terms, the story is of existence independent from God. Each sin closes us off even more from the open connection that we once had—but to which we can aspire again. The *kelippot* are the metaphorical manifestations of that closing off.

"The externalities" are the modes of thought, the forms of perception, that create and sustain our sense of separateness from God.

Levi Yitzhak brings a teaching of the Baal Shem Tov here: the energy in the sin—that which led us to act against our natural and native holiness and connection with God and which we first sense as negative—is actually the potential source of its own destruction. When we sin, our hearts and souls register what we have done, sensing the thickening of the husk over our awareness of God. When we notice that process, ignited by the sin, we can become enflamed with passion to return to a more balanced, more open, more righteous relationship with God and with ourselves. In our returning, in our turning, in *teshuvah*, we burn off the husks, transcend externality, and become one with God once again.

The following is a selection from Zohar III 122a, the source of Levi Yitzhak's opening claim:

> Anyone who trespasses the mitzvot of the Torah causes harm above (as if it could be so) as well as below, harms themselves, and harms all the worlds. Remember the parable of the people on the boat, and one stupid person wants to drill a hole under his seat etc. (cf. Lev. R. 4:6)....
> Yet repentance repairs everything, repairs the world above, repairs the world below, repairs the man himself, repairs the whole world.

Apparently, the recognition of the damage that we do to ourselves, to the whole world, and to the worlds above energizes us to do the work of *teshuvah*.

Again, we must ask if this sort of teaching can help "redeem" some of the gender inequality of the Torah culture, or is any gendering dangerous? Perhaps lifting the person of the "daughter of a priest" (*bat ish kohein*) out of the specificity of family and sin-and-punishment is redeeming—and also challenging. Each one of us, male and female, has a soul, and it is the *bat ish kohein*, and our individual actions, that cloud our hearts and defile our Heavenly Parent. Perhaps this requires too much rereading, but it is worth investigating the possibility, and the challenge.

 ## Questions for Reflection

1. How do you imagine the function of the *kelippot* in your life? Do you sense that following sin they close off your perception of God, or is

God concealed from you? When the *kelippot* become stronger, do they thicken around you? Where? How do you feel this? Where does the movement start that leads to the burning off of the sin inside? How do you feel that point, that moment, the arising of that awareness in you?

2. We might imagine that the psychological dynamic at work here is that a great guilt burns within us and we lash out, reject the sin. Or is it that we wish passionately to be reconciled, closer to God? What is the source, the fuel that feeds your burning enthusiasm for change? Could it be that the force for *teshuvah* comes from within and that it is therefore, to a certain extent, self-regenerating?

3. How do you experience your own soul? Do you sense that it is sullied by sin? When you "sin," does this reflect on anyone else but you? Does it reflect on God, too? How?

Taking It into Your Life

Where Levi Yitzhak presents "sin" as that which separates us from God, we might express this in terms of mindfulness practice as that which separates us from our own, true experience of our lives. Sin would then be that act—word, deed, withholding of information or care—that results from a mistaken perception of our own feelings or experience. We will recognize this in terms of our relationship with other people (and ourselves), but this can be true relative to God as well.

Consider: what causes us to lash out at others? Our first response might be: "They were doing something wrong." That may very well be the case. But when we consider the source of the energy that makes our response forceful—filled with anger, or righteous indignation, or criticism and castigation—we might discover other answers. We may come to recognize that we were responding out of fear: fear for others' safety, surely, but also fear for ourselves. What could be the source of our fear? Fear of being left out; fear of being ignored; fear of learning that our friends might not see the world as we do; fear of being disturbed, of the loss of our own preferred use of time to deal with this issue at hand; fear at being surprised.

When we recognize these possible sources of fear in our own hearts, we are better able to return to the original situation and reconsider what was truly happening. We are able to discern whether our initial anger, righteous indignation, or criticism was rightly placed and appropriate to the situation. Recognizing our own fears—our own discomfort, our own suffering in the face of this situation—we are able to respond to our own hearts with compassion. The energy released there, in our own hearts, can be brought to bear on the situation at hand as compassion for others—while still acting to prevent harm, to respond to danger. Rather than the energy being expressed and directed outwardly in anger or other negative reactions ("externalities"), we can turn it to caring for others and ourselves, in a manner that is more integrative, more whole.

Investigate this process in your own experience. In meditation, when you sense you have developed a degree of balance in your awareness, bring your attention to the images, feelings, and stories that arise in your heart/mind. Without judgment, investigate: what was true at that moment? Look carefully to discern where your self-interest was at stake, where you were afraid, where you were suffering. Notice when you were able to respond with compassion to yourself and when you directed the energy of your suffering outward, toward others in negative emotions or reactions. Consider how you might come to know the signs of your own inner suffering and its causes, so that you might not cut yourself off from it, and so that you might not misdirect the energy outwardly, at others, in unproductive and harmful ways. Always remember to hold your awareness, and this process, with compassion. That is the cauldron in which the energy of sin can be transformed into love and divine service.

> "[And from the day on which you bring the sheaf of elevation offering—] from the day after the Sabbath—you shall count for yourselves [seven weeks. They must be complete]" (Lev. 23:15).

The Sages taught that in this instance "the Sabbath" means the first day of Passover, which negates the view of the Zaddokites (who held it meant the actual day of Shabbat; see Menachot 65b). We need to understand specifically here why the festival day is called "Sabbath."

When an artisan, making something, finishes it, we know why he made it and its true purpose. So when he finishes his work and attains his purpose, he ceases his work (*shavat*). And this (as it were) is the same with God. After six days of creation, God ceased from His work. This is called the Sabbath of Creation (*shabbat bereishit*). But God also created living beings (*chayyot*), particularly those with intelligence (*sikhliyot*), to serve Him and to know that He is the Creator, the Fashioner, God. When finally these beings were completed and acknowledged, there was another cessation (*shabbat*), and it is called Shabbat.

So when the world was created, even though God performed awesome wonders—as with the Flood, and the Generation of the Tower, and overturning Sodom—God's true divinity still was not revealed. No one learned to do *teshuvah* in response to any of these events; they remained in rebellion against God. True, Noah was righteous from the start; and Abraham, who lived in the time of the Tower, was righteous from the start. Still, neither of them came to know the Creator through the displays of God's wonders. But at the Exodus, due to the Creator's beneficence, Israel came to recognize, to understand, and to know (*hiskilu*) the Creator. This was the completion of the creation of the intelligent beings, who served God at the festival of Pesach when these miracles took place.

That is why the day after Passover is called "the day after the Sabbath." That is when the creation of intelligent beings who would serve the Creator was completed. That is why it says, "**You shall count for yourselves**" (*lakhem*), on which the Zohar (III 97b) comments, "For yourselves—specifically!" The creation of the physical worlds was not dependent on us. Rather, it came about by the Creator creating, forming, making, and shaping everything. But the creation of living beings, intelligent beings, who will serve and love and fear God, is dependent on our free will and decision. That is why the verse says, "**You shall count for yourselves**"—specifically! This matter depends on us.

FOR FURTHER THOUGHT

Here is another example of Levi Yitzhak's emphasis on our role in the lower realms, the significance of "arousal from below." It is necessary for God to have created the world so that there might be intelligent beings who could recognize, love, and serve God. But it is not sufficient. In the end, these very beings must do just that; they must raise their consciousness and recognize that there is a God. The full purpose and meaning of Creation was not complete until Israel came out of Egypt and the awareness of God emerged from exile.

In this lesson we are offered another way to understand the two reasons given for the Sabbath: in Exodus we are told to remember the Sabbath as the conclusion of Creation; in Deuteronomy we are told to keep the Sabbath as a commemoration of the Exodus. Both are true, and both are meaningful. Remembering Creation on Shabbat is what brings delight into the day: we lean back into God's sustaining care, relishing our place in God's grand scheme, delighting in all that has been created for our pleasure. Keeping Shabbat, observing its strictures and invitations, is how we testify to our devotion to God, our acknowledgment of God as our sovereign God.

In connecting this lesson to the counting of the Omer, Levi Yitzhak also points us to Shavuot and the giving of the Torah. That, too, is seen in Rabbinic literature as the conclusion of Creation (*Tanchuma, Bereishit* 1): God set a condition with Creation—"If Israel accepts the Torah that has five books in it, it will be well. If not, then I will return you to your primordial state." When awareness came out of exile, when we came out of Egypt, we acknowledged that there is a God, accepted God's sovereignty, and so brought about the completion of Creation—the full expression of Shabbat. The work of the *sephirah*, of noting and moving through each individual day, is that of clarifying our devotion to God and preparing to receive God's sovereignty fully on Shavuot.

 ## Questions for Reflection

1. How do you experience Shabbat: is it for you, or for God? How do you imagine that holding one consciousness or the other affects the experience of Shabbat? Which aspect of Shabbat—"remembering" or "keeping"—is more powerful for you? When, why?

2. The miracles of Genesis—the Flood, the Tower, Sodom—did not induce *teshuvah* among the people. But apparently the miracles of Egypt did. How do you understand this difference? What was the *teshuvah* of the Israelites that distinguished them from the earlier generations? Is this a form of *teshuvah* that you would like to share? Why or why not?

3. How do you feel about the world's existence depending on your opening to awareness of God in the world, of committing yourself to devotion to God and Torah? How is responsibility for freely choosing to do or not do commandments related to consciousness of God and the establishment of Creation? Do you feel that your choices affect the stability of existence, of the persistence of the world? When, how, why?

Taking It into Your Life

In the translation above we have translated *ch-y-o-t* as "beings" and *s-kh-l-y-o-t* as "intelligent beings." We might also have read the words as *ch-y-u-t* (life force) and *s-kh-l-y-u-t* (intelligence). This might lead us to a different understanding of the process of Creation described here. That is, God did create *chayyut* at the start of Creation. Without it, nothing would exist at all. It is God's *chayyut* that keeps all things in existence from moment to moment: "And you enliven [*mechayeh*] them all" (Neh. 9:6). But, that *chayyut* was generic, pulsing through all existence unrecognized. What God needed was for that life force to develop awareness—both self-awareness and other-awareness; reflective awareness and prospective awareness; emotional awareness and analytic awareness. That is the quality of *sikhliyut*. That could not have come into existence with the creation of the physical world. Rather, it had to develop, to evolve, until it manifested in human encounters, in human awareness of divinity.

We are still part of that process. Inasmuch as we are constantly coming out of Egypt, each day, each year, we have yet to come to full awareness of ourselves, our world, and God. While the initial stages seem to be connected to recognizing God's miracles, Levi Yitzhak does also point us beyond. We are called to serve God only for God's sake, to reach beyond our "small selves"—concerned with immediate matters, invested in our individual survival—to our "great selves." That would connect us to all beings, to all existence. Striving to experience our oneness in God, to perceive the unified wholeness of all existence seems to be the engine of evolution.

Shabbat may be the best practice we have to support, sustain, and engender this evolutionary process. Shabbat is coming!

> "[It shall be a sabbath of complete rest for you, and you shall practice self-denial; on the ninth day of the month at evening,] from evening to evening, you shall observe this your sabbath" (Lev. 23:32).

The word *shabbat* signifies negation or cessation, as it says, "The joy of our hearts has ceased" (*shavat mesos libbeinu*) (Lam. 5:15).

So read this verse as follows: "**from evening to evening**" your work shall be to negate and cause to "cease" (*tishbetu*) that which "negates you" (*shabbatkhem*). Who is it who wants you to cease? That must be your accuser. You are to negate him by means of your prayers "**from evening to evening.**"

FOR FURTHER THOUGHT

The context of this verse is the observance of Yom Kippur, which begins before the fall of night at the end of the ninth of Tishrei and ends after the fall of night on the tenth. Our prayers over that extended period have great power. They can nullify the accusations of failure brought by the accuser (*mekatreg*), penned by our own hands.

But the claims of the accuser are caustic. They have the potential to make us lose heart. Moreover, the attacks come constantly, throughout the Day of Atonement. The accuser seeks to wear us down, to make us cease our prayers for forgiveness, our declarations of contrition, our commitment to change.

Levi Yitzhak offers a brief but powerful response: we can negate the accuser; we can stop the stopper. By doing just what the accuser seeks to prevent, we overcome him and accomplish our goal.

This lesson also addresses the somewhat confusing language of this verse. While the JPS translation above is correct, does *tishbetu* really mean "observe"? Shouldn't there be some other way to express what it means? Something like "cease on the day of your cessation"? This is further supported by the start of the verse: "It shall be a sabbath of complete rest." We already know that it is a sabbath; therefore, the end of the verse must mean something different. Levi Yitzhak's play with this odd phrase unpacks the verse in a remarkable and innovative manner, opening up new meanings and possibilities for our observance of Yom Kippur.

Questions for Reflection

1. What do you find to be the most distracting aspect of Yom Kippur? How do you deal with it? Has it changed over time? When, how, why?

2. What do you do to revive your spirits and reconnect with the prayers on Yom Kippur?

3. What do you find to be the most significant impediments to your ongoing spiritual practice?

Taking It into Your Life

The last question above is key to the lesson we might take from this text. All of spiritual practice is to wake up, to know the truth of the moment, the truth of our experience, and so become present to and aware of God. There is a classical list of hindrances that impede our sustained engagement in our practices: aversion, craving, torpor, restlessness, and doubt.

So, for example, when we sit to meditate, we may find ourselves experiencing negative feelings toward our practice. We might find that our bodies ache. Or we may find excuses not to meditate at all. This would be "aversion."

Or we may engage in meditation with an acquisitive mind—looking to have this experience or that, to repeat what we have felt before or to try to attain what we've read in books. We come to our meditation with expectations of outcomes, looking for it to "produce" something. This would be "craving" or "desire."

Or we may find that we fall asleep. Our bodies are sluggish, our minds cloudy. This would be "torpor."

Or we find that we are unable to sit still. Our minds jump from thought to thought, from image to image. We scratch itches, adjust our posture, look at the clock, get a drink. This would be "restlessness."

Or we sit down and sense that nothing new is happening. We wonder if it is worth it. We imagine that we may not be cut out for meditation. We consider that perhaps some other practice might be better—like the one we heard our friend mention or that we saw in a magazine recently. As this runs through our mind and heart, we are not meditating. This would be "doubt."

Pay attention as you engage in your spiritual practice—meditation, prayer, yoga, study, mitzvot—to sense when (if ever) you experience any of these hindrances. You can call them *mekatregim*, accusers, detractors. As you notice them, you might seek to employ one of the traditional antidotes: identify what is pleasant in the practice to balance aversion; bring single-pointed attention to balance the distracting thoughts of craving; investigate with precision some aspect of your practice to awaken interest and balance torpor; extend the movements of practice—extending the breath or holding a pose longer—to calm restlessness; remain present throughout the whole of the movements of practice, sustaining awareness through the whole of a breath or pose to balance doubt.

In all, the fact that we experience hindrances in our practice is part of the practice. What we are called to do, as Levi Yitzhak says, is recognize when we are in danger of ceasing from our practice, letting go of our true fundamental intention, and then respond resolutely, appropriately, with joy and compassion, and go on.

Behar

> "[YHVH spoke to Moses on Mount Sinai:
> Speak to the Israelite people and say to
> them: When you enter the land that I assign
> to you,] the land shall observe a sabbath of
> YHVH" (Lev. 25:1–2).

The AR"I *z"l* taught regarding the verse, "Now, you **speak to the Israelite people and say**: Nevertheless, you must keep My Sabbaths, [for this is a sign between Me and you throughout the ages, that you may know that I *YHVH* have consecrated you]" (Exod. 31:13) (which is also reflected in the *Tur, Orach Chayyim* 281): When Israel were enslaved in Egypt, Moses asked of Pharaoh that the Israelites be given one day out of seven to rest from their labors, and he selected the Sabbath. When, later, they were commanded to observe Shabbat, Moses rejoiced at the portion he received, since he had—of his own consideration—identified this as a day of rest even before it was commanded.

This is the meaning of the verse in Exodus: "*Now*, you speak," since you, Moses, had earlier commanded them to rest on Shabbat. Further, that is the meaning of the phrase "keep My Sabbaths"—we should rest on Shabbat not because this would be rest from labor, but only because the Holy One commanded us to cease labor on Shabbat.

This also is the meaning of "**the land shall observe a sabbath of YHVH.**" It is common for people to plow a field one year and then to leave it alone the next so that it will produce well. Therefore, we have this direct instruction from God, "**the land shall observe a sabbath of YHVH**"—that in the year of release the land should rest, not because it will improve the quality of the land, but because it is "**a Sabbath of YHVH**," because of God's commandment.

FOR FURTHER THOUGHT

This is the only lesson in *Kedushat Levi* on the weekly portion *Behar*. When this circumstance arises, it does invite some speculation about why: paucity of challenging verses in the parashah; no previous teaching on which to rely, from which to draw, against which to comment; levels of complexity beyond the audience of this particular work; lack of access of the author or editor to original materials; nothing came to mind ... I do not know why but feel it is worth noting.

In this passage, Levi Yitzhak relies on some earlier material. The reference here to the writings of the AR"I *z"l* is to *Likkutei Torah* (*Ki Tissa*, s.v. *v'atah dabbeir*) where Luria investigates two aspects of Shabbat observance. Luria reads the verse from Exodus carefully and hears the plural "My Sabbaths" as suggesting two levels of Shabbat: one is our observance of the mitvzot in their concrete practices; the other is observing Shabbat as a spiritual practice, connecting male and female, *Tiferet* and *Malkhut* (the blessed Holy One and the *Shekhinah*), etc. He draws the link between these "two Sabbaths" and the emergence of Shabbat as an Israelite/Jewish institution. First Moses established a day of rest for the people, then God decreed a day of spiritual rest for all creation.

The *Tur* (*Arba'ah Turim*, legal code of R. Ya'akov ben Asher, fourteenth century) antedates Luria, and so his comment may be the source for Luria's teaching. In particular, the *Tur* brings the midrash (essentially what we have in our text) as an explanation of the first line of the middle section of the Shabbat morning *Amidah* (*Kedushat hayom*): "Moses rejoiced in his lot, for You called him a faithful servant." We might think that it is solely in response to God having called Moses a "faithful servant" (Num. 12:7) that Moses rejoices, but R. Ya'akov has another thought. It is because God affirmed Moses's initiative in arguing for a day of rest.

This lesson echoes one we studied earlier, in *parashat Emor*. There are two aspects to Shabbat: it is a day of rest, of cessation from labor, of creative manipulation of creation; it is a day on which we acknowledge God as Creator, as sovereign, and the One source of order and justice. Shabbat is not only "for you" to rest and refresh yourselves. It is also the time on which we can come to acknowledge God, to know God, to rest in God. This extends beyond our personal inner space as well. The land, too, needs and deserves this rest. This serves as both a challenge and a reminder: do what you think makes sense for the good of people and the earth. But remember that there is another consideration: you must also do what God demands of you. Working to preserve the health of the land is not merely for your own self-preservation; it is for the sake of acknowledging God as the owner of the earth, its true master.

 # Questions for Reflection

1. How far should we go in applying "reason" to supporting our commitment to the commandments? Is reason or rational explanation the only rationale for observing the commandments? Can we, should we, change the commandments when the circumstances of the original reason no longer apply or when we find a reason to do something else? What other considerations—beyond what Levi Yitzhak offers—might guide us? What do you consider to be sufficient "spiritual" reasons to change or affirm commandments?

2. Arthur Waskow and others are actively trying to introduce the concept of Shabbat to the broader work world as a way of humanizing our twenty-first-century lives. There is a movement afoot to leave the national forests alone, to protect them from further logging. What does this lesson add to these—and similar—conversations? How will your communities respond to this argument? Is this a useful or persuasive "political" argument? That is, can you bring it to the public square, or is it for internal consumption only?

3. How do you hear God's voice commanding you to do or refrain from doing—especially if it is in concert with your own inclination to begin with (and here, think particularly mitzvah!)? Is it a gift to be commanded? Do you have a sense that what you intend and choose to do is correct because you sense God's commandment? How do you protect yourself from haughtiness: that you figured out what God wants? What if you are wrong, deluded, or self-serving in your intention? What might be the consequences? What tools do you have to check yourself and your inner inclination, to discern more precisely which of your actions are, indeed, God's commandments?

Taking It into Your Life

In the practice of spiritual direction, people work together to sense more profoundly, more directly how God is at work in their lives. When thinking about this practice, many people question the premise: What does it mean to say that God is "calling" you to do something, "moving" in you, "directing" you in a particular way? Isn't this a glorified way of justifying what you want to do anyway? Doesn't this risk devolving into dangerous fanaticism, where any act can be justified by saying, "God told me to do it"?

This lesson invites us to investigate more deeply how we might come to sense God's affirmation (or negation) of our actions. While Moses may have been unique in his relationship with God, we can still learn from his experience (as Levi Yitzhak does here). For the purposes of this exercise we will focus on a decision made in the past, seeking to sense how we might know whether it has truly been affirmed by God.

Settle yourself in a relaxed but attentive position. Bring your attention to your breath to establish a foundation of stability in your body and inner awareness. When you sense steadiness in your mind, allow thoughts of past experiences to arise in your consciousness. Without getting caught up in these memories, you may notice that one or another presents itself with greater clarity, with a stronger charge of interest. Allow this memory to become the focus of your attention. Reflect on the time and place in which it arose. Sense in your body what the feeling tones were when you were making the decisions that affected the outcome of this event. Let these sensations direct you to recollect the issues involved, the ways in which you weighed your options, determined your course of action.

Notice when your body registers tension in response to this memory and where it remains at ease. Note as well your emotional landscape as you rehearse this event. Which emotions are recollection of what you were feeling then, and which are your response to that event from your present perspective? As you look back on that event, how does it fit in your current life? How did it affect the course of your life? Would you have gotten to this stage, this state, without having passed through that event, or was it pivotal? Have you had to repair the outcome of that event, or did it lead to greater wholeness or healing?

As you reflect on this experience, consider how bodily and emotional sensations may be cues to when your actions are in line with the most beneficial, most compassionate, and most just intention. What awareness might have given you more courage or encouragement in the past for the good that you did? What awareness might have led to more caution or alternative actions in the past when you perceive mistakes? How might this awareness of your experience in the past help you seek out God's presence in the present, to sense more clearly how you might act and be more aligned with the divine will?

Bechukkotai

"If you walk in the way of My statutes and
keep My commandments and you fulfill
them" (Lev. 26:3).

Apparently we have some extra language here, since it could have simply
said, "If you keep My commandments, I will give you, etc." But, let us
look at this in light of what we read in the Talmud (Kiddushin 40a):
"The blessed Holy One ties good thoughts to deeds." That is, whatever
we think, taking on ourselves in thought to do some commandment,
the blessed Holy One ties it to deed, as if we had actually done it
in that moment. Taking it a step further, then, when we perform a
commandment honestly, without any self-interest, then it may well be
that we will be able to ascend to another, higher level and then to do
another commandment. And if we are able to do another commandment,
we will then be able to ascend to an even higher level. That is why the
tzaddik is called a "walker," since he goes from level to level. This is the
meaning of "one mitzvah draws another mitzvah after it" (Avot 4:2).

On this basis we can interpret this teaching (Niddah 73a):

It is taught in the House of Eliyahu (or, *Tanna deBei Eliyahu*
teaches): "Whoever learns [*shoneh*] laws [*halakhot*] each day is
assured to have a place in the world-to-come [*olam haba*], as it
says: 'His are the eternal routes [*halikhot olam lo*]' (Hab. 3:6). Do
not read *halikhot*, rather *halakhot*."

This refers to the tzaddik. That is why it uses the term *shoneh halakhot*
to speak of learning. The tzaddik changes (*shoneh*) his ways (*halikhotav*)
each day. Each day he goes from one level to another higher. In this he
is assured of a place in the world-to-come.

So, "**if you walk in the way of My statutes**," that is, if you cleave
to My *chukkim*, then you will become a "walker." "**And keep My
commandments**"—keep (i.e., observe, look out for, as in "his father took
note [*shamar*] of the matter"; Gen. 37:11): moreover, I say—if you "keep"
My commandments, if you even think of doing My commandments,

even though you have not yet done them, it will be as if "you had fulfilled them." That is, I will account it as you had done them, since the blessed Holy One ties good thoughts to deeds, which is the meaning of the phrase "**you fulfill them**."

FOR FURTHER THOUGHT

This Torah portion is filled with "blessings" when we fulfill God's commandments and curses when we do not. It can be terrifying. The possibility of failure in our lives is so great. When we pay attention to the potential outcomes of our behavior, we can indeed witness the "destruction" and "exile" that may come in their wake. Further, we are aware of the question, how will we ever do all that is expected, let alone avoid all that is proscribed? Yet, what a relief! Levi Yitzhak offers us instead this unusual and redemptive lesson. Rather than focusing on what we *have not done*, he focuses on what will come merely of our *positive intention*, not even the good that we might do. Here is a wonderful way out, and up.

The quotation from Kiddushin appears in a section having to do with the qualities of mitzvot and transgressions, about whether only the former or both "produce fruit" (yield outcomes in the future). In particular, the sequel to our quotation is: "Even if one [merely] thinks of performing a precept but is forcibly prevented, Scripture [and so, also, God] ascribes it to him as though he has performed it." So, it is important to develop clear-mindedness, to know truly what we intend, what our deepest intention is in the moment, so that it might be worthy of being sustained.

The image of being a "walker" is common in Hasidic literature. Based on earlier sources, our teacher and others read the following verse from the prophet Zechariah to distinguish between the human, Joshua, and the angels around him: "And the angel of *YHVH* charged Joshua as follows: 'Thus said *YHVH* of Hosts: If you walk in My paths and keep My charge, you in turn will rule My House and guard My courts, and I will permit you to move about [*mah'lekhim*] among these standing ones [*ha'omdim*]" (Zech. 3:6–7). The mystical reading is that Joshua is the walker (moves about) and the angels are the standers. This invites the claim that the spiritual life is (or should be) one of constant movement, rising and sometimes falling, to then rise again, always toward greater awareness of and attachment to God.

This trope is particularly useful to Levi Yitzhak in this lesson, as it makes possible a more literal reading of the opening verse "If you walk in the way of My statutes." It is not only a matter of following the laws; it is of participating in them such that they move us along our spiritual path. And this is a matter of clarifying our intention and our inner movement in keeping the commandments.

The particular interpretation of "keep" (*timshmeru*) that Levi Yitzhak introduces (and which appears frequently in Hasidic texts) is based on the meaning of the verb *sh-m-r* as it appears in Gen. 37:11. There, Jacob observes the interaction among his sons, noting the hatred that is growing between the older ones and Joseph, and the verb there suggests "noting, keeping awareness of." That is what we are invited to do, as well: keep our awareness clear, open, and awake to what is arising and to our deepest intention, that it might be worthy of being enacted.

Questions for Reflection

1. Levi Yitzhak introduces an additional qualification to performing an acceptable mitzvah: that it be performed without any *peniyah*—self-interest, self-consciousness, or ulterior motive. Why is this qualification necessary to move one further along on the spiritual path? What thoughts or feelings might you identify as *peniyah*?

2. I have moved along my own spiritual path, over the years, buoyed by Franz Rosenzweig's idea of "not yet": I accept that there are commandments out there waiting for me yet to perform, but I have "not yet" been able to honestly take them on. Does this fit with Levi Yitzhak's teaching? What happens when "not yet" actually becomes "never"? How do we keep our intention alive, so that we do keep moving?

3. Do you want always to be moving? Can there never be time to reflect, to rejoice in just being where we are for the moment? How will we even know where we are if we don't stop to observe? Could this be what Levi Yitzhak meant to suggest when he quoted Gen. 37:11? How do you reconcile these two needs?

Taking It into Your Life

A contemporary development in sports training is the practice of visualization. That is, before engaging in the particular event (e.g., field events like high jump, shot put, etc.), the athlete runs through the steps that she had practiced in training, envisioning each element, recalling the physical sensation of the act. Further, when viewing internally the earlier practice, the athlete envisions as well her current situation. She sees herself in the stadium, taking her place for the event. In her mind's eye she actually performs the act, not only as she had done in practice, but also as she would do so now, attaining the fullest expression of her performance. She sees her success.

This may be similar to what Levi Yitzhak is inviting us to do in our spiritual (and Jewish) lives. Just like training for an event, engaging in Jewish practices is repetitive. It may come to feel that it is all just doing the same thing over and over again. Instead, we are invited to pause before engaging in the activity and to envision our performance. We can see ourselves doing the act, embodying it fully. Like the athlete, we can see ourselves attaining the fullest expression of that act. Through this inner preparation, we generate the energy by which we may fulfill the act in a manner that is more satisfying, more fulfilling, and different each time we do it, even if it is the "same thing over and over again."

This form of preparation can also be employed to help us move from intention to action. Long before we actually succeed in taking on a new practice, or long before we actually do some ritual, we can prepare for it internally. Seeing ourselves doing it, sensing it in our bodies, feeling the outcome of having fulfilled our intention, we build energy to connect with our intention and fulfill it in action. In this manner, we grow in capacity and awareness. We become walkers, moving and growing in our spiritual lives.

"I will grant your rains in their season,
[so that the earth shall yield its produce
and the trees of the field their fruit]"
(Lev. 26:4).

Scripture brought up the matter of reward for doing the mitzvot (cf. Lev. 25:18ff.), and we have to deal with it here as well. It is a problem, because we know that "there is no reward for fulfilling the mitzvot in this world" (Kiddushin 39b).

We can explain this with the teaching in Avot (4:2): "The reward for doing a mitzvah is doing a mitzvah." Surely there is no reward in this world for doing the mitzvot. But the reward for doing a mitzvah is that it draws an opportunity to do another mitzvah in its wake. That is the sense of the verse "**I will grant your rains in their season**" (in response to your proper behavior), and due to the rains, the world will be blessed. From its abundant produce you then will be able to give *tzedakah*. In this manner, we see that the reward for doing a mitzvah is doing another mitzvah, for one mitzvah brings another in its wake.

FOR FURTHER THOUGHT

It is not clear in the opening sentence what Levi Yitzhak is actually referring to. I have pointed to the verses in the previous chapter, because in *Kedushat Levi* we read, "since *they* have spoken about the reward for a mitzvah." If Levi Yitzhak had intended to refer to his own writing, he could easily have said (as he does elsewhere), "as *we* have spoken." Yet, it does also seem as if this short lesson carries forward the theme of the first lesson in this parashah relating to how one mitzvah brings another in its wake.

In the previous lesson, one mitzvah following another is the dynamic that energizes the ongoing spiritual movement of the tzaddik. Here, however, Levi Yitzhak expands his view to include everyone. This is hidden somewhat in the translation, in the last phrase of the next-to-last sentence. There he actually says, "From its produce *each and every one of you* will be able to give *tzedakah*." Doing mitzvot generates a dynamic by which everyone—at least in potential—can reap the reward of doing more mitzvot.

Because Levi Yitzhak—following Rabbinic precedent and his own predilections—wishes to negate any material reward in this world, he has to grapple with and interpret our verse, which suggests that abundance will follow from observing the commandments. Instead he says that the rain will simply be rain. It will fulfill its natural role, nurturing vegetation and bringing abundance. Whatever blessing may come from this will be in how we use it. When we see the fullness of the world as a resource not for our own benefit or enrichment, but as an opportunity to perform a mitzvah, the source of *tzedakah*, to be used for the benefit of those in need, we will be truly blessed. There is no greater reward.

Questions for Reflection

1. Are you satisfied with a spiritual system that does not offer reward in this world? Do you believe in a world-to-come in which you will receive a reward? If so, how do you perceive this?

2. Are you satisfied with a spiritual system that claims that "virtue is its own reward"? Is that enough for you? Why or why not?

3. What is your experience of "doing a mitzvah brings another mitzvah in its wake"? How does this work?

Taking It into Your Life

In this lesson we learn that the fruitfulness of nature is for the sake of doing mitzvot. We might have known this from considering what is required for us to observe various rituals: we need wine or bread on which to acknowledge the holiness of Shabbat through reciting *Kiddush*; we need an *etrog* and *lulav* to celebrate Sukkot; we cannot fashion tefillin without leather, and we cannot make a Torah without parchment.

But Levi Yitzhak teaches something much more profound, since he does not focus on ritual objects or celebrations. Rather, he sees the response of nature—its dependability, its interconnectedness—as the impetus for us to live engaged, ethical lives. The Torah seems to suggest that the response of nature to our doing mitzvot is a reward of wealth. We will prosper as our crops thrive; faithfulness to God brings material well-being. Levi Yitzhak is not happy with that economy. Material well-being may be nice and is surely necessary for us to live at all. Yet, once that is assured, the fecundity of nature is solely so that we can do mitzvot for the sake of others. Whatever comes into our possession, then, is not for our personal enjoyment, but so that we might do more mitzvot with it.

Hasidic literature is rife with stories of tzaddikim who would give away whatever money might come their way (even to the detriment of their own families). It is hard to imagine them as true models; their behavior seems exaggerated. But, it might be worth stopping to consider again and take their lesson to heart. What do we truly "need" to live? How do we know when we have "extra" wealth? How can we sense when our charitable giving is not a matter of "giving money away" but passing it along?

Consider experimenting with one of these practices:

Put whatever loose change is in your pocket or purse at the end of the day aside for *tzedakah*; notice if you begin to strategize how to maximize or minimize the amount of change you carry.

Build into your monthly charge-card expenses regular donations to charities you favor. What happens to your budget when these expenses just "show up" without a specific action each month?

Notice how the food you purchase gets used. How much gets consumed, thrown away, or ignored? What is your normal diet like, and what are the "extras" that appear but do not truly satisfy or, after the first taste, languish and get stale?

Consider your relationship to your yard (if you have one). How much attention (money, resources, effort) goes into making it look good? What are the consequences (environmental, social, communal) of making it so? How might this slice of "nature" be made a source of *tzedakah*?

Further, consider what Levi Yitzhak is asking of us: recognize the world as God's, offered to us so that we might live, and so that—now living—we might do more mitzvot, we might do *tzedakah*. What do you sense to be the implications of this perspective in terms of how we use the world and its resources? How shall we respond to inequity in distribution of food, water, energy, and natural resources? How can we prepare for the potential dislocations that may come about due to global warming and other changes? What actions can we take so that mitzvot and *tzedakah* will flow from them and from us?

The Book of
Numbers

Bemidbar

"As *YHVH* commanded Moses. And he
recorded them in the wilderness of Sinai"
(Num. 1:19).

Note that it would have made more sense to say, "He recorded them in
the wilderness of Sinai as *YHVH* commanded Moses."

Here's how we can understand this: The Holy One gave the Torah
to Israel, and the soul of Israel is the body of the Torah. The Jewish
people are the six hundred thousand letters of the Torah; thus Israel
is the Torah, since each and every Jew is one letter of the Torah. This
tells us that when Moses counted the Israelites, he was actually learning
Torah.

This is, then, how we should understand our verse, "**as** [*ka'asher*]
YHVH commanded Moses": that is, all of the commands of the
Torah "that [*asher*] *YHVH* had commanded Moses" (Num. 1:54) are
themselves the result of Moses counting the Israelites.

This, in turn, explains what comes later: "Do not on any account
enroll the tribe of Levi or take a census of them with the Israelites"
(Num. 1:49). The Israelites represent the Written Torah, and the tribe
of Levi represents the Oral Torah. That is why "they were recorded by
YHVH" (*al pi YHVH*; 4:49).

FOR FURTHER THOUGHT

There certainly are problems with this verse, grammatically, syntac-
tically, and otherwise. Set apart on its own, it seems to begin in the
middle, out of order. And so notes Levi Yitzhak. Indeed, he brings
Num. 1:54 in contrast to this verse, to heighten the seeming problem
in the structure of our verse. The commentator Hizkuni (R. Heze-
kiah ben Manoah, France, thirteenth century) suggests that the first
phrase ("as *YHVH* commanded") refers backward, to the previous
verse, where Moses and Aaron gather the people, and the second

phrase was only to identify the location of this census. Alternatively, we might suggest that in a very terse manner this verse frames the opening of the book of Numbers. The first verse of the book says, "On the first day of the second month, in the second year following the exodus from the land of Egypt, *YHVH* spoke to Moses in the wilderness of Sinai." Our verse picks up on God's command to take a census, and then notes the place—in the same order as the first.

For all this, Levi Yitzhak sees another lesson in this inverted verse. What is the significance of a census anyway? How does that advance Torah? It cannot be merely a way of finding out how many Israelites there were—God would certainly know this. So, there must be something more. Levi Yitzhak turns to the tradition that the number of Israelites was equal to the number of letters in the Torah. We know that God gave the commandments (and all of the Torah) to Israel, and there must be a relationship between the words that God spoke to Moses and the Israelites he led. In numbering the Israelites, Moses was "reading" Torah, learning more deeply the nature of the relationship between God and Israel. We would then read our verse, "That which God commanded Moses, he recorded by numbering the Israelites in the wilderness of Sinai."

This is not only a solution to a difficult passage in the Torah. It is also a message to Levi Yitzhak's students: you, too, are included in this Torah. It is not simply a record of past events. Just as Moses connected each individual to the Torah so that they found their root in one letter there, so we can find our place in Torah. Connecting to the letters of Torah, we too can learn what God is commanding us now, how we are to live today.

 ## Questions for Reflection

1. There is a custom to point at the Torah scroll when it is lifted, symbolically pointing to one's own letter in the Torah. Beyond this, how do you experience your connection to Torah on a soul level? How do you read yourself in Torah?

2. Is there any way in which "counting" your community—*chavurah*, congregation, family—is a way of "learning Torah" for you? Do you "read" Torah by "reading" your community? How might this be a way in which we can learn Torah today? When does this not work, if at all?

3. What commandments can you learn from counting your community? Can you draw an analogy between your community (or your community as part of the larger Jewish people) and the Written Torah? What—or who—embodies the process that will constitute and produce the Oral Torah in this case?

Taking It into Your Life

The image of all Jews having a letter in the Torah is powerful, and the collectivity of the Jewish people "spelling out" the words of Torah even more so. Levi Yitzhak distinguishes between the body of the Israelites and the Levites as the distinction between the Written Torah and the Oral Torah. It is challenging to work with this image: each of us has a particular, fixed role in spelling out the Torah, yet we also, in our individual lives, as we live out our Jewish lives, interpret Torah, extending it. In that sense, we are all part of the Oral Torah as well.

We might investigate, then, finding ourselves in the Torah, while also making Torah ourselves. As the Hasidic teachers would regularly teach, the Torah cannot be merely stories of what happened in the past; it must relate to what is happening to us now; it must give instructions for how we are to experience God directly in our very lives. It may well be that our capacity to find ourselves in Torah makes it possible for us to make ourselves Torah.

Make a point of reading thoroughly through the Torah portion. As you do, return over and over to the question "Where am I in this story?" Are you being addressed as Moses or Aaron? Do you sense an affinity with one of the tribes? Where do you feel you are encamped relative to the Tabernacle? Will you march first or last in the order of tribes—and why? Do you want to "bring up the rear" to gather and protect the strays, returning lost property to its owners? Do you want to go first, to see most clearly the movement of the cloud directing your travels each day? Do you want to be in the middle, surrounded by friends and family, secure in their company, even when your journey seems confusing, even if you feel lost?

Are you one of the Levites? Are you one who is "formally assigned" (*netunim*; Num. 3:9) to serving God and the people? Do you want to be assigned to your daily tasks, so that you will do them correctly and so also safely? How would it feel to be devoted to service? Do you find when engaging with your work (the holy) that there is danger as well as excitement? What would it be like to be the director of the Tabernacle, assigning all the Levites to their tasks? What would it be like to know where everyone else fit in making for holiness?

These sorts of questions may help bring the Torah to life in yourself. When you begin to feel your deep association with what is happening in the portion, you may also sense how your daily affairs are affected by this awareness. And you will also see how your actions interpret and extend the Torah out into the world. Your life will become Torah.

Naso

"YHVH spoke to Moses: Speak to Aaron and
his sons: Thus shall you bless the people of
Israel. Say to them" (Num. 6:22–23).

This is how it works: the Baal Shem Tov used to wake people up with
the verse "*YHVH* is your shadow" (Ps. 121:5), which is to say, just as
the shadow does precisely what the person does, so does the blessed
Creator (as it were) do just as we do. Therefore, we have to do mitzvot
and give *tzedakah* and have compassion on the poor in order that the
blessed Creator will express goodness toward us as well.

Now, this dynamic is called "**thus**" (*ko*)—since the meaning of *ko* is
"thus," that is, just as one does, so too does the blessed Creator do as well.

It is well known that the blessed Creator desires to do good for His
people Israel, for "more than the calf desires to suck, the cow wants
to suckle" (Pesachim 112a). Therefore, when we stand to pray before
the blessed Creator, reciting the *Shemoneh Esreih* or any other prayers
of supplication, we have to be careful to pray only so that the blessed
Creator will derive delight from our prayers. This is similar to the
mishnah (Avot 2:8): "If you have learned a great deal of Torah, don't
hold it as your goodness, since it was for this purpose that you were
created." That is, everything we do should only be for the sake of
delighting the Creator.

It is also well known that when we pray only for ourselves, we are
in the position of a recipient. When we want to receive something, we
hold out our hands with the backs downward and the palms upward.
But when we pray only so that the blessed Creator will have delight
from our prayers, we are in the position of one who provides, since (as
it were) we are providing (delight) for the blessed Creator. And one
who provides for another holds his hands with the backs upward and
the palms downward.

Now, the Priestly Blessing is recited with hands raised, that is, with
the backs upward and the palms down, toward their faces, just like

one who desires to provide for another. This is the sense of our verse, **"Thus [*ko*] shall you bless the people of Israel"**—you shall bless the people of Israel so that the blessed Creator will have delight from your act. In this way, you will (as it were) provide for the blessed Creator, following which the blessed Creator will provide every good thing and blessing for Israel. This is what we taught above regarding the term *ko*: just as Israel does, so too does the blessed Creator (as it were), providing all good things and blessings, life, and peace. Amen.

FOR FURTHER THOUGHT

The starting point for this lesson is the section of the Torah known as the Priestly Blessing. It was part of the daily service in the Temple in antiquity and remains a part of traditional (primarily Orthodox) practice today. It is recited daily in services in Jerusalem and on the three pilgrimage festivals, Rosh Hashanah, and Yom Kippur outside of Israel. While this passage is part of all statutory services, its dramatic recitation takes place during the additional (*Musaf*) service, before the final blessing of peace (*Sim Shalom*). As the *Musaf* prayer is repeated by the reader/cantor, the *kohanim* (those of priestly descent) and *levi'im* (Levites) retire from the sanctuary. The Levites wash the hands of the priests, and the priests remove their shoes. They then return to the sanctuary, where the priests move up the bimah to stand in front of the ark. When the reader comes to this part of the service, the rabbi or some other leader (and, in some congregations, the congregants themselves) calls upon the priests to bless the people. They then recite a blessing, acknowledging God as the One who "sanctified us with the sanctity of Aaron, and who commanded us to bless His people Israel with love." Facing the congregation with their tallit over their heads, draped before their bodies on their extended arms, hiding their faces, they then recite these three verses word-by-word, led by the rabbi or other leader. At the end of each verse the congregation responds, "Amen." Levi Yitzhak has this image in mind when he talks about the priests having their hands with the backs up and the palms down.

Being a priest who blesses the people is challenging. Despite God's clarification "And I will bless them" (Num. 6:27), there is the risk the priest will claim that role. The ego will do anything to build itself up. Moreover, being the one who blesses others may signify that we are not in need of blessing. Levi Yitzhak wants to turn this around, reminding the priest that God is the source of blessing, and we all benefit from it. Once again we meet the Besht's teaching on "God is your shadow": what we do causes our shadow, God, to do as well. Our behavior affects divine behavior. Levi Yitzhak points to the small word *ko* (thus) that appears in the introduction to the Priestly Blessing as the defining term. "Thus shall you bless them": by doing good, by blessing others, by seeking to bring delight to God, you will bring blessing to yourself. Blessing comes from concern for others.

This is such a simple image, so inviting. Yet, it is also a great challenge. Every movement, each limb, can bring blessing or its opposite. We are challenged to watch not only our intentions but also our every action. Happily, Levi Yitzhak helps us out, reminding us that we can, indeed, bring our intentions and actions into common purpose and so bring blessing for ourselves, but particularly for others.

Questions for Reflection

1. Levi Yitzhak begins by focusing our attention on our actions, particularly that we should "do mitzvot and give *tzedakah* and have compassion on the poor." But the rest of the teaching has to do with the Priestly Blessing. What is the connection? What do those first actions have in common with the Priestly Blessing?

2. The description of how we hold our hands—what positions us as recipient and what as provider—seems sort of mechanistic. Yet, Levi Yitzhak does not seem to mean this only symbolically. Do you have a sense of how this works? Have you had an experience in which you felt—physically—the flow of energy to you or from you according to how you held your hands? When you meditate, pray, or recite the Blessing after Meals (*Birkat Hamazon*), do you think about how you are holding your hands— to be recipient or provider?

3. The Talmud (Baba Kamma 92a) teaches, "One who prays for his fellow and needs the same blessing will be answered first." Is there some relation between this teaching and our lesson? The Talmud suggests that our needs are answered first because we behave in an "other-centered" manner, putting aside our needs for the sake of others. Is seeking to bring delight to the Holy One through our prayers the same as praying

for someone else's well-being (seeking compassion for them, as the Talmud literally says)? If so, is delight what we need in turn? Are "all good things and blessings, life, and peace" the equivalent of God's delight? Does God need delight as much as we need these blessings? How?

Taking It into Your Life

This teaching specifically mentions the *Shemoneh Esreih* (the silent, standing prayer, or *Amidah*), with its specific requests and supplications of God. This is suggestive. It invites us to consider how we understand our prayers of petition. In particular, when we pray for our specific concerns—for our health or that of others, to ease the suffering of conflict, or simply for the welfare of loved ones—what are we asking of God? What is our intention? What is our expectation?

The answers to these questions will be multifaceted. Surely, we are expressing our true desire: may my loved one be healed, may my friend be free of suffering, may my community be safe. In a sense, we are asking that God pay attention to our needs and desires. Yet, more than that, when we express these prayers, we want God to fulfill our prayers and bring these outcomes to pass.

In the moment of our own pain, we call out to God. We see suffering in others, we feel our own suffering, and we want it to end. There is nothing wrong with that. We know that there is nothing separate from God and that therefore illness and healing are in God's being. It is in God that the desired healing also will take place. So we pray to God. Our hope is that what we want will come to pass.

But do we expect that our prayers will bring it about, will force God to do as we request? We know that doctors, medicine, time, and luck bring about healing. We know that attention, company, and interventions can ease conflict. We know that safety comes from diligence and interconnectedness. None of those activities take place outside of God. They are all, also, sustained by God.

When we speak our prayers of petition, they come out as requests. Their underlying meaning, however, is the expression of awareness of the truth: all is not in our hands. There is much that we—and others—can do. But we are not fully in control. We sense in ourselves how much we depend on others and so, in turn, how others depend on us. In putting our feelings into words, we help make clear our intention: to be one who heals, as well as one who brings healing.

We remind ourselves that as hard as we will work to ease the suffering of others (and ourselves), we must not do so while also in contention with that same suffering and its causes. We raise our awareness from our limited, personal concerns, placing them in a larger perspective. In turning to God, we join God in the whole process of life and death, of health and illness. Even before any result may come about, raising our consciousness in this manner helps us connect with God and know God's true desire for the good of all, for the end of suffering, for the end of conflict. We delight in that knowledge. We rejoice at knowing God's ways. Our prayers of petition take on the quality of praise, honor, and joy—even in the presence of our ongoing pain.

Perhaps, in this way, our prayers of supplication are for God's sake, as God delights in our company, in being known by us, in our striving to be like God.

> Another interpretation of "[Speak to Aaron and his sons:] Thus shall you bless the people of Israel. Say to them: … Thus they shall place My name on the people of Israel, and I will bless them" (Num. 6:23, 6:27).

From this we derive the rule that the priests have to say the words of blessing out loud, so that the people can hear them. Hearing the letters of the words the priests pronounce will have an impact on the people. The letters will then light up before them, and in this way they will be blessed.

This is the sense of the verse: "**Thus shall you bless … *Say to them***": you must speak, articulating the letters. It is not sufficient to seek their good through blessing them in thought; it must be through articulating the words and letters of the blessing. That is the sense of "**They shall place My name on the people of Israel, and I will bless them**": that is, God will bless them.

FOR FURTHER THOUGHT

Levi Yitzhak deals with two difficulties in this text: why does verse 23 add the seeming redundancy "say to them," and to whom does the pronoun "them" refer at the end of verse 27?

The Rabbis addressed the latter question directly in an early midrash (*Sifrei Bemidbar, Naso* 43):

Why does the passage end with the words "And I will bless them"? Because you might think that since it says at the start "Thus shall you bless the people of Israel" that the blessing applies only to Jews. But, might the blessing apply to converts, women, and slaves? Scripture tells us, "I will bless them" (too).

Why does the passage end with the words "And I will bless them"? So that the Jews will not think that their blessings are dependent on the priests, Scripture tells us, "*I* will bless them."

And so that the priests will not say to themselves, "We will bless Israel," Scripture tells us, "*I* will bless them." I will bless the Jewish people.

So we know that it is God who will bless the people. What has that to do with how the priests speak to them? It cannot merely be that the priests pronounce certain words in a certain formula; that would be magic. There must be something else going on. Levi Yitzhak brings the key Hasidic focus on the letters of Creation, the letters of human speech that echo God's creative speech. When we say words with intention, we activate the building blocks of Creation. We touch the energy that enlivens and sustains all things. Thus, when the priests pronounce the blessings with full intent, they project the letters out onto the listening people. The people take the letters in, which then transfer their energy to the people. The letters are absorbed and create an impression in them. The people sense the presence of the divine energy in them, generated by the letters of the blessing. That energy manifests as light, shining internally, directed to the core, the soul, where God and humans intersect.

 ## Questions for Reflection

1. What is your intention when you bless others? How will you feel if your blessing does not come to pass?

2. How do you know when your blessing is in line with the most propitious and correct unfolding for the other person? How do you know that is your intention?

3. Have you ever experienced being blessed as being enlightened, having the letters of Torah making an impression in you—your heart or soul? When or how?

Taking It into Your Life

Levi Yitzhak is quite clear: it is not sufficient to think thoughts of blessing. For the words to be effective, they have to be spoken.

Investigate your own experience of thought and speech. Pay attention to the thoughts that pass through your mind. Notice which thoughts you would be willing to put into speech and which you would not. What is the difference between them? Why do the thoughts that should go unspoken arise in you? Where do they come from? What do they mean?

Notice in particular which thoughts of blessing arise in you. Which of those thoughts need to be expressed, and which can remain as thoughts? Why?

When we have spoken about loving-kindness practice, we have noted that the first step is the need to bring awareness of loving-kindness to our own suffering, to our own lives. But we often also witness situations where we would want to express loving-kindness for those affected. We wish them well; we want only the best for them; we want them to feel safe, contented, strong, have a sense of well-being. Do we need to articulate this "prayer" out loud for it to be effective? Is the awareness of our desire for their well-being the core of our prayer? Is it our desire that they know we care for them? Is it our expectation that our prayer will bring them well-being?

When we face a loved one and wish to express our love and concern for them, is it sufficient to think thoughts, or do we have to express our feelings in words? What is it about the intimate relationship that requires speech?

How might we learn from Levi Yitzhak about the power of speech, as well as the power of silence?

Beha'alotekha

"Now, the manna was like coriander seed,
[and in color it was like bdellium]"
(Num. 11:7).

When a person gives *tzedakah*, he provides for/affects the poor person. Yet the Sages also taught, "More than the householder does for the poor person [does the poor person do for the householder]" (Lev. R. 34:8). If this is the case, then the poor person also provides for the householder. There really is no difference in the fact that the householder provides for the poor something tangible, and the poor provides something spiritual for the householder (that is, the Holy One gives him *olam haba*/the world-to-come, holiness and purity).

This is how it was with the manna, too. The manna provided for the Israelites, who ate it, since it had some physical substantiality; and the Israelites provided something spiritual in the manna, as the Sages taught that anything that they wished to taste in the manna they would taste (Yoma 75a). In this sense, the manna received from them something spiritual, that is, the flavor that they desired to taste.

Now *gad* (coriander) is an acronym for *gomel dalim* (helps the poor) (Shabbat 104a). This then helps us to understand what the Torah means when it says "**the manna was like coriander seed**" (*zera gad*): the manna had a quality like one who is *gomel dalim*, where one side provides something tangible and the other provides something spiritual in return. This is how it was with the manna. The manna provided something physically sustaining for the Israelites, and the Israelites in turn provided it with something spiritual. This is the meaning of *zera gad*: like the "sowing" (*zeri'ah*) of *gomel dalim*, since we know that "sowing" is *tzedakah*, as the Sages taught on the verse, "Sow *tzedakah* for yourselves" (Hosea 10:12; see Baba Kamma 17a).

FOR FURTHER THOUGHT

What an interesting turn of thought. We might have expected Levi Yitzhak to suggest that the spiritual reciprocation that the Israelites provided was giving delight to their Creator, in thanks for the life-giving wonder of the manna. But that would have been difficult on two grounds: it would have been gratitude for receiving something (and the opposite of "not in order to receive a reward") and the Israelites were not all that grateful for the manna, in the end. But here the consumption of the manna did offer something back, something reciprocal to the manna: the flavor that the Israelites "tasted" back into it.

This teaching is grounded in the idea of the cyclical and reciprocal nature of spiritual life. That is, initially everything derives from God and depends on God's initiative (*itaruta dele'eila*—arousal from above). But, ultimately, the greater expression of spiritual awareness and action is when we initiate action and awareness (*itaruta deletata*—arousal from below). God may give to us, but we also give to God by receiving God's goodness and then responding in gratitude and prayer.

It is worthwhile reading the whole of Lev. R. 34:8, but here is the relevant section for our lesson:

> R. Kohen and R. Yehoshua son of R. Shimon said in the name of R. Levi: In the past when a man did a mitzvah the prophet used to record it, but now if a man does a mitzvah who records it? Elijah and the King Messiah, and the blessed Holy One signs for them. This is as Scripture says: "In this vein have those who revere YHVH been talking to one another. YHVH has heard and noted it, [and a scroll of remembrance has been written at His behest concerning those who revere YHVH and esteem His name]" (Mal. 3:16).
>
> R. Yehoshua taught: The poor man does more for the householder than the latter does for him, as evidenced by the fact that Ruth says to Naomi: "[Her mother-in-law asked her, 'Where did you glean today? Where did you work? Blessed be he who took such generous notice of you!' So she told her mother-in-law whom she had worked with, saying,] 'The name of the man for whom I acted [*asher asiti*] today is Boaz'" (Ruth 2:19). It is not written, "Who did for me" but "For whom I acted" (*asher asiti*), by which Ruth

intimated to Naomi: I have done many services and favors with him today for the morsel that he gave me.

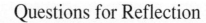

Questions for Reflection

1. In our lesson, who or what is the "householder" when it comes to the manna (i.e., God, the Israelites, or the manna)? Who or what receives the benefit of the spiritual blessing? How might this carry over into the other ways we are blessed in our lives—that is, who is the "householder" then? How do you feel about always being in the position of the *dal* (poor)? Does it help you to think that you can actually do something in return for the One who provides for you?

2. Levi Yitzhak tells us that the provider (*mashpia*) is also a recipient (*mekabbeil*). How do you understand that the *mashpia* is also a *mekabbeil*? Do you feel better, more satisfied, more whole doing for another (being provider) or receiving the benefit from the other (as *mekabbeil*)? Is being *mashpia* or *mekabbeil* a matter of intention or action? When someone comes to comfort you, can you receive their expression wholeheartedly, without hiding your discomfort as a *mekabbeil*? How well do they receive your "blessing," your willing receipt of their comfort? Can you do one without the other?

3. Is the reciprocal benefit that the poor person provides for the one who gives *tzedakah* "real"? Does it matter, in the end, that the Israelites "thought" a flavor into the manna? Does the "reality" of our action depend on our intention? If we apply Levi Yitzhak's teaching to our relationship with and actions in the world, how might this change the way we experience our lives, even if it is not "real"? Might it change how we behave? How?

Taking It into Your Life

What do you make of the "spiritual" quotient we provide to the manna? Does this open up a new realm of "the spiritual," a different way of thinking about it? Might this teaching encourage you to pay more attention to how you eat?

During your meals, set aside some time to practice tasting your food. Start with a clean palate, so that there is no other taste in your mouth. Begin by smelling your food. Notice where you perceive the aroma and when. How close does it have to be to your nose for you to smell it? Do you smell different tones of aroma at different distances?

What is your reaction to smelling the food? What happens in your body when you aroma something you like? What happens emotionally?

When you place the food in your mouth, do not begin to chew immediately. Let the food rest on your tongue. Notice where you taste different aspects of the food, where different parts of flavor (sweet, sour, bitter, hotness, etc.) are sensed. Notice texture and temperature.

Begin to chew, slowly. Notice how the food breaks apart and where it moves in your mouth. Do not rush to swallow, but notice the changes in texture, temperature, and flavor as you chew and as the food moves in your mouth.

Notice as well how you respond to the taste of the food, where you register it in your body. What is the nature of aroma and flavor? How dependent is it on your attention? How do you contribute to the experience of the food, giving to it as much as it gives you?

"[And Joshua son of Nun, Moses's
attendant from his youth, spoke up]
and said, 'My lord Moses, restrain them!'
But Moses said to him, ['Are you
wrought up on my account?] Would that
all *YHVH*'s people were prophets, [that
YHVH put His spirit upon them!']"
(Num. 11:28–29).

We hold that tzaddikim are able to annul negative decrees and to change the unfavorable to the good. But, in truth, this is only the case so long as the decree has not been written by the prophet. If, however, the prophecy has already been written down, it is impossible to annul it. Otherwise, people would accuse the prophet of having given false prophecy and having written it down.

This creates a problem for us: how is it possible, then, to pray for annulment of the travails of the time of the Messiah that are written in the books of the prophets? There is a way to deal with this, based on Rambam's writings. He argues that we do not know with certainty from the prophets how it will be before the coming of the Messiah (may it be soon and in our days). Now, since the travails of the Messiah are not known from the prophets, and the details are not given, we can pray to annul them.

If this is so, then what difference does it make? That is, if the travails of the Messiah are not written clearly in the prophets, we are able to request their annulment. And if the travails of the Messiah are indeed written about and hinted in the prophets, but we cannot now understand them, then only when the Messiah comes (may it be soon) will he explain the meaning of the prophets. But, even if the travails of the Messiah are written clearly in the prophets, when the Messiah arrives all Jews will attain the level of prophecy! Scripture confirms this, as it says: "[After that, I will pour out My spirit on all flesh;] your sons and daughters shall prophesy; [your old men shall dream dreams, and your young men shall see visions]" (Joel 3:1); "[No longer will they need to teach one another and say to one another, 'Heed *YHVH*';] for all of them will know Me, [from the least of them to the greatest, declares *YHVH*]" (Jer. 31:34). In that case we will be able to seek to annul the decrees. Once all Jews are prophets, there will be no concern that they will claim that the prophet prophesied falsely. They, too, will be prophets, and they will know that the prophet prophesied in truth, but they will also know that the tzaddikim of previous generations annulled the decree before the arrival of the Messiah.

So, Joshua said to Moses, "**Restrain them**," because they had prophesied, "Moses will die and Joshua will bring Israel into the Land" (Sanhedrin 17a). It would have been impossible to annul this [*something is missing here*] since it was written in the Torah. That is why Moses replied, "**Would that all *YHVH*'s people were prophets**." That is, when once all of the Jews will be prophets, they will then be able to annul this decree, even though it is written. Once all the Jews are prophets, they will understand that tzaddikim are able to annul decrees. Even if it is given to a prophet directly from God, tzaddikim are still able to annul it.

That is what the Sages intended in their teaching on the verse "[Hear, O Israel,] you are about to cross the Jordan" (Deut. 9:1): Moses opened an avenue for them to seek mercy for him from God so that he might enter the Land (Deut. R. 3:11), even though Moses himself had already declared, "For I must die [in this land; I shall not cross the Jordan. But you will cross and take possession of that good land]" (Deut. 4:22). Surely, the Israelites believed that Moses's prophecy was true. But Moses trusted that even if the Israelites had sought to annul the decree against Moses, they never would have doubted (heaven forbid) any of Moses's prophecies, for they all held that his prophecy was complete truth, even as they realized that the Jews, through their prayers, are able to annul the decree, turning it to the good.

FOR FURTHER THOUGHT

In this lesson, Levi Yitzhak weaves together a number of threads, all having to do with the power of speech in prayer, Torah, and prophecy. Intentional human speech shares some of the power of divine speech: it has effect; it changes the world. This is particularly true of these three forms of speech. Prophecy is the human expression of divine intent. When it issues from the mouth of the prophet, it has the power to transform hearts and bring about *teshuvah*, in which case the decree would not be enacted. However, if that change does not come about, and particularly if the prophecy is written down, then the decree exists independently of the prophet, and it must come about without fail.

Yet, the power of *teshuvah* is great. Even today, long after the prophecies of the travails before the coming of the Messiah, the power of prayer and the workings of the tzaddik have the capacity to annul and reverse negative decrees. The problem with this, however, is that in annulling the decrees through prayer or the intercession of the tzaddik, the possibility arises that people will think that the original prophetic decree was false and so all prophecy is untrustworthy. In the end, this would even undermine people's trust in the Torah itself. Yet, for Levi Yitzhak, the possibility must exist that the tzaddik can annul a heavenly decree, even if it has been written in the Bible. That is one of the primary roles of a tzaddik: to bring health, well-being, and mercy to his people through direct intervention above.

This passage in the Torah offers Levi Yitzhak an opportunity to reflect on the nature of prophecy and the intervention of the tzaddik or community through prayer. Eldad and Medad begin to prophesy in the camp, and Joshua implores Moses to stop them. He fears that their prophecy (not recorded in the Torah, but invented by the Rabbis) will be irreversible. Moses hints to him that he need not fear: tzaddikim may be able to annul it, as may the people through prayer. Moreover, when the people attain the level of prophecy themselves, they will understand the necessary and life-giving dynamic of prophecy and intervention.

Questions for Reflection

1. How do you relate to the prophecies regarding the coming of the Messiah? Does the fact that the Messiah has not come make you doubt the prophecies of a Messiah? Do you look forward to the coming of the Messiah? How does this figure in your spiritual life?

2. How do you understand Levi Yitzhak's claim that at the coming of the Messiah everyone will attain the spiritual level of prophecy? Is that something that you hope for or strive for personally? What qualities of prophecy would you want to attain?

3. Levi Yitzhak assumes that prophecy is not determinative, because it is subject to *teshuvah*, prayer, and the intervention of the tzaddik. Does it surprise you that he (and the Hasidic tradition) places the tzaddik higher than the prophet? What does it mean to you that outcomes are indeterminate, that prophecies can be changed?

Taking It into Your Life

Faith is a fundamental, and problematic, aspect of spiritual life. It is necessary to ground our efforts in practice. Faith is what sustains us during times of uncertainty, fatigue, listlessness, and confusion. Yet faith can also prevent us from seeing clearly in a given moment. Faced with new data, presented with unfamiliar circumstances, we may proceed on the basis of our faith without investigating further, without determining whether our faith is appropriate to the circumstances.

For faith to be both spiritually sustaining and alive to new circumstances suggests that it is most true and dependable when it is "verified faith." That is, faith is well grounded when we have investigated it to determine, through our own experience, that it is meaningful, dependable, and true. Because we work on knowing the foundations of this faith directly—even if we cannot "prove" that in which we have faith—it remains active, alive, and dynamic in our lives. We both rely on the faith we have developed and continue to investigate it, seeking to know its limits, its extent, its possible development and evolution. This faith would be the sort that Levi Yitzhak attributes to the people when they attain to prophecy: they would both trust the veracity of prophecy and know the power of *teshuvah* and prayer.

Spend some time checking in with your own inner experience of faith. When did it develop? How did that come about? What are the foundations of your faith, and how has it sustained you over time? Has your faith ever been shaken? When, how? How has your faith been strengthened? When, why? Have you ever found that your faith has kept you from seeing something important, because it conflicted with your faith? When, how? Has your faith ever prompted you to see something new, to grow even beyond the faith itself? When, how?

Shelach Lekha

An alternative interpretation: "Send for yourself [*l'kha*] [men] to scout the land of Canaan, which I am giving to the Israelite people; [send one man from each of their ancestral tribes, each one a chieftain among them]" (Num. 13:2).

Commentators before me have already commented at length on the significance of the word *l'kha*, "**for yourself.**" The intention of the blessed Creator was to send reverent and whole men whose sole intention would be to serve the Creator and certainly not to scout out (*latur*) the land of Israel in its physicality. Rather, the blessed Creator commanded Moses to send ahead servants of God who will be able to make an imprint there through their divine service, through study and prayer; to extend vitality and plenitude from the supernal land to the lower land, so that the land itself will desire that the children of Abraham, Isaac, and Jacob should come to dwell in it.

This is the meaning of *shelach* (usually translated as "send"): read this instead to mean "extend," as "Pharaoh's daughter sent her handmaid" (*vatishlach et amatah*) (Exod. 2:5; the Sages read "her handmaid/*amatah*" as "her limb/hand," imagining that Pharaoh's daughter extended her arm over the waters to reach Moses). That is, the men should expand their humanness, to attain the status of Moses. That, then, is the sense of the phrase "**send for yourself [men]**" (*shelach lekha anashim*): let them expand their humanness, stripping off their physicality, until they attain the status of "you" (*lekha*), your station. They should not come into the land of Canaan to scout it in its physicality (heaven forbid!). Rather, immediately upon their arrival there they should devote themselves to Torah study and prayer. This is the meaning of *veyaturu* (**to scout**)—related to the word *torah*: when we engage in Torah and mitzvot, we attain a portion in the Land of Israel, beyond our ancestral inheritance, acquiring this portion through our own efforts in study and performing mitzvot.

This is the sense of the phrase "**which I am giving**"—in the present tense. That is, when we engage in Torah and mitzvot, God continuously gives the Holy Land to us. This was not the consideration of the mindless appointees. The scouts thought that Moses sent them to assess the land in its physicality, and so in turn Moses prayed on Joshua's behalf: "May God save you [*Yah yoshi'akha*] from the plan of the scouts" (Sotah 44b)—that he not join in their intention simply to be scouts in the physical sense, rather that he should have the true intention of *veyaturu*—related to Torah.

FOR FURTHER THOUGHT

Once again, in classical Hasidic style, Levi Yitzhak removes the source text from its "historical" context to apply it to his time, to the immediate life experience of his students. The challenge facing the scouts did not have to do with planning for battle or assessing the productivity of the land. Rather, it had to do with their powers of perception, their spiritual acuity: would they be able to see past the physical contours of the land, to perceive its true nature, connected intimately with God and Torah? This is our challenge as well. Can we see clearly in our lives, can we train our hearts to perceive what is true in this moment, can we meet God in truth? How can we escape being trapped in or seduced by the very concrete and immediate manifestation of the physical, to more clearly respond to (and effect) the spiritual?

Levi Yitzhak explains that it could have been for the scouts, and so also for us, that whenever we study Torah we receive an inheritance in the Land of Israel. In this he offers another example of classical Hasidic teaching: the Land of Israel is both the physical place and a spiritual state. Whenever we study Torah or do mitzvot, we enter the holiness of the Land, a symbol of the *Shekhinah*. In some sense (and despite the love of the Land of many early Hasidic rabbis) this approach undermines the importance of the actual physical existence of the Holy Land. This is a dramatic, and challenging, reminder of what the Land of Israel meant to Jews before Zionism, and certainly before the existence of the State of Israel. And perhaps it is also a warning to us as we sometimes struggle with the "physicality" of the actual state and its attendant problems: we must not forget its potential and the necessity to strive to attain the spiritual blessings of the Land, both there and in our own souls.

Questions for Reflection

1. Consider the Rabbinic imagination as it was applied to Pharaoh's daughter. There are manuscript illuminations that depict her hand extending like the comic-book character "Elasticman" to reach for Moses in the bulrushes. What would it take for us to be able to stretch our hands out beyond our physical limits to save someone in need? How can we project ourselves and our intention into the world? How can we expand our humanness? How can we become like Moses? What is the spiritual component of such a personal extension/expansion?

2. Levi Yitzhak teaches, "When we engage in Torah and mitzvot, we attain a portion in the Land of Israel, beyond our ancestral inheritance, acquiring this portion through our own efforts in study and performing mitzvot." Does entering into the realm of holiness—through Torah and mitzvot, for instance—feel to you like inheriting the Land of Israel? Is that a "homecoming" of sorts? What is this portion, and how is it related to the actual possession of the Land of Israel?

3. What can we recover from Levi Yitzhak's teaching about the importance of leaders whose power is found in freedom from physical ties and concerns? And perhaps those who are free of emotional/ego and familial ties or status concerns as well? Who are the leaders today whose claim to authority is in "Torah and mitzvot"—that is, in devotion to God, to self-restraint, love, and compassion? To the good of the cosmos over the good of the group? Will they, can they, have greater success now than Caleb and Joshua did? Is our era any less physically oriented or materialistic than the generation in the desert? How are we like that generation and how are we not?

Taking It into Your Life

This teaching is an invitation to persevere in spiritual practice, to remain mindful of the spiritual in the midst of a very physical/material world. The contrast between Moses's goal—that the men should engage in Torah (*veyaturu*)—and the danger God notes in the closing paragraph of the parashah is well known: "That shall be your fringe; look at it and recall all the commandments of *YHVH* and observe them, so that you do not follow [*taturu*] your heart and eyes in your lustful urge" (Num. 15:39). This challenge, which is Levi Yitzhak's, remains for us today.

The lesson teaches that we have to learn how to see clearly. We can turn our gaze on anything, at any time, and get caught up in what appears to be happening. How we perceive the object—if we are not mindful, if we are not seeing clearly—will be shaped by our reactions: Do we feel it to be pleasant or unpleasant, desirable or undesirable? Does it fit our perception of how things are supposed to be, or do we perceive it as wrong, out of place? Does it arouse fear in us, does it generate craving in us? In all of these instances, what exists, what we see before us, is processed through our ego concerns, self-interest, fears, anxieties, biases, and preferences.

But we will not have seen the object, we will not have perceived the events truly. That requires awareness on a different level, one that can separate between the object and our perception of it. We are invited to learn to say, "Here is a city. Here are its inhabitants. They are strong. Their cities are fortified. I experience fear, but it is only a sensation, a projection of my own insecurities, not a reflection of what is happening in the moment. I am not under attack; I only fear its possibility in the future. Recognizing my fear, how can I see more clearly?" In this process, we remain connected to what we see, investigating without bias what is happening, learning to say what is, rather than give in to the story that our hearts generate about what we see.

Mindfulness practice—this practice of learning to see clearly—is much like Torah study and doing mitzvot. It requires clear-headedness. It demands intention. It connects us to the truth of the moment: this is what I am called to do right now, in this moment. Moses intended to send men who were balanced in their hearts and minds, who used Torah study and doing mitzvot as mindfulness practices, so that they might respond in the moment skillfully, with wisdom. His prayer for Joshua was that he, too, might maintain mindful awareness.

What tools do you have (like Moses's prayer, for instance) to encourage yourself and others to fulfill the true intention of *veyaturu* and be protected from the way of the "mindless ones"? How would you use prayer, mitzvot, and Torah study as means to maintain a balanced heart and mind, to remain present to what is, as opposed to the story you might tell in the moment?

"[When Moses sent them to scout the land of Canaan, he said to them,] 'Go up there into the Negeb and on into the hill country, and see what kind of country it is. [Are the people who dwell in it strong or weak, few or many? Is the country in which they dwell good or bad? What are the towns they live in like? Are they open or fortified? Is the soil rich or poor? Is it wooded or not? And take pains to bring back some of the fruit of the land]'" (Num. 13:17–20).

The principle is: when we wish to raise up a spark, we have to connect ourselves to the quality (*middah*) of *YHVH*, the quality of loving-kindness (*chesed*). This is implied in "**Negeb**," which is in the south of the Land of Israel and signifies *chesed* (the right side).

Alternatively, we have to break the desires generated by the evil inclination (*yetzer hara*). This can be accomplished in light of the verse "Your commandments make me wiser than my enemies; they always stand by me" (Ps. 119:98). This verse teaches that we are to say to the *yetzer hara* (which is our "enemy"), "You try to seduce me to follow your desires, principally to bring me pleasure. But isn't the greatest pleasure in serving God? If so, then it would be better to serve God! The greatest difference between these two approaches is that the pleasure in serving God is eternal; the pleasure that you provide is a passing thing." So this is how we should understand the verse: "From my enemies"—that is, from the *yetzer hara*—"I am made wiser; in your commandments I find eternal pleasure."

We can read this in our original verse: "**Go up ... into the hill country**"—the *yetzer hara* is called "hill" (*har*). We learn this from the Sages (Sukkah 52a):

R. Yehudah taught: In the time-to-come the blessed Holy One will present the *yetzer hara* and slay it in the presence of the righteous and the wicked. To the righteous it will appear like a high mountain, and to the wicked it will appear like a thread of hair.

Read the verse, then, to mean that from the seductions of the *yetzer hara* we can derive the pleasure of serving God, and in this manner we can raise the spark and shatter the husk.

Alternatively, we can raise the things of this world to the state of nothingness (*ayin*). We can see those things as if in the state of *ayin*, the source from which are hewn all souls. In this manner we can raise up the spark. This is inferred in the phrase "**What are the towns**" (*umah he'arim*), since "what" (*mah*) signifies *ayin*, as the Sages taught (Chullin 89a):

> Rava said (others say R. Yohanan): Greater is that which is said of Moses and Aaron than that which is said of Abraham. Abraham said, "I am but dust and ashes" (Gen. 18:27), whereas Moses and Aaron said, "We are nothing" (*venachnu mah*) (Exod. 16:8).

In these three ways we can raise the spark and subdue the evil.

FOR FURTHER THOUGHT

In this lesson, Levi Yitzhak employs Moses's instructions to the scouts to identify three practices by which we might resist the seduction of the *yetzer hara*, to raise up sparks from within the material world, wresting these sparks from within the husks. In this, he once again ignores the specific context of the biblical narrative to present the Torah text as immediately applicable to the lives of his students.

The three practices are as follows:

1. God's loving-kindness has the quality of expansiveness and freedom, as opposed to God's rigor. When we bind ourselves to the quality of God's loving-kindness, we are able to loosen the grip of the husks holding the divine sparks, releasing them to then rise up to God.

2. When we see through the blandishments of the *yetzer hara* to recognize that the only true, eternal pleasure is serving God (rather than the *yetzer hara*), we connect to the divine sparks in the material world, releasing them from the husks and returning them to God.

3. When we connect ourselves to *ayin* and then also connect the physical world to *ayin*, we dissolve that which separates

the sparks from God, freeing them from the realm of the physical.

Our internal orientation determines the state of existence. The clarity of our perception and the intention of our hearts affect our capacity to reunite sparks with their source. Our ability to discern the insubstantiality of the physical garments behind which God is hidden allows us to then connect directly to the Divine in the material world. When we see clearly, the world is aligned more perfectly.

Levi Yitzhak cites a teaching of the Sages that seems to compare Abraham and Moses, but he does not present the text in its entirety. I have quoted the passage that he seems to reference, yet it may be that he is citing Pesachim 88a:

> R. Eleazar also said: What is meant by the verse, "And many people shall go and say: 'Come, let us go up to *YHVH*'s mountain, to the house of the God of Jacob'" (Isa. 2:3)? The God of Jacob, but not the God of Abraham and Isaac? Indeed, the site not as Abraham perceived it, as Scripture connects him to "mountain": "As it is said to this day, 'In the mountain where *YHVH* is seen'" (Gen. 22:14). Nor as Isaac experienced it, as Scripture connects him to "field": "And Isaac went out to meditate in the field in the evening" (Gen. 24:63). But like Jacob, who called God "house/home": "And he called the name of that place Beth-el [God's house]" (Gen. 28:19).

In this passage there is no reference to Moses, as there is in Chullin. Yet, note: here Abraham is associated with "mountain." This may not be the passage that Levi Yitzhak meant to cite, yet it is suggestive, in that it presents Abraham as one who struggled with his "mountain"— for example, the *yetzer hara*—and overcame it. Still, he was not as perfect as Moses, who had no sense of self, not even enough to say, "I am." His only awareness was *"venachnu mah—we are nothing."*

Questions for Reflection

1. What does it mean to you to connect to God through the quality of *chesed*? Is it in the experience of loving-kindness that you sense God? Is it in enacting *chesed*? Is it witnessing loving-kindness? How do you imagine that your connection to *chesed* helps raise sparks?

2. What is your response to being reminded that your personal enjoyment of any of the world's pleasures is really serving the *yetzer hara*? How does

connecting fully to this world help you connect to God? When do material and worldly pleasures distract you from God?

3. Levi Yitzhak reminds us that all worldly pleasures are limited in their duration, while delighting in God is eternal. What experience do you have of sensing an enduring, eternal pleasure? How, if at all, is that related to your spiritual work?

Taking It into Your Life

Surely much of what Levi Yitzhak teaches here is presented in brief. We would benefit from unpacking each of the elements of this lesson. Nevertheless, the primary concern here is the emphasis on practice. To that end, let us investigate how to enact these practices.

"When we wish to raise up a spark, we have to connect ourselves to the quality [*middah*] of *YHVH*, the quality of loving-kindness [*chesed*]." Imagine: we are facing an object or immersed in an activity, and we are aware that this presents an opportunity to raise up a spark, to redeem the innate holiness in the world by connecting it once again fully to God. Levi Yitzhak instructs us to extend our awareness out to connect with the quality of God's loving-kindness, the awareness that God loves all creation, and it is this love that flows constantly into the world and sustains it. So we are invited to experience, in our own lives, the presence of God's love in ourselves. The experience is both of the love and of the expression of that love; that we are loved and that God loves. When we sense that inner awareness, we can then extend it to that which we observe and recognize in it God's sustaining love, and know that God extends love to it as well. In that manner, we both reveal and make known God's love in this instance, in this object and moment. It is the love we perceive, and not the object. We dissolve the seeming distance between this thing, this moment, and God.

"From the seductions of the *yetzer hara* we can derive the pleasure of serving God." We are instructed to let go of our grasp on the material world, our insistence that it is "all that is." Surely there are many things in life that are pleasurable, and the Sages castigated anyone who did not enjoy all that God created and is permitted to us (cf. Ta'anit 11a). But more significantly, the Baal Shem Tov reminded us that everything comes from God, everything is God, so everything, even the blandishments of the *yetzer hara*, can lead us to God. The challenge is to notice the inner movement of our heart and our desires: When we feel desire, what is its source? How is this our habitual reaction to fear, sadness, anger, yearning, confusion, etc.? When we can see clearly, we are more able to make wise choices; we can be more skillful in our actions. Noticing the movement of our hearts can help us direct our energies and efforts toward God.

"We can raise the things of this world to the state of nothingness [*ayin*], … the source from which are hewn all souls." Mindfulness meditation supports mindful awareness. An aspect of mindfulness is the awareness of the fundamental emptiness of all existence that claims to be independent, self-sufficient, and self-generating. Mindful awareness helps us see objects as they are in themselves, not as we wish to perceive them, not as we react to them, not as we know them in relation to other things. We see them not as objects, but as subjects in themselves, knowing them as they know themselves. Mindfulness meditation helps us perceive the world as only a garment covering its true expression: all is God. Directing our attention to *ayin*, and so connecting all we see to the *ayin*, we make God more manifest in our own lives and in the world.

"YHVH, slow to anger [and abounding
in kindness; forgiving iniquity and
transgression; yet not remitting all
punishment, but visiting the iniquity of
fathers upon children, upon the third and
fourth generations]" (Num. 14:18).

When the Israelites made the Golden Calf (cf. Exod. 32 ff.), they sinned against God. But here they sinned against themselves, marring the image of the people of Israel. They did not believe that they had the power to change their circumstances through prayer.

The quality (*middah*) of compassion (*rachum*) is when the blessed Holy One spontaneously reaches out to connect to the lower realms (as it were). This is similar to the wealthy person who has compassion for the poor person and has to connect himself to the suffering of the poor person. In doing so, he finds compassion for himself as well.

The quality of graciousness (*chanun*) is that we find grace (*chein*) in the eyes of the blessed Holy One.

Here, when the people sent out the scouts (and when they learned of God's displeasure), they neither believed in the quality of compassion—that the blessed Holy One would connect directly to the people of Israel—nor in the quality of graciousness, that we are viewed with grace by God. That is why, here, Moses did not included compassion and graciousness in his appeal to God, only that God is **slow to anger**.

FOR FURTHER THOUGHT

Following the incident of the Golden Calf, God taught Moses how to appeal to God for forgiveness. The Sages imagine God instructing Moses, "Whenever Israel sin, perform this rite and I will forgive them" (Rosh Hashanah 17b). The "rite" was to be the recitation of God's attributes of mercy (Exod. 34:6–7) So, we would have expected Moses to employ that precise formula in this moment of crisis. He does, and he doesn't. That is, he seems to quote God directly, but he leaves out the declaration that God is compassionate and gracious (*rachum vechanun*). This is surprising, particularly as the original formulation is known as God's Thirteen Attributes of Compassion! Why, when God has threatened to wipe out the whole of the people, would Moses not employ the complete formula and not call on God to be compassionate?

Levi Yitzhak is surely aware of the views of the Sages, seen in Rashi's comment on Num. 14:18 and the passage in the Talmud on which it is based (Sanhedrin 111a–b):

> When Moses ascended on high, he found the Holy One sitting and writing "slow to anger." He said to God, "Sovereign of the Universe! Slow to anger with the righteous?" God replied, "Even to the wicked." He said, "Let the wicked perish!" (Ps. 37:20). God retorted, "See now what you ask for." When Israel sinned (with the scouts), God said to him, "Did you not say to me, 'Let Your patience be for the righteous only'?" Moses responded, "Sovereign of the Universe! Did you not assure me, 'It extends even to the wicked'?" Hence it is written, "Therefore, I pray, let my Lord's forbearance be great, as You have declared" (Num. 14:17).

For the Sages of the Talmud, apparently, it is more important that God be "slow to anger," that is, disposed to hold off punishing the guilty, than that God be known as compassionate. The possibility of experiencing God's anger, known too directly through the destruction of the Temple and the exile, was too awful to contemplate and too real to dismiss. So the Rabbis emphasized God's forbearance.

But for Levi Yitzhak, God is not a punishing God. He, along with his Hasidic colleagues, regularly misquotes Lam. 3:38: "Nothing bad issues from the mouth of the Exalted One." God is the source of all good, and only good. In the wilderness, following the report of the scouts, the people lost sight of this "truth," and perhaps Levi Yitzhak's listeners did as well. His message is that God can and *does* seek to hold us with compassion; God can and *does* deal with us with grace. If we can hold our hearts steady in that awareness, we will be able to approach God in prayer and activate those qualities of the divine heart. We will be able to change the circumstances of our lives. If we do not remember that God is compassionate and gracious, then all we have left is that God is slow to anger, and all we can hope for is that God will restrain the forces of judgment and punishment until such time as we may merit blessing. That may have been all that Moses and the people could muster in the wilderness, and it may have been sufficient for the Sages of the Talmud, but it was not enough for Levi Yitzhak, and perhaps it should not be enough for us either.

 ## Questions for Reflection

1. We have met the image of the wealthy person connecting in compassion to the poor before. It is only when directly connected to the suffering of the poor person that the wealthy one is motivated with purity of heart to care for the other and can discover compassion for himself. This suggests that God's extension of compassion to us helps God experience compassion for God's self. How do you understand this? Why would God need to experience compassion reflexively? What might be the consequence (for God) of our unwillingness or inability to recognize that God reaches out in compassion to us?

2. What is the relationship between the capacity to pray that misfortune be overturned and knowing God's compassion and graciousness? How does sensing—and trusting—these qualities in God help energize the spirit in prayer? How might the inability to sense these qualities affect the nature of our prayer?

3. The midrash (Num. R. 20:10) reports a popular saying: "People say to the hornet: Neither of your honey nor of your sting." If we come to God in fear and can rely only on God's long-suffering nature, is it likely that we

will want to remain in relationship? If we cannot rely on God's compassion, will we want to risk God's displeasure? How do you experience this in your spiritual life? How do you work with this in relationship with other people—whether in your interpersonal relations or in your spiritual conversations?

Taking It into Your Life

Once again, we are invited to practice loving-kindness and compassion. Only when we can respond with love and compassion to ourselves—even when we make mistakes, even when we fall into the same habitual traps that stymie us in our attempts to live more fully with ourselves and others—will we be able to extend love and compassion to others.

This is a form of meditation practice. After settling yourself in your body and your breath, bring the image of yourself to your mind's eye. See yourself clearly, but if possible also in an image that is neutral and perhaps even pleasant and at ease. Hold that image in your mind's eye until it is settled and you can sustain it with ease.

Now you will want to develop a feeling of loving-kindness, the love that you feel spontaneously when your heart is most open. Recognize that this love may not be directional; you may simply sense that your heart feels love. This love is the desire for the well-being of all life, of all existence. It is content-less. You may not know, perhaps cannot know, what will be the fullest blessing for all existence. Instead, you can work to generate this type of love by repeating these sentences:

> May you feel protected and safe.
>
> May you feel contented and pleased.
>
> May your body support you in the unfolding of your life.
>
> May you experience your life with ease of well-being.

Repeat these phrases over and over, and as you repeat them, sense that this desire is directed to your own self.

You may experience questions and challenges arising in your mind or heart: What about that time that you did thus-and-so? What about the fact that you are always this way or that? What about your sense that you have failed to finish a project / lose weight / read a book / whatever? These questions are irrelevant to whether you, as a person, are deserving of the love that you are expressing. Yes, there may be things you have done for which you feel badly or for which you need to do some *teshuvah*; all the more reason for you to extend loving-kindness to yourself, the energy from which you can act with honesty and purpose.

There is no one more deserving of your love and compassion than yourself. Developing this quality in our hearts can be the foundation from which we can extend it to all others.

"And *YHVH* said, 'I pardon, according to your words'" (Num. 14:20).

Rashi comments: "**According to your words**"—because you said, "Lest they say, 'It is because *YHVH* is powerless, etc.'" (cf. Num. 14:16).

What is it that Rashi comes to teach us? This appears to be his intention: Moses prayed to the blessed Holy One for Israel's sake, arguing that there not result a desecration of God's name (heaven forbid), as it says, "When the Egyptians hear, etc." (Num. 14:13). But this is confusing. Are not all human thoughts in God's hands, directing people's paths according to the divine will? And since that is so, let God direct the thoughts of the nations so that they not say, "It is because *YHVH* is powerless, etc.," and there will be no desecration of God's name!

But this is the matter: the speech of a tzaddik has effect both above and below, as it says, "You will decree and it will be fulfilled" (Job. 22:28; cf. Mo'ed Katan 16b). That being so, the very fact that Moses said in his prayer that (heaven forbid) there might be a desecration of God's name if God destroyed Israel (heaven forbid), he made it so! That is what Rashi taught: "Because you said, 'Lest they say, etc.'": your words have effect, and so then surely they will say so. But had you not spoken so, then the nations would surely not have said this. Since you yourself said that they would say this, and "you will decree and it will be fulfilled," they certainly would say so [and therefore I have pardoned the people].

FOR FURTHER THOUGHT

Speech is a central concern in Hasidic spirituality. In the midrash (e.g., Gen. R. 65:21), the "voice of Jacob" is identified with prayer and study, which are the sources of Jewish power. The Hasidic emphasis on prayer and Torah study follows in this vein but heightens the power of speech. Humans share the capacity for speech with God, and when employed with intention, it has the potential to be as powerful as divine speech. It is the medium through which Jews participate with God in revealing the divine life force in all things.

Levi Yitzhak often emphasizes the importance of guarding one's speech, noting that what we do and say here below has an effect above. It is not often that he offers an example of the negative impact of speech, particularly when voiced by a "tzaddik." Apparently this problem troubled him, because he not only develops it here in its place, but he also refers to this same teaching back in *parashat Lekh Lekha*. There, Abraham spoke words of doubt ("O Lord *YHVH*, what can You give me, seeing that I shall die childless"; Gen. 15:2). Having said these words, making his inner doubt a fact, he forced God to act on his behalf. Levi Yitzhak reads God's response—"The word of *YHVH* came to him to say [*leimor*]"—to mean that God told Abraham "to say" what follows: "That one shall not be your heir; none but your very own issue shall be your heir"(15:4). Even though the language is awkward, Levi Yitzhak reads it as if it could have been Abraham's speech. God insisted that Abraham speak these words in order to counteract the effect of his original doubting speech. This subsequent declaration would then become the new fact.

While God can do anything, the Hasidic view understands that the preferable, most effective, more desirable process is for God to be energized through human initiative. God seeks the intervention of the tzaddik to effect the good, perhaps particularly when the tzaddik creates the negative condition through careless—or doubting—speech. Levi Yitzhak may have intended this lesson to demonstrate the power of the tzaddik. But having addressed it to his students, and so also to us, he invites us to consider our own speech and to recognize the intrapsychic as well as interpersonal power our words carry.

 # Questions for Reflection

1. Levi Yitzhak describes a familiar interaction. One person speaks his or her fear or concern, and the other acts on that basis, often making things worse. Have you ever had this experience? What is it like to be the one who speaks and then gets acted upon? What is it like to be the one who responds to the difficult speech? What does it take to undo this sort of misunderstanding?

2. Levi Yitzhak leads us to think that God did not really mean to wipe out the Israelites and that it was Moses who overreacted in his speech. Does this make sense to you? Have you ever been in a situation where someone threatened to act, not really meaning it, and then others responded as if the threat were real? What was the outcome? What does it take to unravel this sort of interaction?

3. When do you know that your words have effect? What is required—in terms of relationships, perceptions, circumstances—to be in a position that your speech has power? What do you do to make sure that your words have only positive effects?

Taking It into Your Life

The situation that Levi Yitzhak describes is when a tzaddik expresses doubt in God's beneficence, that God's intention is that all unfold for the good. This raises an interesting question: what is the difference between a *tzaddik* entertaining these doubts and expressing them? Clearly the latter is more problematic, because speech is so powerful; the words of a tzaddik have effect. For Levi Yitzhak, this means that by saying something a tzaddik makes it so.

This may be a step beyond our conception of "how things work," yet perhaps not so far. Haven't you had the experience of witnessing the impact of your words on others—of saying something and knowing internally that you shouldn't have? In moments that reveal our most "superstitious" selves, do we not sometimes attribute something bad that happens to us to some word or another we spoke unthinkingly?

This suggests a practice of paying attention to our speech, particularly in relation to our inner thoughts, particularly thoughts of "doubt." For a period of time, bring your awareness to what you say. Notice when you express doubt: doubt in your own ability to do or accomplish something; doubt in the capacity of others to do what they say; doubt in the ultimate possibility of good to emerge from the current situation. As you notice these sorts of expressions, pay attention to your inner experience. What is the source of your doubt? When does it emerge from fear? What it the source of that fear? When does it emerge from frustration? What is its root? When does it emerge from heart pain? What produces this? When does it emerge from pride and a desire for power? Where is this in your heart? What other emotions do you sense relative to your doubt, and what might be their roots?

As you discover the roots of your doubt, you need not squelch or deny or seek to uproot them. Rather, pay attention. Notice them as they arise. Notice how they prompt speech. As you see them rise to the surface as speech, see whether you can hold back for a moment. Consider: I know I feel this way, but do I need to speak my doubt? There are times that doubt may be a form of caution, and not speaking might be unwise. But there are other times that doubt is just doubt, and it might not need to be spoken. Observe what arises in place of your expression of doubt. Perhaps it is pain. Perhaps it is fear. Perhaps it is frustration. Perhaps it is loss. Notice. Stay with that awareness.

In response to whatever arises, you can bring compassion—to your own heart, to others, to the rest of the world. Notice what sort of expression arises out of compassion, in place of doubt. How does that change your perception of the situation, your perception of others, and your capacity to act wisely? How does compassion help keep you connected to trust and faith? How might this practice help your words have effect?

Korach

"Now Korah, [son of Izhar son of Kohath
son of Levi,] took, [along with Dathan
and Abiram sons of Eliab, and On son of
Peleth, descendants of Reuben]" (Num.16:1).

There is one sort of tzaddik who serves only to bring delight to the blessed Creator. For this tzaddik, it makes no difference if she brings delight to the blessed Creator or some other tzaddik brings delight to the blessed Creator. But someone who wants to receive a reward for his service will be one who desires that he alone brings delight to the Creator.

This is the meaning of "**Now Korah took**"—that is, he wanted to be the one who "took" and not any other. This is what Rashi explained (cf. Sanhedrin109b, in the name of Resh Lakish): "He took a bad bargain for himself," challenging Moses and wishing to become the high priest. If, however, he had desired to serve only to bring delight to the blessed Creator, he certainly would not have disputed, claiming that he (alone) should be the high priest.

Rashi's report that Korah was jealous of the leadership of Elizaphan ben Uzziel (Rashi on Num. 16:1; cf. Num. 3:30) is unclear on its surface. Why did he not challenge Moses at the time of Elizaphan's appointment, waiting till this moment instead? The explanation is that before the event of the scouts, all of the people were fit to enter the Land of Israel immediately. Korah therefore reasoned that Elizaphan would serve in his role for only a limited time, since very soon they would enter the Land. But after the incident of the scouts, when Korah understood that God had decreed that they would remain in the wilderness for forty years, he then became jealous of Elizaphan, seeing that he would serve as leader for forty years.

FOR FURTHER THOUGHT

Rashi cites the *Tanchuma* on our verse:

> Against what did Korah rebel (in what way did he separate himself from the community/Moses)? Regarding Elizaphan ben Uzziel, his father's brother who had been appointed *nasi* of his family, as it says, "The chieftain of the ancestral house of the Kohathite clans was Elizaphan son of Uzziel" (Num. 3:30). Korah reasoned, "My father had four brothers, as it says, 'The sons of Kohath were Amram, Izhar, Hebron, and Uzziel' (Exod. 6:18). Amram was the firstborn, and (through him) Aaron and his descendants merited to serve as priests, and Moses the role of leader. But who actually has more right to this second office? Would it not be the second son? I am the son of Izhar, and I certainly am worthy of being the leader (*nasi*) of my family. Yet he (Moses) made the son of Uzziel (the leader)! Should the younger son of my father's younger brother be greater than I? If this will be the case, then I challenge and negate all that he (Moses) has done." This was his challenge and disagreement.

Let us unpack this explanation. Jacob's son Levi had three sons: Gershon, Kohath, and Merari. Kohath had four sons: Amram, Izhar, Hebron, and Uzziel. Aaron was the eldest son of Amram, Kohath's eldest son, and so he could rightly claim the high priesthood. But Moses, Aaron's younger brother, also held a key role as prophet and leader. So perhaps the role of the high priest should rotate among all of Kohath's descendants. Instead, the rest of the descendants of Levi became the clans of the Levites, the assistants to the priests in the Tabernacle and Temple. Again, if the descendants of Amram were elevated to the priesthood, perhaps then the descendants of Izhar, Kohath's second son, should have had a unique or at least some elevated role among the Levites. But, instead, Elizaphan, the son of Uzziel (the youngest of Kohath's sons!), was given a particular and elevated role among the Levites—not a descendant of Izhar, like, for instance, Korah.

Korah has two claims. One is that he was passed over in Moses's appointing Elizaphan and should at least have served as the *nasi* of the Kohathites. The second claim is that this indicates that all of Moses's appointments are unworthy/illegitimate. Korah reasons that if that is the case, and Moses, the son of Amram the firstborn, is going to remain as unchallenged/unchallengeable leader, then why shouldn't the firstborn of the second son serve as priest?

And in the end, as the midrash unfolds, Korah is presented as challenging Moses in fundamental ways. He questions the rationality of the tzitzit (why would a tallit that is completely colored *tekhelet* still need a thread of *tekhelet* to be kosher?), as well as the mezuzah (if a house is filled with holy books, why would it still need a mezuzah containing only two short passages?). Having called Moses's lawmaking into question, suggesting that the laws were all Moses's invention, he then challenges Moses's authority altogether.

Korah's initial intention and desire were properly motivated: he wanted to serve God. Further, he wanted to follow the rules, including that of primogeniture. But he was frustrated in his quest and did not know how to deal with his inner turmoil. He could have connected his spiritual yearnings to the good of the whole people. He could have recognized that his role was to bring all of his energy to his work as a Levite and so support and engage the whole of the people in divine service. In that manner, he would have been like the tzaddik whose sole intention is that God derive pleasure, no matter who causes it. Instead, he allows his frustration to energize his ego, his unique need and desire, and so he acted to satisfy himself, at the expense of Moses, the people, and God.

 ## Questions for Reflection

1. In your experience, in your inner sense of your self, what is the seat of selfishness? What helps you let go of self-concern to act solely "for the sake of heaven"? What practices might we engage in to help us discern the most subtle movements of self-concern, to help us become truly grateful in every instance?

2. These two lessons appear in *Kedushat Levi* as separate teachings. Yet they seem also to be interconnected, developing a theme. How do you see the connection between these two teachings?

3. If we were to poll the Jewish community, it is likely that we would find a fair amount of sympathy for Korah. Rashi's comment regarding Elizaphan's appointment—where he says specifically that it was "according to divine instruction" (*al pi hadibbur*)—makes Korah's argument against self-service and arbitrariness seem even more persuasive. How well do

you deal with situations in which the justification really seems like a rationale—that is, when there is no clear logic or rational explanation for why things are the way they are? Are you able to keep your cool, to rejoice in what is? Can you recite a blessing even over the bad? What, if anything, can you accept as "God's word"?

Taking It into Your Life

It is so hard to be selfless! Even in the moments when we think that all of our interest, concern, and delight is in the good that comes to another, we sense niggling selfishness: "I hope that they notice my happiness for them"; "When did I last feel as happy as they are today?"; "Did I spend enough on this present?" And then, when we've done our job well, for its own sake, we sense troubling self-concern: "I know that I did this because I chose to do it, but I sure hope that someone notices"; "I did such a good job on this, investing a lot of time and effort—it would be nice if they added something to my fee."

Can we really blame Korah if we are not so clean? Levi Yitzhak's teaching directs us to the spiritual practice of finding joy in the success and well-being of others. It is a quality of heart that is related to loving-kindness and compassion. That is, when we are aware of our love of all beings, of our fundamental compassion for their suffering, and of our desire only for their good, we will be inclined to delight in their well-being. In a sense, this requires that we both recognize our interconnection with all beings—that our desire to end our own suffering is inextricably connected to ending all suffering—and that we recognize that what we see happening around us is not "all about" us. What happens to others is simply what happens. When good fortune falls on someone else, it implies neither that we are undeserving nor that the other is somehow better than us. Rather, it is an invitation to us to be pleased in their good fortune, without reference to our own state.

As you move through your day, pay attention to the movement of your heart as you witness other people's joy or well-being. Notice when jealousy arises; when anger or frustration arises; when joy, happiness, or delight arises. Do not judge your response; simply note it. When you sense something other than joy in others' good fortune, remain with that feeling; notice where it sits in your body; notice what other associations arise in conjunction with it. Perhaps you can discern where the block is to your delight in others' good fortune: your own sense of loss; your fear that you will not have good fortune; a sense that you do not deserve such happiness. In response to this awareness, you can bring some loving-kindness or compassion to your own heart. This response may loosen your own heart, ease it, and make it more possible to experience joy in others' well-being.

> "[You and your sons shall be careful to
> perform your priestly duties in everything
> pertaining to the altar and to what is
> behind the curtain.] I make your priesthood
> a service of dedication (gift); [any outsider
> who encroaches shall be put to death]"
> (Num. 18:7).

Now, when we serve God, it is not a gift because it is our obligation. But when we raise up sparks, this is our gift to God.

This is the meaning of the question "Have you engaged in business faithfully [*nasata venatata be'emunah*]?" (Shabbat 31a). When we engage in business (lit., *masa umatan*, "taking/lifting and giving") with a gentile and profit from this business, we then are able to serve God even more, thereby raising up sparks from the nations. This is the sense of the phrase *nasata* (i.e., have you taken or lifted)—this means raising up—*venatata be'emunah* (and then given faithfully). This is our gift to God, when we raise up sparks.

This is the source of converts to the Jewish people from the nations. They come to connect with Israel when we raise up the sparks in them (as above). This is service that is a gift.

FOR FURTHER THOUGHT

There seem to be two points to this lesson, both challenging in positive and negative ways. The first is that performing the mitzvot, and thereby serving God, is not considered "a gift" to God. The second emphasizes the separation between Jews and gentiles, the former having the power to raise sparks trapped within the latter.

Regarding the first lesson, it is interesting to introduce into our spiritual vocabulary the idea of a gift to God. What, at all, can we give to God? Job says, "If you are righteous, what do you give Him;

what does He receive from your hand?" (35:7). According to Levi Yitzhak, apparently, even our obedience is no gift; it is merely fulfilling an obligation. Rather, what we have to offer is our awareness and intention. So when we act with intention—making of our deeds more than mere performance, directing our attention toward bringing God delight—we offer God a gift. The gift is in returning the divine to its source, making clear that there is nothing, and no place, in which God is not present.

If nothing is devoid of God, then we should be able to recognize the divine soul in all people, too. Our ancestors did not see this, and not without reason. Levi Yitzhak considered it possible for a divine spark to be present in gentiles, but he could not conceive of that spark enlivening their lives in a positive way. It could only be trapped, imprisoned in their coarse bodies. But we need not, cannot, carry this bias forward. Instead, when we recognize the divine spark in all things—in ourselves, in other people, and in inanimate objects—we will acknowledge divinity in all of creation. In this manner, we would raise sparks by raising our consciousness, not by separating the spark from some lower domain.

In turn, this might also transform our understanding of what attracts people to Judaism. That is, when gentiles find that they are met by people truly interested in them, people who affirm that they have a divine soul and who offer practices and community through which this soul can be nurtured, they will want to become part of that community. Rather than redeeming souls that have been lost, we will be enlivening souls that yearn to be connected with God. And as much as this may apply to "non-Jews," it surely applies to Jews.

 ## Questions for Reflection

1. How do you understand the relationship between raising sparks and giving God gifts? What are we "giving to God"? How, if at all, do you see it as different from "simply" serving God?

2. Levi Yitzhak plays on the Hebrew idiom for "business" to connect "lifting" (*masa*) to "giving" (*matan*), arguing that in raising sparks, we give God gifts. But perhaps he means to teach that we are to transform doing business into a religious and spiritual practice. How do you understand this connection?

3. How do you understand the possible place of "raising sparks" in the work of *keiruv*, bringing people near to Jewish life and practice?

Taking It into Your Life

The sparks that we seek to raise up are "holy sparks." Their holiness derives from their source in divine emanation. They, like all divine emanations, are both from God and of God; they are divinity. These sparks are trapped in the mundane realm so long as they go unnoticed as divinity and so long as they are not employed in divine service. The latter can be accomplished through consumption: we eat something and use the energy derived from that food for divine service—the sparks contained in that food are raised up by our dedication of them through our actions. Alternatively, the consumption may come about through the use of an object: when we use a tool, wear a garment, or otherwise imbue something with holy intention, with awareness of God, or in divine service, we raise up the sparks in the object. And this proper use applies to money as well. Doing business honestly, and applying what we earn to holy tasks, is another way of raising sparks.

Some sparks can only be raised through appreciation. You may recall Levi Yitzhak's teaching where he speaks of the view of appreciation versus the view of possession. When we look upon an object, and particularly a person, and recognize not only that God is present in this person/thing, but also that God's presence enlivens, sustains, and makes possible the existence of this person/thing, we value them not for our benefit but simply because they exist. This, too, is a form of raising sparks, as it is the means by which we elevate our relationship from subject-to-object to that of subject-to-subject; from I-It to I-Thou.

Here is where Levi Yitzhak's association of business with raising sparks might be suggestive and meaningful. Remember the Hebrew idiom for negotiating business: *masa umatan*—raising and giving. When we are able to recognize God's presence in the other, we raise them in our own estimation. We relate to the spark of divinity, and so our interactions take place on that higher level. We are elevated, but so also is the person over against us. That we relate to the other in this manner raises them and is, in turn, a gift to them. We give to the other the awareness—consciously or unconsciously—of God's presence in them. We make known to them the presence of the divine spark that sustains and animates them.

In this manner we raise the spark in the other person. As opposed to consumption or use, we do not remove the spark from the thing or the person. Rather, we make its presence more evident; we raise our conscious-ness—and the consciousness of the other. Rather than utility in negotiating relationships, doing the business of life, it is in mutuality and in apprecia-tion that we raise sparks in other people and in ourselves.

Practice.

> "[All the sacred gifts that the Israelites set aside for *YHVH* I give to you, to your sons, and to the daughters that are with you, as a due for all time.] It shall be an everlasting covenant of salt [before *YHVH* for you and for your offspring as well]" (Num. 18:19).

This was declared after Korah's rebellion. Korah had wanted that he and his fellows should all be priests (*kohanim*) and not Levites (*levi'im*). Now, *kohein* signifies loving-kindness (*chesed*; cf. Zohar I 148b), and *levi* signifies rigor (*din*; cf. Zohar I 236a). Korah wanted all to be loving-kindness (*chesed*).

But in truth, both rigor and compassion (*rachamim*) have to exist together in this world. Ramban taught that salt is the heat (*eish*; fire) in water. In that sense, then, the power of salt derives from both fire and water, which are analogous to rigor and loving-kindness. These two together are the forces that guide the world.

This was declared after Korah's rebellion to demonstrate that his effort—to make all loving-kindness—had been nullified. This is not the case, as the world must be directed by both rigor and loving-kindness.

FOR FURTHER THOUGHT

Levi Yitzhak continues to work through balancing the fact that God is a loving, compassionate, and good God, yet in that goodness God also manifests judgment (as limitation, rigor, or punishment). He hears in Korah's declaration in Num. 16:3—"For all the community are holy, all of them, and *YHVH* is in their midst"—a claim that the Levites should be *kohanim*, symbolically arguing that God be manifest only through the quality (*middah*) of loving-kindness. As beautiful as this wish sounds, and as desirable as it may seem to be, Levi Yitzhak reminds us that unbounded love is dangerous. The Sages taught that for the world to survive, God's love needed to be limited, so that it might be experienced without being overwhelming (cf. Gen. R. 12:15). This perspective is reflected in the dynamic system of the *sephirot/middot*.

Here is Ramban on Lev. 2:13:

> The verse reports that this is a "covenant of your God" (*berit elohekha*) and not "a covenant of *YHVH*"—using the name that has been consistently used throughout Numbers 18 and as it appears with regard to all of the sacrifices. Nor do we find that the verse calls this "the covenant of *YHVH* your God." This being the case, I surmise that this is what it means: "salt" here means salt water. Through the sun's force in the water, it becomes salty. Water in its original form moistens the earth from which plants grow. But if the water becomes salty, it will destroy the land it touches, burning it so that it cannot be sown and will not produce. In this manner, the covenant contains all of the *middot*: water and fire are present in it. "It shall come to you, the former monarchy will return" (Micah 4:8), that is God's rule. Just as salt enhances the flavor in food and preserves it, it can also destroy food with its saltiness. In this way salt is like a covenant. That is why Scripture states: "Surely you know that *YHVH* God of Israel gave David kingship over Israel forever— to him and his sons—by a covenant of salt" (2 Chron. 13:5), for this quality also applies to David's rule.

Ramban sees "salt" pointing to something else: water. Water is considered, in the mystical writings, to be a symbol of loving-kindness (*chesed*), which flows freely in all directions. But in this case we see salt water (indirectly) associated with rigor or limitation (*gevurah*) through the name of God (*elohim*). This leads Ramban to remind us that the *middot* are all present in the world at the same time; the *middot* are interconnected, and the potential for one or another to be manifest depends on our actions. So water will at times be life-sustaining (*chesed*), but it can also turn destructive (*gevurah*). But in the end, water will still be life-sustaining. It is possible to dilute the salt and to revive that which has been burned by it.

That is also the nature of the covenant: destruction may be the consequence of failure to fulfill the covenant, but in the end, God maintains faith with the people, as with the Davidic line, to return them and it to full force and well-being. The midrash (cf. Lev. R. 24:2, end) consistently links the eternal nature of the priestly covenant of salt with that of God's covenant with David and his descendants (as in the verse from 2 Chron. 13:5). That these covenants are eternal does not mean that there may not be periods of destruction. Rather, the balance of loving-kindness and rigor (*chesed* and *gevurah*) promises that eventually health, balance, and well-being will be restored.

This, of course, is Levi Yitzhak's key point. The world cannot survive on love alone; it must be balanced by rigor. But love will prevail in the end. It must be nurtured, it must be elicited; it cannot be mandated. Korah may have been well intentioned, but he was wrong to ask that the quality of *din* be negated. It must be present so that *chesed* can be productive.

Questions for Reflection

1. How do you hear Levi Yitzhak's reworking of Korah's claim? Does this make his challenge to Moses any less compelling? Why or why not?

2. Do you wish that there were only loving-kindness and no rigor or limitation in the world? How do you respond to Levi Yitzhak's claim that there must be rigor and limitation? Are you satisfied? Why or why not?

3. How do you respond to Levi Yitzhak's interpretation of the covenant of salt? Is it a helpful metaphor for the balancing of the *middot* in all things for you? What works and what does not? How might you apply it in your life and work?

Taking It into Your Life

One way to understand the role of *gevurah* relative to *chesed* is that the former provides a form, a vessel, in which the latter might be contained so that it can be recognized. If love were to extend without limit, it would not be perceptible. We see that in the midrashic explanation of the origins of the divine name *shaddai* (Gen. R. 5:8):

> R. Natan commented in R. Abba's name, and R. Berekhiah in R. Yitzhak's name: "'I am *el shaddai*' (Gen. 17:1). It was I who said to the heavens and earth, 'Enough' (*dai*). For had I not said '*dai*' to the heaven and the earth, they would have continued to extend even until now."

This is an opportunity to investigate your own experience of how you contain, limit, and express your love for others, for the world, for God. The challenge is to discern when you hold back your love so that it does not smother or overwhelm another, when you hold back your love out of fear or uncertainty, and when you provide a form for your love so that it can be recognized and experienced.

Love is a powerful emotion, to feel, to express, and to receive. Notice when you sense love arising in your own heart. When you notice it, do you nurture it? Do you hold fast to it so that it does not dissipate? Do you turn away from it? When you recognize that your love is related to another person, do you always let them know? When do you hold back, and what allows you to express that love? What forms are most effective for expressing love? Is it always in words? Is it always in action? What calculations help you understand which form is best? When do you find that these calculations impede your expression of love? How is your love received? Are there times that it is not recognized as loving? When, why? Are there times that it is rejected? When, why? Is it possible that your love might be better received if it were expressed in a different manner?

How have you found that expressing love for God is different from and the same as expressing it to other people? Are there any limits to expressing love of God? If love for God cannot be bounded, are there still forms that you need in order to recognize your own love of God? How do you recognize others' love of God? What forms, if any, help you perceive that love?

Chukkat

"This is the law of the Torah that *YHVH* has commanded, saying: ['Instruct the Israelite people to bring you a red cow without blemish, in which there is no defect and on which no yoke has been laid']" (Num. 19:2).

In general, the reasons and meanings of the Torah and the mitzvot are hidden from everyone. We have only to do and fulfill all of the Torah because it is God's command that falls on us: to do and fulfill the commandments. This is the sense of the phrase "**This is the law** [*chukkat*]: (it is) **the Torah**." All of the Torah and the mitzvot are to be considered like statutes (*chukkim*), since nothing of the reasons for the mitzvot has been revealed to us. The essential thing is that our fulfillment of the Torah and mitzvot is because "**YHVH has commanded, saying**"; because God's commandment obligates us to do them and fulfill them.

This explains why God commanded us to perform this ritual of a cow, to purify those impure from contact with the dead. The soul and vital force that energize us, hewn from under the Throne of Glory, wish to serve God always, without ceasing for even a moment. But the body prevents this; there is a constant struggle between the soul and vital force and the body. When we merit, we can overcome the body so that it will act according to the will of the soul.

Why doesn't the body wish to fulfill the Torah and mitzvot? Because it does not perceive the reasons for them. If it knew the reasons for the Torah and mitzvot, the body would want to fulfill them as well. It is only this ignorance that prevents it. But the soul is hewn from beneath the Throne of Glory and therefore perceives the reasons for the Torah and mitzvot, and thus always desires to do them, fulfilling them without ceasing even for a moment. In one who merits, the soul overcomes the body so that it does and fulfills the Torah and mitzvot. So when someone dies, their soul ascends above and the body remains on its own, and it conducts impurity. That is why the graves of tzaddikim do not make one impure: their bodies were so transparent that their bodies of themselves sought to fulfill the Torah and mitzvot. Their bodies no longer made others impure.

That is what our verse says: "**This is the law:** (it is) **the Torah**"— because the Torah appears to us as a statute whose reason is not revealed, and the body resists fulfilling the Torah, the body therefore is defiling when it dies. That is why God commanded us to perform the ritual of the red cow, to purify us from the impurity of the body alone, since it is the body that defiles in death.

FOR FURTHER THOUGHT

We see in this lesson the tension within Hasidic teaching between the compassionate acceptance of the body as a potential source of knowledge of God and its negation as what separates the holy soul from its source. On the one hand, we see here the identification of the soul with divinity. Its sole desire is to serve God, because it is intimately connected to its source. The soul, directly, intuitively, by nature, knows the meaning and reason for the mitzvot. The body, however, does not know God as directly and so does not understand the meaning of the commandments. It sees no reason not to do as it wishes. The soul has the capacity to instruct and direct the body, and in so doing to purify it, to make it transparent to the divine will. As the body experiences the alignment of intention and action in the divine light, it more easily and willingly turns to do the divine will. The body that is less in touch with its divine source, which is less able to fulfill the divine will, is corruptible in death and so defiling. The body that is more aligned with the divine will, which naturally and spontaneously acts in line with God's intention, is pure and so does not defile.

Levi Yitzhak presents the difference between the body and soul and the source of impurity in death as intersecting in the rules regarding the Red Heifer. This ritual was required to purify those who had come into contact with death: handling a corpse or being with it in the same room, touching a bone, or walking in a cemetery. The ritual itself is puzzling, as the pure person deputized to purify the impure becomes impure himself. Handling the water of lustration makes one impure; yet that same water, when sprinkled, effects purification. This ritual is identified as a "statute" (*chok*), a rule for which there is no rationale or rational reason. The soul may not need any reason, but the body seeks it for inspiration. When a person—embodied—is able to willingly undertake this ritual (and others like it), the body aligns itself with the soul. Engaging in this ritual, accepting God's will without need for reasons, purifies the body such that in the end it itself becomes pure. This body will not defile when it dies. The purification of the ritual of the Red Heifer comes about not through the details of the actions per se, but through the direction of the body to its fulfillment, accepting the commandments without need for reason.

And once one is able to behave this way with regard to *chukkim*, the laws for which there is no rationale, one may then be able to do so with regard to the rest of the Torah and so become more transparent to the divine light, more pure. In that sense, Levi Yitzhak is inviting us to consider all of the Torah and its instructions to be of the order of *chukkim*: "This is the law [*chukkat*]: it is the whole of the Torah."

Questions for Reflection

1. How do you sense your desires and passions? Do they arise in your body, in your mind, in your heart, in your soul? Which part of you do you feel to be most in line with the divine will?

2. Is it your goal to divine God's will? Does your sense of spiritual practice mean understanding what God wants of you? How? When? If this is how you understand your spiritual practice, then do you also need to understand the reason for God's will for you?

3. When do you sense that your soul is compelling your body to behave properly—whether doing the mitzvot or otherwise?

Taking It into Your Life

Mindfulness practice helps us connect intention to action. Mindlessness is when we simply react to whatever is before us; we do whatever comes to mind or to hand without awareness. It may be that connecting intention to action is what Levi Yitzhak means when he speaks of the soul compelling (or directing) the body to act. When we pay attention to what is arising in the moment—to our physical, emotional, intellectual, and spiritual experience—we may gain the freedom to choose wisely how to act skillfully in the moment, acting with compassion and aligning ourselves with God's will.

Meditation is a practice by which we can learn to discern our intention more clearly and to sense our alignment with our intention. It may be helpful to practice in a manner that makes this concrete. Two suggestions are walking practice and eating practice.

Walking practice: Begin in a standing position. Feel the sensation of your feet on the floor. Notice the feeling of being erect; check your posture; feel the sensation of the air around you, the sounds and movements in your vicinity. Bring your attention to your feet and to your intention to walk. Pay close attention to that intention. Break the movement of walking down into its component parts. Notice the intention to lift your foot—and then lift your foot. Notice the intention to move your foot forward—and move your foot. Notice the intention to set your foot down—and set it down. Keep returning your attention to your intention and the action associated with it. When distracted, notice your distraction, and bring your attention back to the sensation of your feet. Begin again, always associating your intention with the act.

Eating practice: Begin with your meal in front of you. Pay attention to your experience of hunger at the moment. What motivates you to eat this meal right now? What do you desire? What appeals to you? As you notice these sensations and thoughts, notice where they are located in your body. Where does the energy to begin eating start? Pay attention to your intention. Connect this intention with the movement of your hand to pick up your fork, with the movement of the fork toward the plate. Notice what you intend to select to eat; notice the movement of the fork toward that food. Feel the fork in your hand selecting the food, raising it from the plate, bringing it to your mouth. Sense the intention to open your mouth and place the food in it. Feel the food in your mouth and your intention to chew, to taste, to enjoy the food. Notice the arising of the sensation of the desire to swallow the food; swallow.

Working in this manner, we can build our awareness of the connection of intention to action. We can become more aware in the moment of impulse in the body and the reactivity in the heart and mind. When we notice the arising of an action, we can ask: what is my intention in this moment, in this action? Asking this question may make more possible our choosing wisely what to do and when. At times of uncertainty, of uneasiness or lassitude, we can investigate with some clarity: what is my intention now? In this manner we may be able to more clearly align our intention with our actions, our heart and mind with our body, and all of them with our soul.

> An alternative explanation of: "This is the law of the Torah [that *YHVH* has commanded, saying: 'Instruct the Israelite people to bring you a red cow without blemish, in which there is no defect and on which no yoke has been laid]" (Num. 19:2).

In our explanation, we will also interpret the verse "He sets the childless woman (*akeret*) among her household [as a happy mother of children. Hallelujah]" (Ps. 113:9). From a worldly perspective it appears to us as if we were created to engage in the things of this world. But in truth that is not the case. The primary reason (*ikar*) that we were created was to recognize the unity of the blessed Creator. That is the sense of "He sets the childless woman among her household": when the Redeemer comes (may it be soon), the reason for our creation will be revealed, that we might come to recognize the oneness of the blessed Creator.

That is the mystical sense of "**This is the law of the Torah**": There are mitzvot that reason compels us to perform. When we do them, we do not sense so strongly that we are performing them because the Creator commanded these mitzvot. That is why the blessed Creator gave us commandments that reason does not comprehend. When we do them, we more readily recognize that we do them only because of God's commandment. That is the sense of "**This is the law [*chukkat*] of the Torah**": this is why the Creator gave us commandments that are statutes (*chukkah*), where reason does not compel action—so that it will be more apparent "**that *YHVH* has commanded**" us to do so. We are to know that we perform the mitzvot only because of the Creator's command.

FOR FURTHER THOUGHT

On the surface, this lesson approaches the issue of the *chok*, the statute for which there is no reason or rationale, as the core matter of this parashah. But once again Levi Yitzhak expands the range of its meaning. He focuses on the effect that performing the *chukkim* has on our spiritual awareness. Rather than training the body to perform with purity of intention, here the matter has to do with training our awareness to recognize the unity of the Holy One, the fact that there is nothing but God. When we obey God's commandments without question, without needing a reason to convince us to do so, we display our devotion to God, taking on the yoke of the divine rule. In so doing, we enthrone God; we demonstrate our acceptance of God's sovereignty. We make clear to ourselves, to others, to all creation that God rules: "Your dominion extends through all the worlds" (Ps. 145:13); "Your sovereignty extends through all creation" (Ps. 103:19).

To make his claim, Levi Yitzhak refers to Ps. 113:9. The Zohar cites this verse as follows:

> Rabbi Eleazer opened, "He settles *aqeret ha-bayit*, the barren woman, in her home, as a joyous mother of children (Ps. 113:9). He settles *aqeret ha-bayit*—Rachel, (*iqqara de-veita*), essence of the house. As a joyous mother of children—Leah.
>
> *He settles aqeret ha-bayit*—Sabbatical, essence of this world, by whom it is conducted. [Rachel symbolizes *Shekhinah*, also known as Sabbatical. *Shekhinah* conducts the lower world.] *As a joyous mother of children*—Jubilee, on whom depend all freedom and joy of all worlds. [Leah symbolizes *Binah*, the Divine Mother, also known as Jubilee.]
>
> This verse is totality of all, encompassing all in holy mystery; so the verse concludes: *Hallelujah!* [The verse spans the higher and lower *sephirot*, from *Binah* to *Shekhinah*. Its concluding exclamation, *Halelu-Yah*, "Praise Yah," alludes to *Shekhinah*, known as Praise, and to *Hokhmah* and *Binah*, symbolized by the divine name *YaH* (*yod-heh*).] (Zohar I 154a; Daniel C. Matt, trans., *The Zohar*, Pritzker ed., vol. 2 [Stanford, CA: Stanford University Press, 2007], p. 361)

Here, this verse is used to demonstrate the unity of all creation, the extension of God's presence through all of the *sephirot*. The Zohar invites us to recognize this in the unity that is symbolized in the connection between Rachel/*Shekhinah* and Leah/*Binah* (and even the supernal *sephirah* of *Chokhmah*), "the totality of all, encompassing all in holy mystery." The lesson that Levi Yitzhak takes from it is "the unity of the blessed Creator." The purpose and goal of spiritual life and practice are to recognize that unity and to live in response to it.

When Levi Yitzhak employs Ps. 113:9, he uses it as a signifier of the coming of the Messiah. That is when the *Shekhinah* will find her rest; she will be reunited with her Lover. The truth of God's existence will no longer be hidden by a physical realm that garbs and conceals God. There will be no chance—and no need—to mistake the existence of the material world as distinct from God, to experience ourselves as separate from God. That awareness will allow us to know and do God's will spontaneously, aligned in our deepest beings with God's deepest being. Performing the laws for which there is no reason or rationale, the *chukkim*, trains us in this practice even in this world, in this time before the Messiah.

Questions for Reflection

1. What is your spiritual attitude toward the matters of this world? Do you sense that you were created to engage with them or not? Is it a matter of degree or of orientation? How?

2. What does it mean to you to "recognize the unity of the blessed Creator"? Is that different from declaring, *Shema yisrael*? How? Why or why not?

3. How do you sense when you are doing God's will? Where does that awareness arise, and where does it rest in you? Does it vary from act to act, from time to time? How?

Taking It into Your Life

The authors of the Zohar are masterful in their use of verses and images from the Bible in dramatically new and revealing ways. That they identified the "childless woman" of Ps. 113:9 as Rachel and the "mother of children" as Leah is such a touch. But the connection of Rachel to *Shekhinah* and Leah to *Binah* makes this even more striking. In this light, this verse takes on a deep teleological cast: more than a metaphor, this is the actual promise of the end of exile and the unification of all creation.

That these *sephirot* are hidden, as it were, in the figures of Rachel and Leah suggests other hidden figures working toward redemption, like the thirty-six pious ones on whom the world depends. This tradition has roots in Rabbinic literature (Sanhedrin 97b). It also echoes in the traditions of the hidden tzaddikim (*tzaddikim nistarim*), those pious ones who devoted themselves to the good of all people, yet who were not recognized as particularly saintly or powerful by others.

As a form of seeing God's unity in the world, we might want to train our eyes to see what is less visible, less evident. We can seek out the *tzaddikim nistarim* of our time. Let us not be seduced into thinking that we know what we are looking for: piety, humility, religious fervor, inner power. We most likely do not know what acts are required in this moment to maintain the world's existence. The smallest act, the most subtle gesture, may be the world's redemption.

Train yourself to see clearly, in a focused manner, all of the people around you. Pay attention to who attracts your attention, who would otherwise have escaped your notice. Let your gaze remain on that person from whom you would otherwise have turned away. Investigate closely how they conduct themselves, how they seem to look at the world, how they respond to the people they pass, the animals they see, the air they breathe. Imagine that anyone you see, any person whose path you cross, may be a hidden tzaddik. You may not be able to perceive how they are saving the world, but in the very moment you see them, they may reveal something to you that will inspire your own act of kindness, of compassion, of justice. Learn to recognize in each moment how it is precisely the "childless woman," the "stone despised by the builders" (Ps. 118:22), who is to be raised up and will bring about redemption.

Maybe it will be you.

> "['Take the staff and assemble the
> community, you and Aaron your brother,]
> you are to speak to the rock before their
> eyes [so that it gives forth its water. Thus
> you are to bring out for them water from
> the rock, that you may give drink to the
> assembly and to their cattle.' So Moses
> took the staff from before *YHVH*, as He
> had commanded him. Moses and Aaron
> assembled the congregation in front of the
> rock; and he said to them, 'Listen, you rebels,
> shall we get water for you out of this rock?'
> And Moses raised his hand and struck the
> rock with his staff twice, so that abundant
> water came out and the community and

their cattle drank. Now, *YHVH* said to Moses
and Aaron,] 'Because you did not trust Me
enough to treat Me as holy in the sight of
the Israelite people, [therefore you shall not
bring this assembly into the land that I am
giving to them']" (Num. 20:8–12).

Rashi and Ramban differ regarding Moses's sin. One argues that it was
because Moses said to the Israelites, "**Listen, you rebels, [shall we get
water for you out of this rock?**]" (Ramban on Num. 20:7), and one
argues that it was because Moses hit the rock (Rashi on Num. 20:12).
We shall see that there is only one reason, since one act caused the other.

There are two types of teachers who admonish people, urging
us to do the will of the blessed Creator. One reproves with pleasant
words, telling each of us our elevated status; the source from which
our soul was hewn (since our souls are taken from beneath the Throne
of Glory); how much pleasure the blessed Creator derives (as it were)
from the mitzvot performed by each of us; how much joy fills all the
divine realms because we fulfill the command of the blessed Creator. In
this manner, he inclines our hearts to do the will of the blessed Creator,
to take on the yoke of God's sovereignty. On the other hand, there are
those who admonish people with harsh words, humiliating words,
until they are compelled to do the will of the Creator.

This is the difference between them. The one who admonishes us
with goodwill raises our souls higher and higher. He always reminds us
of our righteousness and greatness, and how powerful our influence is
above. For this reason, he is fit to be appointed as a leader. But the one
who admonishes with harsh words is nothing like this. Indeed, the one
who admonishes us with goodwill, reciting our greatness and goodness,
creates the conditions such that all creation fulfills our wishes of its own
accord. It does that for which it was created, to provide for us. But if one
does not tell and laud the goodness of the people, then creation must be
compelled with great effort to fulfill its purpose, to do our will.

And here, Moses said, "**Listen, you rebels,**" admonishing Israel with
harsh words. Therefore, he had to strike the rock to compel it to do
what it was created to do. But if he had praised Israel, as above, which
was the intention of the blessed Holy One in the instruction "**speak to
the rock,**" he would have said to the rock, "You were created for the
sake of Israel, who are great in spirit. You have to do that for which you

were created: to provide water for Israel." But now that he chastised Israel with harsh words, saying, "Listen, you rebels," he was compelled to hit the rock to force it to do Israel's will. In this manner, one thing led to the other, and they are really one matter.

This is the meaning of "**Because you did not trust Me enough to treat Me as holy in the sight of the Israelite people.**" The one who admonishes with goodwill is able to bring the people to the same state of awareness. This is the implication of the phrase "**to treat Me as holy in the sight of the Israelite people**" (*lehakdisheini l'einei benei yisrael*): the Sages said, "(The men of the Sanhedrin are) the eyes of the community" (Song Rabbah 1:64, on Song 1:15). The wise ones of the community would have been able to attain this state of awareness.

FOR FURTHER THOUGHT

Once again, where the traditional commentators pay attention to the details of the narrative to determine how exactly Moses sinned, Levi Yitzhak pays attention to the inner workings of the mind and heart to locate the sin. The problem was not the words that Moses spoke, nor his act, but the inner experience of the moment. Moses lost his composure, and rather than seeing the good in Israel, he saw only their failings, and he gave voice to his anger and frustration. We have to be careful as well to see clearly in the moment so that we can admonish in such a manner that we encourage rather than intimidate.

This lesson is emblematic of the rejection by Hasidic preachers of the negative, chastising style of the contemporary leaders of the Jewish people. The latter were obsessed with fear of sin. They thought that only by engendering fear in others could they bring compliance with Torah and commandments. The Hasidic leaders, while attentive to the importance of and the power of fear of heaven, recognized the greater potential of love and compassion to bring about change in others. Part of their strategy, and of their appeal, was their understanding of the people and their capacity to connect with them through love. This is based in the teaching of the Baal Shem Tov that no place, no moment, no act, no thought, no experience is devoid of God. Therefore, all moments have the potential to become moments of connection with God, a God who is loving and who desires our loving response.

Questions for Reflection

1. What is your experience—do you attract more bees with honey or with vinegar? Does your answer change with the circumstances? When do you find that you admonish with honey and when with vinegar? What is your inner experience with each one? What prompts each one?

2. What do you make of the fact that Levi Yitzhak spends so much more time describing the manner and outcome of admonishing with goodwill? Whom is he trying to convince? The preachers in his community whose tradition was harsh admonishment? Potential Hasidim who might doubt the integrity of the Hasidic teacher? His own Hasidim? Or could he have another agenda?

3. Do you see the second sort of tzaddik—the one who admonishes harshly—as a real tzaddik? Is there a role for such a person in our communities and our lives? Is it important to have such a tzaddik around to balance the other one, perhaps to keep the "self-esteem" he promotes in check and grounded? When, how, why?

Taking It into Your Life

Levi Yitzhak invites us to consider how we speak to other people. There are few interactions in which we do not or cannot play a role as *mokhiach*— one who encourages another person to change. In every instance, how we speak to another person, how we relate to them, makes it more or less possible for them to attain their fullest potential or express their full being.

As you interact with others, observe how you frame your speech. When do you offer compliments? When do you acknowledge the good in another person? When do you withhold this from them?

When do you frame your comments in such a manner that they are self-promoting, including nonessential information in order to "score points" or establish power or authority? How is it possible to acknowledge relative status—in power, authority, knowledge, competence, etc.—without "putting down" another person?

When someone speaks to you in a manner that seems to undermine your self-esteem or challenges your self-image, how do you respond? Is it possible to allow such comments to pass without revenge? Is it possible to internalize such comments without being demoralized, but instead inspired to be better? How?

When it is necessary to rebuke or criticize another person, what does it take to make this a positive experience, one in which there will be greater energy for positive change?

Balak

"The angel of *YHVH* said to him, 'Why have you beaten your ass [these three times? It is I who came out as an adversary, for the errand is obnoxious to me']" (Num. 22:32).

Why was the angel angry that Balaam beat his ass? So long as Balaam had not seen the angel, he had every right to strike his animal to make it follow the path.

Therefore, when Balaam saw something surprising and unexpected—when his ass lay down under him, something it had never done before (as it says, "Have I been in the habit of doing thus to you?"; Num. 22:30)—it would only have been right for him to reconsider what he was doing, to see that it was God's will that he return and not proceed. Now remember God's precise instructions to Balaam: "[Since it is to call you that the men have come, arise, go with them;] but only the word that I speak to you, that you must do" (22:20). He was instructed to pay close attention and to use his intellect to discern God's will so that he could do it. Therefore, he should have taken things to heart and not have beaten his ass. But in beating his ass he revealed his true wickedness: even though it was God's will that he not go, nevertheless he continued on his way, and he beat his ass in anger because it delayed him in his journey. This is why the angel was angry with him, saying, "**Why have you beaten your ass?**"

FOR FURTHER THOUGHT

Levi Yitzhak applies the lesson of Balaam to our lives in general. God instructs Balaam to do only as God commands. To fulfill God's commandment means not only to do the specific act, but also to do it in such a manner that reveals our true intention to fulfill God's will in the moment. Thus, if there are impediments on the way to completing the commandment, we must consider the possibility that these obstacles are meant to redirect us, to announce that there is a new instruction, a new way we are to fulfill this commandment.

This lesson expands the range of meaning of the term *mitzvah*. That is, God not only has instructed us to obey the rules of the Written and Oral Torahs, but also continues to instruct individuals to do things that are unique to them, to their circumstances and situation, to their specific time and place. Not only from day to day but also from moment to moment we are instructed to move, to act, to respond. We are always on the path that God instructs us, and we must always be attentive to knowing what God desires of us in this instance.

From this lesson, we might be tempted to think that meeting obstacles automatically means that God is telling us to change course. But there is nothing automatic about the process of discerning God's will. It requires clear attention and investigation in the moment to know what is called for. Consider the following extended narrative, a composite of a number of midrashim regarding Abraham and Isaac on the way to the *Akedah*:

> And while Abraham and Isaac were proceeding along the road, Satan came and appeared to Abraham in the figure of a very aged man, humble and of contrite spirit, and said to him: "Art thou silly or foolish, that thou goest to do this thing to thine only son? God gave thee a son in thy latter days, in thine old age, and wilt thou go and slaughter him, who did not commit any violence, and wilt thou cause the soul of thine only son to perish from the earth? Dost thou not know and understand that this thing cannot be from the Lord? For the Lord would not do unto man such evil, to command him, Go and slaughter thy son." Abraham, hearing these words, knew that it was Satan, who endeavored to turn him astray from the way of the Lord, and he rebuked him that he went away.
>
> And Satan returned and came to Isaac, and he appeared unto him in the figure of a young man, comely and well-favored, saying unto him: "Dost thou not know that thy silly old father bringeth thee to the slaughter this day for naught? Now, my son, do not listen to him, for he is a silly old man, and let not thy precious soul and beautiful figure be lost from the earth." And Isaac told these words to his father, but Abraham said to him, "Take heed of him, and do not listen to his words, for he is Satan endeavoring to lead us astray from the commands of our God."

And Abraham rebuked Satan again, and Satan went from them, and, seeing he could not prevail over them, he transformed himself into a large brook of water in the road, and when Abraham, Isaac, and the two young men reached that place, they saw a brook large and powerful as the mighty waters. And they entered the brook, trying to pass it, but the further they went, the deeper the brook, so that the water reached up to their necks, and they were all terrified on account of the water. But Abraham recognized the place, and he knew that there had been no water there before, and he said to his son: "I know this place, on which there was no brook nor water. Now, surely, it is Satan who doth all this to us, to draw us aside this day from the commands of God." And Abraham rebuked Satan, saying unto him: "The Lord rebuke thee, O Satan. Begone from us, for we go by the command of God." And Satan was terrified at the voice of Abraham, and he went away from them, and the place became dry land again as it was at first. And Abraham went with Isaac toward the place that God had told him. (Louis Ginzberg, *Legends of the Jews* [Philadelphia: Jewish Publication Society, 2003; digital edition], p. 226ff)

Clearly, it is neither obstacle nor ease of movement that signifies the sign of God's will or desire. Indeed, it may be impossible to create clear rules by which we may determine when and if we are doing what God wants of us in the moment. The practice of spiritual direction offers a context in which we might, in the company of another person (or several), investigate how God is working in us at the moment, what God may wish of us. In any moment we may discern that ease is deceptive—"Satan" leading us astray—or an invitation to follow God's path, that obstacles are "Satan" seeking to prevent us from doing God's will or messages from God that we are meant to change course. Acting and refraining from acting are ultimately both actions, both ways of following God's will or resisting it. We cannot know in this moment what will be called from us in the future. We can only pay attention in this minute to what is before us, what we are called to do, and then observe the outcome, so that we might see more clearly what God wants of us now.

 ## Questions for Reflection

1. How do you relate to signs (*simanim*) and hints (*remazim*)? In some circumstances we would phrase the question as "How superstitious are

you?" Is there a distinction between a *remez* (like Balaam's ass crouching beneath him) and a superstitious "rule" (black cat crossing your path; spilled salt; red ears)? What is the difference? How do you experience it—when does it come into play in your life?

2. Do you think that Levi Yitzhak would accept as normative practice striking one's recalcitrant ass? Is not God in all things? How do we raise the sparks in animals (aside from eating them)? Is it only when they are doing something for a holy purpose? What work do animals do that is not for a holy purpose (even serving us)?

3. Have you ever had a conversation with an angel? Who has served to open your eyes to what was before you, to how you have repeated the same mistake over and over? Could this person have been an angel? Have you ever served in that capacity for someone else? What keeps angels from being annoying noodges and unwanted advice givers?

Taking It into Your Life

Mindfulness practice helps us pay close attention to the truth of the moment—to see through or around the habits of mind (and body and spirit) that keep us from being compassionate, just, and free in our lives. There is a profound way in which this is similar to what Levi Yitzhak is seeking: to know what God wants of us in this moment. To be aligned with God's will is to be free of personal reservations or preferences, to know deeply what is called for in this moment, and to be able to do it without contention. Seeking to follow God's command from moment to moment demands great curiosity; it requires us to stay awake. To remain attentive to what God desires of us, we cannot simply do what we have always done, continuing what we set out to do without checking in to notice: is this still the right thing to do?

It may be that this practice can also be framed in terms similar to "time management." Stephen Covey taught us to look at our work and efforts, evaluating each activity to determine in which of four quadrants it should be placed. The quadrants have to do with urgency and importance. Something can be urgent but unimportant, or urgent and important; it could be important but not urgent, or unimportant and not urgent.

Use this framework to view what you do from day to day. Become accustomed to discerning what is important and what is urgent, considering when and where they coincide, and when the urgent precludes doing the important. Notice when the important is supplanted by another important matter, and sense when the second is truly more important and when it is only more urgent. When you feel comfortable making these distinctions, notice as well when you turn your attention to what is important but not urgent and when you spend time doing what is neither important nor urgent.

What do you sense God calls you to do: the urgent or the important? Is the urgent always more demanding than the important but not urgent? Why or why not? How can you sense when God is impeding forward action—redirecting you to what is important—and when it is "satan" deflecting you from doing what is important, to do the urgent or the unimportant?

Reflect.

> "[He took up his theme, and said: / From Aram has Balak brought me, / Moab's king from the hills of the East:] / Come, curse [for] me Jacob, / [Come, tell Israel's doom!]" (Num. 23:7).

This is how it is: Each nation has to have some good quality, and it is this which is the vital force that sustains them. The Jewish people, however, are endowed with all of the good qualities.

Here, this wicked man sought to do ill to Israel, who are endowed with all of the good qualities. So, he sought to discern for himself which of those good qualities his people shared with Israel, to be able to use that power to do them ill. That is the significance of his words "**curse [for] me**" (*arah li*), where the verb *arah* has the sense of "plucking (selecting) figs" (*oreh bete'einim*). So he wanted to select out that quality that he had among the good qualities of the Jewish people. That is the meaning of "**curse [for] me Jacob**": he wished to cull out that quality that he has from Jacob and by that means "**tell Israel's doom.**"

> "[Taking up his theme, he said: / Word of Balaam son of Beor,] / Word of the man whose eye is closed" (Num. 24:3).

There is a "good eye" that seeks to pour out goodness on Israel. But "God made both this and that" (Eccles. 7:14), which means that there is a "bad eye" that draws its strength from the realm of the husks (*kelippot*). Balaam had this sort of "bad eye," that drew its strength from the husks, but he was not able to use it against Israel, since God did not permit him to do so. Therefore, he had no power from his "bad eye." At the same time, he was not able to draw power from the "good eye," realm of the holy, since the blessing he offered Israel was against his will and not from his true desire. God compelled him to bless them; since it was not his intention, he could not draw power from the realm of the "good eye."

That is why he described himself as a "**man whose eye is closed**," as he was made "blind" in this manner. He was neither able to draw power from the realm of holiness, the "good eye," nor from the realm of the husks, the "bad eye." Thus, he was blind in both eyes. That is why he describes himself later as "fallen, whose eyes are unveiled" (Num. 24:4): his eyes were unveiled from having "fallen," that is, the "bad eye"; the realm of the husk is called "fallen," as we know from the teaching of the Sages regarding the signs of the "bad eye." Therefore, now that he was not able to draw power from the husk of the "bad eye"—because God had not permitted him—he became blind.

FOR FURTHER THOUGHT

These two selections address the nature of the person who would curse another. In the first case, we learn of Balaam's strategy. Levi Yitzhak knows of the following midrash (Num. R. 20:7; *Tanchuma, Balak* 4) in which the verb *arah* is first used by Balak in his petition to Balaam to come curse Israel:

> "Come then, curse for me [*arah li*] this people" (Num. 22:6). What is the significance of the words *arah li*? I may be able to overcome them a little, as one who picks [*oreh*] figs. "Since they are too numerous for me" (ibid.): Not that they are strong men and their armies are numerous, but they conquer with their mouth! This is a thing that I cannot do.

Fig trees are prodigious and produce fruit continuously through their season. One might pick enough for a meal or to sell, and there will still be more left on the tree. The midrash thus imagines Balak saying that no matter how he tries, he will not be able to overcome all of Israel's power—particularly as it resides in their words of prayer and Torah study.

Levi Yitzhak reads this image in a mystical manner. The plethora of figs on a tree represents the *middot*, the divine qualities of the *sephirot*, or possibly the spiritual powers that characterize the different nations. While one or another of these qualities or powers is found in all nations, Levi Yitzhak asserts that all of them are present in the Jewish people. In his petition to Balaam and in Balaam's efforts to curse Israel, the idea was to find a connection between the one quality in Balak or Balaam and those in Israel and to use that association as a means to curse Israel. Balak, like the evil inclination (*yetzer hara*), wishing to bring about Israel's downfall, will use even the least connection to cause self-doubt or to find fault.

This is possible only when one willfully chooses to see only the worst in another, refusing to see them as a whole being. This personality type is recognized by the Sages and reflected in this mishnah (Avot 5:19):

> Whoever possesses these three things is a disciple of Abraham our Father, and whoever possesses three other things is a disciple of Balaam the wicked: a good eye, a humble spirit, and limited desires—these are the possessions of the disciples of Abraham; an evil eye, a haughty spirit and expansive desires—these are the possessions of Balaam the wicked.

The Sages, reading Scripture carefully, recognize that much of Balaam's power had to do with his vision. He both needed to see the people he would curse and was able to receive divine illumination. His vision, though, was limited, selfish, negative. God prevented him from employing this power, and so he was "blind" in his "evil eye"; unwilling or unable to bless Israel, he was "blind" as well in his "good eye."

Taken together, these two lessons direct our attention to our own experience of viewing others. We are invited to notice how we use connections, similarities, and sympathetic understanding to gain power over others. We are directed to investigate our own inner process of selectivity—how we discern and relate to the core of holiness in the world or its opposite. We are made aware of how, even in our seeing, we are often blinded by our own inner desires, fears, jealousies, and closed-heartedness. And, we are then given the opportunity to choose to live with a good eye, selecting the good in the other for their sake, for the sake of blessing.

Questions for Reflection

1. What prompts you to look for what you have in common with other people? When do you resist seeing that commonality? Why? What do you gain from commonality, and what do you gain from uniqueness? What do you lose from each?

2. How have you used your knowledge of the qualities of other people to gain advantage or power or to assert authority? How have you used your knowledge of the qualities of other people to help them develop their own self-awareness and power?

3. What do you understand to be the "signs of the bad eye"? What is the source of energy that motivates the "bad eye"?

Taking It into Your Life

In these texts we hear echoes of Levi Yitzhak's teaching regarding the "gaze of appreciation" versus the "gaze of appropriation." We use our eyes both to take in the world and to reach out to it. They are the initial means by which we engage in the world, how we first investigate the location and nature of holy sparks around us. But often our looking is not neutral. When our attention is drawn to something we find pleasing or attractive, we reach out with our eyes to possess it. When we see something unattractive or repulsive, we turn away, internally negating it, nullifying its existence.

We employ our vision in even more refined and demanding ways. Without even being aware of it, we notice subtle facial movements, hints of expression that may themselves be unintentional. We observe the dynamics in a group, sizing up the leaders, the followers, the ones who stand to the side, and those who seem lost. We watch the interactions between parents and children, between longtime partners and people on their first date. We use our eyes to gain information about the world we live in, but most especially about the people with whom we work and among whom we move.

Yet often we are unaware of the assessments we make of what we see, appraising highly or lowly the people we are watching. Still, this is going on all the time. The challenge of these texts is to become more aware of the inner process of assessment that is initiated by our seeing. Again, notice when your gaze comes to rest on an object or a person. Pay attention to your body sensations: Do you lean forward or back? Do you sense excitement or lethargy? As you notice yourself watching others, investigate your emotional response: Do you sense what you are seeing as pleasant, unpleasant, neutral? Have you formed an opinion about what you are seeing based on that response? Give heed to the inner response of "I like that" or "I don't like that."

Notice what it may take to turn your connections to people and things into efforts for the good of others. Notice what it takes to make how you see what you see a means of blessing.

"My message was to bless: But when He blesses, I cannot reverse it" (Num. 23:20).

We learn in the Talmud (Megillah 25a):

> One who says "May (only) the good bless You": this is the manner of heresy; "May Your mercies reach the nest of a bird," "May Your name be mentioned for doing good"; "We give thanks, we give thanks"—he is silenced.

Rashi comments:

> One who says "Your mercies reach the nest of a bird and You have commanded us, 'Do not take the mother bird along with her young' (Deut. 22:6), so may You pay attention and be merciful to us" is silenced, since he suggests that all of God's qualities are mercy, but they are only the decrees of a king to his servants.

Further, the *Tosafot* asked: If this is the case, why would the liturgical poet (Kalir) have written:

> They fulfilled the decree "Him and his child you shall not slaughter in one day" (Lev. 22:28); Your thoughts are to be merciful to us, Your deeds to exalt us.

This is as if to say that the Holy One has compassion for the animal and its child, when this instruction is meant only as a decree.

At the same time, the Sages taught (Shabbat 151b):

> R. Gamaliel Beribbi interpreted this verse: "And He shall show (give) you compassion, and have compassion on you, and make

you increase" (Deut. 13:18): he who is compassionate to others, compassion is shown to him by heaven, while he who is not merciful to others, mercy is not shown to him by heaven.

The root of this lesson is found in the Zohar (III 31b): "Arousal from below awakens acts above." Therefore, when we are compassionate to others, we arouse the quality (*middah*) of compassion, and compassion flows to us as well. It is well known that "God's love [*chasdei YHVH*] has not ceased [His compassion is not run out. They are renewed every morning—Your faithfulness is great [*rabbah emunatekha*]! 'YHVH is my portion,' I say with full heart, therefore will I hope in Him]" (Lam. 3:22–24). The blessed Holy One constantly pours out love and compassion and goodness. And when sometimes we are bereft of good things, we are the obstacle preventing that goodness from reaching us; we are not fit to receive that goodness.

But, the blessed Holy One, out of compassion and love, is able to transform our hearts, to give us a pure heart, one powerful and courageous enough to serve God in truth, and then we will be fit to receive that goodness. That is the meaning of our prayer (in *Tachanun*; cf. Ps. 40:12): "You, O God, do not hold back your compassion from us [*mimmenu*]"—let not the obstacle to your goodness be "from us" (due to us; *mimmenu*)—"Your love [*chasd'kha*] and your truth [*amit'kha*] always protect us [*yitzrunu*; this could be read 'form us/create us']." The blessed Holy One creates us anew in each moment, as the Sages taught, "Let everything that has breath praise *Yah*" (Ps. 150:6)—with each and every breath praise God (cf. Gen. R. 14:9). Thus, we see that God can make us anew and give us a pure heart.

We know that when the blessed Holy One makes a decree that the tzaddik can annul it (cf. Mo'ed Katan 16b). This lies behind the verse (from the prayer *Unetaneh Tokef*): "Your throne is established in love [*chesed*], and You sit on it in truth [*be'emet*]." When the blessed Holy One establishes His throne in love, arousing compassion and love for Israel, then He sits on the throne "in truth" (*be'emet*), since no tzaddik can annul this decree. But when the opposite prevails (heaven forbid), then the tzaddik can annul the decree, and the blessed Holy One is compelled to rise from the throne of Judgment and sit in the throne of Compassion—and so, God had not been seated "in truth" (*be'emet*).

Now, when the blessed Holy One commanded us not to take the dame and her young, it was not because of God's compassion. Had it been from God's compassion, God would not have had to command us; God alone would have been able to save the mother, for great spaciousness and salvation is God's. Rather, God's intention was that we might arouse God's quality of compassion when we show compassion to the bird's nest, as above. This also helps us to understand the poet: "Your thoughts are to be merciful to us, Your deeds to exalt us"—You have commanded us so that we might arouse compassion, so that You might be compassionate to us.

Thus, when the tzaddik blesses Israel, he surely does so with a full heart, out of the compassion and love that he has for them. And so heaven blesses him in turn, as we learned above: "he who is compassionate to others, compassion is shown to him by heaven." But Balaam knew in himself that he would not bless Israel wholeheartedly, that the blessed Holy One placed a hook in his mouth to prevent him from cursing Israel. Therefore, he knew that the blessings he pronounced would not redound to him. That is what he meant when he said, "**My message was to bless**"—I took blessings from the blessed Holy One to bless Israel—"**But when He blesses, I cannot reverse it**"—I cannot turn the blessings so that they come back to me.

FOR FURTHER THOUGHT

Why would Levi Yitzhak go to such lengths to show that the commandments are not an expression of God's compassion for us? Do we not wish to know and benefit from God's compassion and love? The issue seems to be that if the commandments are an expression of God's compassion alone, then that represents "arousal from above." When God acts without having been stimulated or moved to do so by our actions, the direction, focus, and force of God's act is not fully felt by Israel. God's goodness flows equally over the whole of the world, affecting the wicked equally with the good. Levi Yitzhak teaches that it is much better, even necessary, that we perform the mitzvot to bring delight to the Creator, so that the expression of God's love and compassion in response may be more effective.

In this lesson, Levi Yitzhak plays with the terms "love" (*chesed*) and "truth" (*emet*). God's love is most truly expressed when it flows directly. That love flows most directly when it arises in response to our actions. When we act lovingly and compassionately toward others, God responds with love and compassion for us. So that we are able to act in that manner, God creates us anew in each moment, forming us with love and truth. With these newly transformed hearts, we are able to fulfill God's commandments—"the decrees of a king to his servants"—without reservation, solely to bring God delight and to do good for others. True, when we fail to do so and God issues a negative decree in judgment, the tzaddik can reverse the decree. But, the love that flows in that instance is not as effective; it is not "true" love.

The compassion that we express to others, the consequence of our performing the commandments for God's delight, returns to us as blessing from God. The compassion we express to others must be wholehearted; it cannot be forced or result from ulterior motives. Balaam did bless the people, but since his blessing was imposed on him by God, he could not benefit from it in return. Balaam, as always, serves as a foil, a negative example from whom we can learn.

Questions for Reflection

1. What is your experience: would you prefer that God extend love and compassion spontaneously but without direction or that God extend love and compassion with intention but dependent on your behavior? Why? How does that affect your behavior, if at all?

2. How do you respond to Levi Yitzhak's assertions about what constitutes "true love"? How might his use of the phrase from *Unetaneh Tokef* change your experience of that prayer next year?

3. When have you felt that the blessings you extended to others were truly heartfelt? How have you felt blessed in the blessing of others? When? Have you ever sensed being blessed by the fact that you blessed others? When, how, why?

Taking It into Your Life

A key to this lesson is that God creates us anew each day, an important Hasidic teaching. God's love and compassion are renewed faithfully each day, manifest in our renewed capacity to express love and compassion.

We might practice with setting intention. Each morning, as you start your day, pause for a few moments to internalize the possibility of being a new person today. You are free in this day to be most fully who you are, without the burden of your remembered faults and mistakes. You are free this day to act as you truly wish, unencumbered by your internalized self-limitations and fears.

From this place of awareness, set your intention: As this day is new, so am I made new; may I use my body, mind, heart, and spirit to extend love and compassion to all of God's creatures. May I notice even the least of all creatures and know that it, too, basks in God's love and compassion. May my life be a blessing to all I meet.

Reflect.

"How fair are your tents, O Jacob, your dwellings, O Israel!" (Num. 24:5).

Consider this verse in light of the mishnah: "Shammai taught: Establish fixed times for Torah study; say little and do much; receive all people with welcome" (Avot 1:15).

Jacob signifies a lower spiritual level, and Israel signifies a higher one. This is why the word "**your tents**" (*ohalekha*) is associated with Jacob: you should make the time you allot to your work temporary, passing; "**your dwellings**" (*mishkenotekha*) is associated with Israel: make your Torah study fixed.

FOR FURTHER THOUGHT

There are many ways in which we might understand the difference between "tents" and "dwellings." Levi Yitzhak picks up on the difference between the temporary, passing nature of a tent versus the permanent, fixed quality of a dwelling. To this he brings the distinction between Jacob and Israel, the former signifying a lower status. This is reflected in the following passage from the Zohar (III 73a):

R. Eleazar asked his father, R. Shimon, this question: "We know that it is forbidden to teach Torah to a gentile, and the Companions in Babylonia have done well to connect this to the verse 'He has not done so for any other nation' (Ps. 147:20). But in the preceding verse it says, 'He issued His commands to Jacob'—why does it then conclude, 'His statutes and rules to Israel'?"

He replied, "Eleazar, come and see: how fortunate are the Jews, that the blessed Holy One planted this supernal holy portion in them, as it says, 'I give you good instruction' (Prov. 4:2)—to you and not to idolaters. Now, since God's own holy, supernal name is hidden, so too is the Torah both hidden and revealed in the mystery of God's name. And in this manner as well are the Jewish people in two degrees, both hidden and revealed. We have taught: these three degrees are all connected one to the other, the blessed Holy One, Torah, and Israel, and each one is made up of degrees, hidden and revealed. The blessed Holy One is both hidden and revealed, as is the Torah. Israel is also composed of these levels. This is as Scripture says, 'He issued His commandments to Jacob, His statutes and rules to Israel': two degrees, Jacob and Israel, one revealed and one concealed. ...

"To the simple Jew we teach those things in the Torah that are on the surface, the letters and the plain contents and the precepts, and no more. This is indicated in the words, 'He issued His commandments to Jacob.' ... But if a Jew rises to a higher grade, then 'His statutes and rules to Israel': these are the allegories of the Torah and the hidden paths of the Torah and the secrets of the Torah, which should only be revealed to those of a higher degree."

Levi Yitzhak brings the theme of the Zohar and its configuration of Jacob/Israel into relationship with that which is temporary and that which is permanent. The Torah study of the "Israel" Jew comes from dedicated study, day and night, with full attention. It is that goal toward which Shammai points us. It is what is represented by the "dwelling." When we are dedicated to that goal of engagement in Torah, whatever distracts us—our daily affairs, our employment and work—can only be attended to sporadically. This is the temporary nature of the "tent." And surely the one who devotes more time to what is of passing importance, ephemeral when compared to Torah, can only attain the degree of Jacob.

 ## Questions for Reflection

1. When you think about Jacob and Israel, do you make the sorts of distinctions that the Zohar and others make? How do you relate to the person of Jacob, and how is that different, if at all, from the person of Israel?

2. In many ways, the Jacob of the Torah is the most developed of the Patriarchs. His "work life" is more fully realized. How do you see this fact reflected in our lesson, if at all? Does that make you more or less positively oriented toward your own work life? When, how, why?

3. How do you sense the Torah is planted in you?

Taking It into Your Life

Consider the story in the Talmud (Shabbat 33b) of R. Shimon bar Yohai and his son R. Eleazar, who secluded themselves in a cave for twelve years to escape the wrath of the Roman emperor. This is purportedly the same R. Shimon and R. Eleazar of whom we read in the Zohar.

> So they went and hid in a cave. A miracle occurred and a carob tree and a well of water were created for them. They would strip their garments and sit up to their necks in sand. The whole day they studied; when it was time for prayers they robed, covered themselves, prayed, and then took off their garments again, so that they should not wear out. Thus they dwelt twelve years in the cave.
>
> Then Elijah came and stood at the entrance to the cave and exclaimed, "Who will inform Bar Yohai that the emperor is dead and his decree annulled?" So they emerged. Seeing a man plowing and sowing, they exclaimed, "They forsake life eternal and engage in the passing matters of this world!" Whatever they cast their eyes upon was immediately burnt up. Thereupon a *bat kol* [heavenly voice] came forth and cried out, "Have you emerged to destroy My world? Return to your cave!" So they returned and stayed there twelve months, saying, "The punishment of the wicked in Gehenna is twelve months."
>
> A *bat kol* then came forth and said, "Leave your cave!" They came out, and wherever R. Eleazar wounded [with a glance of his eyes], R. Shimon healed. He said to him, "My son! You and I are sufficient for the world."
>
> On the eve of the Sabbath before sunset, they saw an old man holding two bundles of myrtle and running at twilight. "What are these for?" they asked him. "They are in honor of the Sabbath," he replied. "But one should be enough for you!" He replied, "One is for 'Remember' and one is for 'Observe.'" Said he to his son, "See how precious the commandments are to Israel." With that their minds were set at ease.

In this story, R. Shimon and his son learn that as important as Torah study may be (it sustained them for thirteen years!), it cannot supplant the matters of this world completely. "The passing matters of this world" (*chayyei sha'ah*) have their place. Indeed, as we learn in the conclusion, it is those activities that create the wherewithal by which we can adorn and enjoy the commandments.

Still, it takes practice to maintain an honest balance. Shammai sought to guarantee that Torah would get its due by teaching, "Establish fixed times for Torah study." Hillel taught, "Do not say, 'When I have leisure I will study' for you may never find leisure" (Avot 2:5). Rabban Gamaliel, son of Rabbi Yehudah HaNasi said, "It is good to combine Torah study with some worldly occupation [*derekh eretz*], for the energy devoted to them both helps us forget sin; all Torah study that is not combined with some trade [*melakhah*] in the end is wasted and leads to sin" (Avot 2:2).

Observe carefully how you spend your time. What constitutes "free time"? How do you use it? How is it distinguished from the time you devote to Torah study? What aspects of your life do you consider to be devoted to the passing matters of the world (*chayyei sha'ah*) or that which is temporary? What is devoted to that which is eternal? How do you experience your connection to "Israel," the eternal, supernal aspects of Jewish life? When, in the midst of your daily affairs, do you realize that even those matters can be devoted to God, made spiritual? When are the commandments "precious" to you, and how can you expand that experience?

Reflect.

Pinchas

"Pinchas, son of Eleazar son of Aaron the priest, has turned back My wrath from the Israelites by displaying among them his passion for Me, so that I did not wipe out the Israelite people in My passion" (Num. 25:11).

"Pinchas is Elijah" (Zohar II 190a); and Elijah lives on forever (Zohar II 197a). How is this so? First, understand that our physical bodies are not deeply connected to divine service, since the body tends to look out for its own needs. But our soul is always attentive to the fear of heaven. The body is not like the soul, and therefore it is corruptible and dies. Nevertheless, if the body could similarly serve God at all times, no one would die, and this is how it was before the first human (*adam harishon*) sinned.

Now Pinchas committed his life to taking this act, as the Sages taught, and thus his body demonstrated that it gave no thought to its own physical needs. It was devoted solely to serving God just like his soul. His body, when he did what he did, was as if it did not exist, since he had accepted his own death to fulfill the divine will. In this manner Pinchas's body was completely purified, and so he still lives. This is suggested in the midrash (Num. R. 21:1): "'Pinchas son of Eleazar son of Aaron the Priest': The Holy One said, 'It is only right [*badin hu*] that he should receive his reward.'" This accords with what we have taught above: his body was as if it did not exist when he did what he did, as if it was hidden. Now this is hinted at in the midrash where it says, "It is only right" (*badin hu*): *hu* (i.e., "he" or "it") is the third person pronoun, meaning the one who is hidden. And his body was hidden—and therefore it is only right that he should indeed receive his reward.

FOR FURTHER THOUGHT

In Hasidic works, in general, there is an ambivalence toward the body. Hasidic teachers received all of the teachings of the Middle Ages that treated the body as negative, corrupt and corrupting, a distraction from the work of the soul. But the Baal Shem Tov taught that we not only can but must serve God in every manner, including in the most basic embodied experiences: eating, drinking, having sex, doing business. In our lesson we hear some of both themes.

Levi Yitzhak suggests that one might be able to train the body, direct the body, and come to know the body and its perceived "needs" that it too might serve God in purity at all times, like the soul. The soul so desires to serve God that had it no other constraints (like working with a body) it would spontaneously do God's will in purity. The body can attain that status as well, when its self-concern—primarily for self-preservation—is nullified. The instinct for self-preservation is powerful and exerts its force on subtle levels. It is the source of the energy that leads us to lash out at others when we feel threatened—because someone has taken the last piece of cake that we wanted, because someone has challenged us in our expertise, because we fear that our "inadequacies" will be revealed.

The clearer our self-knowledge, the more possible it is that we might resist the instinctive reaction, instead to respond skillfully and wisely. Again, the metaphor of transparency might be helpful: the whole of our hearts, souls, and bodies will be known to us, and so there will be less likelihood of getting stuck in a habitual reaction. The divine light will pass through us, and our actions will manifest its purity more fully.

And we might even recognize this in people we know or of whom we have heard. There are those who are able to act without consideration of their personal needs for the sake of others or who act for the sake of heaven (martyrs, those who offer their lives for others). There are those who can so focus the mind in the present moment that their physical beings cease functioning in "the normal manner"—think of Ghandian, nonviolent passive resistors whose bodies do not stand in the way of doing what is right.

So our lesson is actually an invitation to pay attention to the body for the sake of heaven. The process, apparently, will lead us to relate to our own bodies in the third person, as if they were not present, as if their needs did not always take precedence over what is called for in the moment. We will treat our bodies with the same care and concern we show to others, but not more (and not less). Whatever needs to be done will flow naturally, without self-concern, for the sake of heaven.

Questions for Reflection

1. Have you ever had an experience in which your body—your awareness of your body and its physical needs—fell away and the whole of your person was concentrated on the moment? Are you able to describe the "feeling"? Can you replicate the moment? Do you want to?

2. Many of us have a difficult time squaring Pinchas's zealotry and God's particular blessing (as did the Rabbis). Levi Yitzhak suggests that the reason that Pinchas received this blessing was the purity of his being—he had transcended physical needs or concerns and was completely devoted to God. Does this redeem zealotry, particularly in an age of "suicide martyrs"? Is there any way that we can accept Levi Yitzhak's view and not step onto a slippery slope? Or is he so circumspect as to say, "Don't try this at home, kids"? How do you understand this lesson for yourself?

3. There is a Hasidic tradition that the bodies of tzaddikim are so connected to God that they spontaneously do what God wants. For that reason, for instance, Abraham had to "send out" his hand to grab the knife with which he intended to sacrifice Isaac—his hand "knew" that was not what God wanted and had to be forced. Would you want to bring your soul/mind/body so into line with God that you spontaneously did what God wanted? What reward would you receive for your actions then? What would your body be like then? Would it be anything like what Levi Yitzhak is suggesting about Pinchas?

Taking It into Your Life

One way the Hasidic and mystical tradition has of talking about this experience is "the negation of the physical" (*bittul hayesh*). The goal is to raise one's consciousness toward God, seeking to so cleave to God that one loses awareness of the physical, separate existence. Indeed, one moves from "somethingness" (*yesh*) to "nothingness" (*ayin*). Still, in this experience, the assumption is that one returns again to the status of *yesh*. Indeed, this is the dynamic process by which the tzaddik induces the flow of blessing to the people: moving between the realm in which all is present and all is potential (*ayin*), where all is perceived as good, drawing that goodness down into the realm of *yesh*.

This is suggestive for mindfulness practice. While our goal may be to maintain mindful awareness all the time, it is hard to do. But we may move in and out of such awareness. When we are able in a moment to stop, pay attention, let go of biases and preferences, see clearly and not create a story, we may find that our bodies are at ease and able to respond with energy and calm. Practice this—right now—by taking a breath, feeling yourself sitting in your chair, sensing the ease that comes of awareness of how, in this moment, it cannot be otherwise. Notice the freedom that arises, inviting clear-sighted, purposeful action without fear. Perhaps this is the spirit of Elijah moving in you.

Practice. Reflect.

While we're at it, it would be worthwhile to explain the question of the Zohar: how is it that Pinchas was appointed a priest? Is not a priest who has killed someone is disqualified from the priesthood! After all, the quality that characterizes the priesthood is love (*chesed*) and not judgment (*din*). Further, in this manner we can explain the phrase "the one who was killed with the Midianite woman" (Num. 25:14), which seems extraneous. These two matters will explain each other.

Consider this: evil thoughts displace the holy soul (*neshamah*); bad words displace the holy spirit (*ruach*); bad deeds displace the holy lower soul (*nephesh*). In this light we can understand this verse: "The name of the Israelite who was killed [*hamukeh*], the one who was killed (*hukah*) with the Midianite woman" (Num. 25:14): immediately as they began to sin, before Pinchas killed him, the man entered the state of being "the one who was killed" (*mukeh*), a wicked corpse smitten (*hukah*) along with the Midianite woman. He actually died when his holy *nephesh* departed. From this we learn that Pinchas merely killed a dead man and so was still fit to serve as a priest.

For Further Thought

In a post-9/11 world, an age of suicide martyrs and reactionary religious impulses, it may be that we should not teach this text. It presents the story of Pinchas to further minimize the consequence of his zealotry, possibly dulling our revulsion at such acts even in our own time. Still, not to teach it would deprive us of the creative lesson with which Levi Yitzhak frames his message. He connects three spiritual realms—intention, sound, and endeavor—with three realms of action—thought, speech, and deed—and three levels of soul—*neshamah, ruach,* and *nephesh.* To become one who is truly "dead in this life," one would have to lose all three of these aspects of soul. But even before this outcome, Levi Yitzhak points us to the awareness that mistaken thoughts, misplaced words, and thought-less acts not only harm others, but they also harm us by diminishing our souls.

Here are some of the relevant texts behind our lesson (Berakhot 18b):

> "But the dead know nothing" (Eccles. 9:5): These are the wicked who in their lifetime are called dead, as it says: "And to you, O wicked one who is slain [*challal rasha*], the prince of Israel" (Ezek. 21:30). Or if you prefer, I can derive it from here: "At the mouth of two witnesses shall the dead be put to death [*yumat hameit*]" (Deut. 17:6). But is he not still alive! What it means is: he is already counted as dead.

In this passage, we have the classical teaching that "the wicked in their lifetime are called dead." To be alive is to be aware of acting before God's presence. It is possible to do evil only by denying God's existence or God's knowledge of and care for the world. This, in turn, is to become dead to the world—and to bring death into the world.

It is worth noting how the Zohar addressed this issue (Zohar III 221b):

> "The name of the Israelite who was killed, etc." R. Yitzhak said: This verse should have read, "The name of the Israelite who Pinchas killed" and not "who was killed, the one who was killed." This verse was expressed in a closed, secret manner.
>
> But R. Eleazar taught this: Once the blessed Holy One raised up Pinchas to be the high priest, He did not wish to recall Pinchas in connection with the death of a man, as this is not fitting for a high priest. Before He had raised him up to be high priest, Scripture did

mention him by name: "When Pinchas, [son of Eleazar son of Aaron the priest,] saw this, [he left the assembly and,] taking a spear [in his hand, he followed the Israelite into the chamber] and stabbed both of them, [the Israelite and the woman, through the belly]" (Num. 25:7–8). But once He elevated him to be high priest, Scripture did not recall his name in association with killing, since it was not befitting him. The glory of the blessed Holy One cared for him, since it is not fitting that a high priest should be associated with killing. And this is why Scripture also later speaks indirectly, saying: "The name of the woman who was killed, etc."

Questions for Reflection

1. Have you ever had the experience of meeting someone who you sensed was "dead" in the midst of his or her life? When? What led you to feel this way? How did this affect your interaction with this person?

2. Have you ever had the experience of meeting someone who you sensed was fully alive in the midst of his or her life? When? What led you to feel this way? How did this affect your interaction with this person?

3. When have you felt most alive? What contributed to that experience? When, if ever, have you felt a deadness in your heart or soul? How did you respond? What brought you back to life?

Taking It into Your Life

One goal of spiritual practice is to live our lives most fully. We neither create fantasies nor hide from realities. We strive to be fully present to what is, to see clearly and respond with compassion. Levi Yitzhak offers us a framework for "checking in" and becoming aware of our lives: noting thought, word, and deed. In terms of mindfulness practice, this means setting an intention to guide us in how we speak and act as well as how we respond after we have spoken or acted. Thus, beyond word and deed we want to pay attention to the content of our thoughts without being caught up in them; notice where we have been led astray by our thoughts without judging. In all of this, the goal is to distinguish between what is happening right now and how we are remembering the past or projecting into the future.

Regarding thought: Note when your mind runs to rumination, rehearsing past events, retelling old stories. Note as well when your mind turns to imagining what will happen in the future. While it is important to learn from the past and plan for the future, rumination and worry are quite different. When you notice these sorts of thoughts, bring your attention to the breath. Become more grounded in this moment's experience, and ask: But what is true now?

Notice when your thoughts turn to self-denigration or self-congratulation. While it is important to recognize mistakes and acknowledge skills and abilities, guilt and overconfidence are quite different. When you notice these sorts of thought, bring your attention to the breath. Become more grounded in this moment's experience, and note: This is true, but what am I called to do now, and how can I do it?

Regarding speech: When you feel prompted to speak, check in with yourself. Ask: Is this true? Is it helpful? Is it useful? Does it need to be said now? In this manner, we might more skillfully discern when we are speaking truly for the good of others and when it is for ourselves. We will speak words that will elevate our souls and those of others, as we will more likely speak out of wisdom, compassion, and love.

Mindfulness practice, tied to awareness of thoughts and speech, will also impact our actions. We will more likely be aware of what we are doing from moment to moment and recognize when our actions are misapplied, misdirected, or wasteful of our energies or those of others. Our actions will come more in line with our words and our thoughts. We will more truly be alive.

"Now Zelophehad son of Hepher had no sons, only daughters. [The names of Zelophehad's daughters were Mahlah, Noah, Hoglah, Milcah, and Tirzah]" (Num. 26:33).

The essence of devotion is grounded in fear and love (*rachimu udechilu*), which is love and fear (*ahavah veyirah*; the two *middot* of *chesed* and *gevurah*). When one serves God out of love, it has the quality of delight. But when one serves God out of fear, that is not so much the case, rather there is more a sense of shame.

This is implicit in the name **Zelophehad** (*Tzelophechad*): it means "shadow of fear" (*tzel pachad*); **the son of Hepher** (*Chepher*): it is related to the phrase "Then the moon shall be ashamed [*vechophrah halevanah*], [and the sun shall be abashed. For *YHVH* of Hosts will reign on Mount Zion and in Jerusalem, and the Glory will be revealed to His elders]" (Isa. 24:23). He had nothing but daughters.

(The rest is missing.)

FOR FURTHER THOUGHT

As noted, this lesson is incomplete, and it is problematic. Apparently, Levi Yitzhak had in mind associating the product of fear with "daughters" and so the product of love with "sons." Once again, we are challenged by this gendered aspect of Jewish mystical thought and discourse. The gendered association of "fear" with the left side and with the feminine creates associations that lead to the exclusion of women, the devaluing of the blessing of daughters.

There is no good way to "explain away" this dynamic here. However, it should not prevent us from noting the larger concern that Levi Yitzhak seems to wish to address: the danger of serving from fear, unbalanced by love. Surely, Levi Yitzhak does not mean to denigrate the spiritual power of fear of God. In many instances he acknowledges that the "higher fear"—recognizing God's exalt-edness and awesomeness—can lead to love of God. Turning one's attention to the amazing intricacy of all creation, the immenseness of time and space, the awesome fact that what is *is*, engenders this higher fear of God. And that this very God—the One in whom all of this exists, from whom all of this exists, and without whom nothing would exist—allows, even wants, to be known and loved by us is overwhelming. Yet, it is also an invitation to relationship, and one of love.

The lower fear—fear of punishment—cannot lead to love. Its only product is grudging and half-hearted obedience, and even worse, shame. When this is how we experience our lives, we live in the shadow of fear; there is darkness and no light. Even the sun and moon, who see everything at all times, both day and night, will be ashamed of our behavior—abashed at our internalized guilt and shame. Nothing productive will come of this fear. This is not the stuff of relationship, and surely not of love. It can only be enlivened by bringing God's love, and the possibility that we might legitimately and fully love God, into our hearts.

This is a powerful lesson. Levi Yitzhak may have given this sermon to counterbalance the teachings of the non-Hasidic preachers around him. It is no less important today, when fear is so much the currency of politics, so much the chastening rod of "cultural guardians." Fear of things is debilitating and prevents common cause and peacemaking. Fear of God and love of others are energizing and may make possible the resolution of conflict and ways of peace.

Questions for Reflection

1. What makes you afraid? How do you respond to this fear? Is this fear ever uplifting? When, how, why—or why not?

2. How have you experienced the difference between the two forms of fear: lower fear and higher fear—fear of punishment or suffering and fear of God's exaltedness? What has been the consequence of this difference in your life?

3. What do you imagine it might take to transform lower fear to higher fear?

Taking It into Your Life

The term "fear of God's exaltedness" comes with a cost. It orients us vertically, reinforcing the hierarchical aspect of the "King" metaphor. Yet we still can recognize aspects of this sort of fear. Johnny Cash once sang, "Because she's mine, I walk the line." Out of concern for the feelings of his beloved, he trains himself to behave differently, to avoid doing what would be hurtful to her. The midrash tells of Joseph seeing the image of his father in the moment before he might have succumbed to the wiles of Potiphar's wife, and so avoiding sin. Reminded of his responsibility to honor his father, and out of concern for his own well-being, he controls his behavior even to his own disadvantage. In these two instances we see how fear of hurting another, fear of the consequences of our actions on the well-being of another—and not fear of punishment or personal suffering—can positively change behavior. This is an aspect of "fear of God's exaltedness."

There are a variety of ways to think of God in a nonpersonal manner. We might find God in the community of Israel, Jewish peoplehood. We might find God in the amazing dynamism of the ecosystem, in the process of evolution, in the existence of life at all. We might find God in those moments of deep communion with another person. In each of these instances, it is possible to experience God's awesomeness. When we consider that we are part of the Jewish people and its history, that we exist as part of all creation, that it is possible to open our hearts fully to another and to have that reciprocated, we are overwhelmed —and we respond with love.

Reflect.

"Let *YHVH*, the God of the breath of all flesh, appoint [someone over the community]"
(Num. 27:16).

Here is the guiding principle: we are to defend (*lilmod zekhut*) the Jewish people when they do not fulfill the divine will all the time like the angels, because they are busy making a living. Now, Abraham embodies the quality of loving-kindness, and he defended the Jews when he fed the angels. He demonstrated to them the needs of flesh-and-blood people, so that the angels would not indict the Jewish people.

This is also implicit in what Moses said: "O God, **the God of the breath of all flesh**! [When one man sins, will You be wrathful with the whole community?]" (Num. 16:22). That is: human beings, because they are flesh-and-blood mortals, have need for income and sustenance, and therefore they sometimes do not serve God constantly. This, too, is what he meant here, saying, "**Let *YHVH*, the God of the breath of all flesh, appoint**"—that is, "appoint a judge and leader who will always defend Israel, just as you defend a person who does not serve you constantly." In this manner Moses requested that God stand up a leader for the Jews who would defend them.

That is the meaning of "**Let *YHVH*, the God of the breath of all flesh, appoint**": just as You are **the God of the breath of all flesh** and You defend them, so should You **appoint someone over the community**. Let the leader of Israel be someone who will defend them as well.

FOR FURTHER THOUGHT

The key to this lesson is the unusual appellation that Moses gives to God: "the God of the breath of all flesh." In this, he emphasizes that this is the God who understands and defends human beings, who are subject to the demands of flesh and therefore cannot devote themselves solely to serving God continuously. Behind this lesson is the attitude of the Sages, who emphasized the preeminence of human beings over angels. They told stories in which the human protagonist demonstrated that the humans gain even greater merit for observing the commandments and exercising freedom of choice to do so. They also told stories in which the angels accuse the Jewish people of failure, only to be censured in turn. In our lesson, we have Abraham symbolically arguing in favor of the Jewish people, demonstrating to the angels what it means to be human—to have to eat and find the means to eat—and that despite those pressures, people can express the divine quality of loving-kindness.

In turn, the verb *yiphkod*—in the sense of "appoint"—may also suggest to Levi Yitzhak a term for "remembering," noting (as in "*YHVH* took note [*pakad*] of Sarah"; Gen. 21:1). He hears in this an appeal to God to remember the all-too-human needs of the Israelites and to remember them for good. Noting their inability to serve God continuously, and so the potential that they may not compare well with the angels, Moses appeals to God to remember to appoint someone who will remind God of the true devotion of the Jewish people, even if they have to turn their attention to making a living and seemingly away from God. In that sense, we can read the opening verse as follows: "Let *YHVH* remember that He is the God of those who are spiritual but also bound by the needs of the flesh, and so appoint a leader who will remind God of this fact, defending the Jewish people, arguing in their defense."

Questions for Reflection

1. How do you understand the relationship between finding a leader "who shall go out before them and come in before them, and who shall take them out and bring them in" (Num. 27:17) and one "who will always defend Israel"? What are the similarities and what are the differences?

2. What are the qualities of leadership that you would expect from or connect with someone inspired by "*YHVH*, the God of the breath of all flesh"?

3. One of the innovations of the Baal Shem Tov was the concept of *avodah shebegashmiyut*—divine service carried out in the world, in the course of daily affairs. Yet Levi Yitzhak did not argue that the people were engaged in this form of divine service. Could it be that making a living is a form of service? How? How would we recognize it as service of God and not ourselves?

Taking It into Your Life

The role of the tzaddik, the leader, is to defend the Jewish people: *lelamed zekhut*. This term has its origins in the courtroom, and it means to offer arguments for acquittal, noting extenuating circumstances, questioning the capacity of the witness to have seen the act truly, challenging the veracity and authority of the witnesses, or demanding an oath of a claimant to test commitment to his or her testimony. The circumstance here is that the Jewish people have been accused—perhaps by the angels—of failing to serve God fully and truly. Someone needs to rise to their defense, particularly as it appears that the accusation is accurate.

How do you play the role of *melameid zekhut*, the one who argues for or defends the Jewish people? Can you do so, even as you recognize that their actions may be flawed, even wrong? When, if ever, is the behavior so painful to witness that you cannot bring yourself to defend it? When, if ever, is the behavior so offensive that you fear not rising to their defense? How do you maintain your balance in this process?

How does it feel to acknowledge mistakes in others, and yet feel compassion for them, even recognize how the act came about, its origins and rationale? In defending them, are you condoning their behavior? How is it possible to defend offensive behavior and also invite, even compel, change in the offender? How do you maintain a balanced heart, a compassionate heart, and a connection to offenders in this process?

How do you deal with your own mistakes? Can you both acknowledge your misdeeds and argue in your own defense? Can you be compassionate toward yourself, while also making amends and changing your behavior? What does it take to honestly admit mistakes without generating guilt? What is the role of love and acceptance in this process, and how can they be misapplied or abused?

Mattot

"[If a man makes a vow to *YHVH* or takes an oath imposing a prohibition on himself,] he shall not break his pledge; he must carry out all that has come out of his mouth" (Num. 30:3).

Anyone who does not make his or her words profane (*chullin*) has the power to make repairs with **all that comes out of his** or her **mouth**: he will decree it and it shall be fulfilled (see Job 22:28), for the tzaddik rules over God (see 2 Sam 23:3). And it is accomplished through guarding the covenant of the tongue.

This is the association between the opening verse of the parashah, "Moses spoke to the heads of the Israelite tribes (*mattot*), saying: This is what *YHVH* has commanded" (Num. 30:2) and our verse. The word *mattot* signifies "inclining, directing." So the heads of the people have the power to "incline" (*lehatot*) the qualities of the blessed Holy One from judgment (*din*) to compassion (*rachamim*).

FOR FURTHER THOUGHT

The translation above—where *yacheil* means "break a pledge"—reflects the interpretation of the Rabbis, found in *Sifrei Bemidbar, Mattot* 1. Levi Yitzhak also accepts that interpretation and simply repeats it: "*lo yacheil devaro* [he shall not break his pledge]—*lo ya'aseh devaro chullin* [he shall not profane his words; he shall not empty them of meaning]." This version reads the verb *yacheil* as related to the root *ch-l-l*, which we know in the word *chol* (weekday, mundane, profane), but also *chalal* (a corpse; a body emptied of its spiritual vitality).

There is an alternative reading of the verb, suggesting that we not let our words "grow old" by not acting in a timely manner. This "aging" of our commitment is the inverse of the sense that we often meet in the verb *yacheil*: to wait, to hold on, to hope. We find it in Ps. 130:7: "O Israel, wait for *YHVH* [*yacheil yisrael el YHVH*], for with *YHVH* is steadfast love and great power to redeem." By placing our trust in God, we demonstrate—as well as gain—the trust and steadfastness to wait hopefully for redemption.

Taking all this together, it is possible that Levi Yitzhak wanted to deepen our appreciation of how the tzaddik makes his words effective. It is a given in Hasidic teaching (grounded in the Talmud) that the tzaddik has the power to annul or reverse adverse divine decrees. We would like to understand how that is possible. The verses quoted to prove the tzaddik's power suggest that he overcomes God, overturning the divine intention. For his speech to have such power, it must not participate in any manner in the realm of *chullin*: removed from the mundane world, in no way profane, fully alive. It must be full with conscious intention. And while fully trusting in God's love, it must not wait but respond immediately to the needs of the people. The needs of the people are great, and they cannot be satisfied by invitations to patience and pious waiting.

Questions for Reflection

1. How do you understand the "covenant of the tongue"? What are the terms of that covenant? What are we to do—and not do—with our speech? What is God's response to our commitment?

2. The leader's staff (*mateh*) comes to represent the collective of his followers, and so the tribe (*mateh*). How does the image of the staff help you understand how a leader "inclines" or "directs" (*noteh*) his people?

3. The Talmud (Rosh Hashanah 17a) speaks of God having compassion for sinners by saying, "The One who is abounding in love [*rav chesed*] inclines toward love [*mateh kelapei chesed*]." If this is God's natural inclination, how is it, then, that the tzaddik energizes this process, so that God turns from judgment to love and compassion? What does it take to turn God, to make God incline in a particular manner? Can you participate in that process? When, how?

Taking It into Your Life

The verb *n-t-h* is multivalent. It can mean any of the following: incline, stretch out, rest against, lean, turn toward. In our lesson, it signifies a movement that brings about a change of perspective, a new way of seeing things. The intention is that God, and so also we, incline toward love and compassion.

As you make your way through the day, notice when you experience confrontation, contention, conflict, or resistance. In any of these occasions, consider changing your perspective. Shift your position. Lean over or lean back. Turn around. Look up, look down. Stand in your opponent's place, and consider the situation from that perspective. Turn to see yourself, and investigate precisely where you are standing. Is the position you are holding the actual one in which you are standing?

Notice how inclining yourself toward your opponent, coming closer, shifts your feelings. Consider how stretching yourself may change the situation. What might happen if you simply rested in the circumstances that are so challenging without working so hard to change them? Might something new arise? Might some new awareness develop? How might turning toward your opponent with a different heart change the situation?

Practice. Reflect.

> Another interpretation: "[If a man makes a vow to *YHVH* or takes an oath imposing a prohibition on himself,] he shall not break his pledge; he must carry out all that has come out of his mouth" (Num. 30:3).

The midrash interprets "**If a man makes a vow to *YHVH***" in light of the verse "Our days are like a passing shadow" (Ps. 144:4). The explanation for this is the teaching in Nedarim 10b that it is prohibited to say "for *YHVH* an offering" (*YHVH korban*) and only "an offering for *YHVH*" (*korban YHVH*), lest, in the first instance, one die between the divine name and the word *korban* and so express God's name in vain (heaven forbid). Now here, our text says, "**a vow to *YHVH***" (*neder YHVH*; Num. 30:2) and not "to *YHVH* a vow" (*YHVH neder*), lest he die before completing the vow. This is what the midrash was getting at in commenting, "Our lives are like a passing shadow."

And further, there is a debate in the Talmud (Nedarim 9a) regarding whether it is good to make a vow even if one fulfills it. R. Meir holds that even if one fulfills the vow, it is not proper to make an oath. This is the meaning of the verse: "**If a man makes a vow,**" he must make certain to say "**a vow** [or offering] **to *YHVH***," and not "to *YHVH* a vow"—lest he die before he can utter "an offering" or "a vow." Now, we are instructed that we are not to fail to fulfill even one thing that we say, yet how can we be certain that we will actually fulfill "***all* that has come out of** [our] **mouth**[s]"? In this manner, our text teaches us that it is not proper to utter a vow at all.

FOR FURTHER THOUGHT

Once again Levi Yitzhak presents a profound spiritual teaching while seemingly explicating a legal principle. That is, why would it be better not to utter a vow? Isn't there something important in recognizing our inner intention, our desire to move closer to doing the divine will or serving God more fully? Why shouldn't we commit ourselves in a concrete manner, through the words of our mouths?

Part of the answer, Levi Yitzhak tells us, is that for all of our intention, we cannot know that we will succeed. "Do not boast of tomorrow, for you do not know what the day will bring" (Prov. 27:1). Levi Yitzhak examines our verse precisely and realizes that in the repetition of the word for "making an oath / an oath" (in Hebrew one could say *ki yidor*, "when he vows," and not have to repeat *neder*, "a vow"), there is something meaningful we might have missed. This repetition and the order of words in the verse recall the teaching in Nedarim regarding the proper form of an oath and the midrash connecting this verse to the uncertainty of life. This makes our teaching all the more profound: we do not know, from moment to moment, if we will survive. That awareness may make us more careful about what we commit to do and how we fulfill our commitments in the moment. Do it now … you never know.

 Questions for Reflection

1. Do you have any reservations about uttering a vow or dedicating yourself to serving God in a particular way? Are you ever concerned that you might not succeed in fulfilling your vow? There is a traditional practice of saying "without making this an oath" (*beli neder*) when one offers to do something for another person or commits to attending a meeting or the like. Does this practice speak to you? When or how?

2. What do you make of the principle in Nedarim 10b regarding the order of words in an oath and the concern about not taking God's name in vain? Isn't it a bit cartoonish? In normal circumstances, does anyone speak so slowly that they could not complete such a short phrase in one breath? What do you think the Sages are getting at here?

3. R. Mendel of Lisk is cited as teaching, "Don't talk more than you have to, since the total number of words you will speak during your life is determined by heaven. Why should you spend your life-words on speech that is not connected to a mitzvah, that brings you nothing in the end?" If you knew that your words were numbered, that when your quota of words was used up, you would pass away, how would you behave? Is there a connection between this teaching and that of Levi Yitzhak? How do you see it?

Taking It into Your Life

This lesson teaches us something about the moment-to-moment uncertainty of life. We might think that it is impossible for us to hold such a precise awareness of each moment, of our intention and actions, and still get anything done. Yet that is one goal of spiritual practice: to wake up to this moment and all that is present in it, and not waste it looking backward to what was and will be no more, or to the future that cannot be known. It is to be aware in each moment of our true intention, to acknowledge when we are in line with it and when we are off course. Seeing clearly in any moment makes it possible for us to choose how we truly wish to live.

In a sense, we might frame this lesson in the form of a question: if this is the last day of your life (or moment, or breath), are you using it consciously? Are you doing in this moment what you consider to be valuable, meaningful, important? Have you agreed with yourself, and with your loved ones, that this is how you should spend your time? Have you said, "I love you," to the people you love, in case that is the last word you speak to them?

Practice each day in this light. Consider what you are doing, how you are doing it, and how to make sure that what you are doing is connected to your truest intention.

Mase'ei

"Moses recorded the starting points of their travels as directed by *YHVH*. These are their travels according to their starting points" (Num. 33:2).

Why does the text change? It begins with "**starting points**" and then mentions "**travels**," but then it shifts, with "**travels**" preceding "**starting points**." The answer is well known—all of Israel's travels in the great and awesome wilderness were directed by God in order that they might cull the divine sparks that had fallen into husks there; to remove that which had been swallowed by them. This is the reason that Israel would camp in one place for an extended period, while in another for a short time. That is, their encampment was according to the work required to cull the sparks in that place.

Now regarding the spies that Joshua sent into the Land of Israel, Scripture says, "They have come to spy out [*lachpor*] the whole land" (Josh. 2:3). What is the significance of the word "to spy out" (*lachpor*)? The key to the conquest of the land came about through the performance of mitzvot and good deeds wherever the people went, doing those acts that were needed to conquer the land. The people served the blessed Creator with the fear of God's exaltedness (*yirat haromemut*) and true love (*ahavah ha'amitit*) and thereby raised up all the wicked fears and loves there in the land of Canaan. Moses established this principle back in Egypt when he said, "For we will select from [our own livestock] for the worship of *YHVH* our God; for we shall not know with what we are to worship *YHVH* until we arrive there" (Exod. 10:26). This worship is to connect oneself with true fear and love, raising the sparks that are in that place to holiness. The land was compelled to submit, abashed before the Israelites compelled to do their will, for the one who receives is abashed before the one who provides. This then helps us to understand the phrase "they have come to spy out [*lachpor*] the whole land" when we read it in light of the phrase "Then the moon shall be ashamed [*chaphrah halevanah*], [and the sun shall be abashed. For *YHVH* of Hosts will reign on Mount Zion and in Jerusalem, and the Glory will be revealed to His elders]" (Isa. 24:23). The whole of the land was ashamed before the Israelites when they did mitzvot and good deeds and served the blessed Creator with true fear and love; it was compelled to do the will of the Israelites.

Now, among the forty-two journeys that Israel journeyed it says, "They encamped in Haradah" (Num. 33:24), "they encamped in Mithkah" (v. 38), "they encamped at Mount Shepher" (v. 23). When Israel camped in a location at which were located debased fears (may the Merciful preserve us), they would then serve the blessed One with fear of God's exaltedness, trembling before God's awesomeness and glorious power. Thus, it says, "they encamped in Haradah [in trembling fear]," that is, the quality (*middah*) of fear, and they there had to serve the blessed Creator with that *middah*. And when they encamped in a place at which was found debased love that had fallen in the original shattering, they would then serve God with true love. Thus, it says, "they encamped in Mithkah [sweetness]," in the *middah* of love. So also, "they encamped at Mount Shepher [beauty]," in the *middah* of beauty (*hitpa'arut*; *tiferet*). In this manner, they would raise up all the sparks that had fallen there, to their source, to the source of holiness. This was the primary purpose of Israel's travels in the wilderness.

This is why Moses used the term "**starting points**" (*motza'eihem*, related to the word for "bringing out" and "finding"): this refers to the process of raising the sparks that they found and bringing them out from their husks. "**Their travels as directed by *YHVH***": this teaches us that their endeavors were directed by God through their travels. "**These are their travels**": that is, these are the travels that Israel made in the wilderness, informing us that the primary purpose of their travels was for the sake of "**the starting points**," to bring out the sparks and to raise them to their holy source.

FOR FURTHER THOUGHT

We generally think of Israel's travels in the wilderness as "wandering," as just a way of "killing time" until the generation of the Exodus died off. Instead, here we are told that the travels were intentional and that Israel accomplished great work on the way. They traveled from place to place, there identifying and connecting with a particular divine spark buried, hidden, swallowed up in the husks of the wilderness. They used different techniques to raise up each different sort of debased spark, to return it again to its holy state, according to its source. Would Israel have been able to accomplish the same repairs in the wilderness if they had entered the Land quickly, as originally had been intended?

Levi Yitzhak is building from teachings of the Baal Shem Tov (see the teachings in *Degel Machaneh Efraim* on this parashah), and older sources. However, he develops it further, both in the puns on the place-names he identifies (linking them to *ahavah*, *yirah*, and *tiferet*) and in the association he makes with the conquest of the Land. In this manner, he expands the realm of identifying sparks trapped in the husks from the wilderness to the Land itself and perhaps even to his own hometown. Further, as we have seen elsewhere, he hints at the power that Israel has in the world: it was created for them, and when they fulfill their role in redeeming creation, it responds by supporting and sustaining them.

Questions for Reflection

1. This lesson focuses on the practice of "raising sparks." The *middah* (even though debased) of the spark determines the *middah* by which it is raised. Does this reflect the ancient beliefs that lie behind homeopathy—that cures come from sources similar to the affliction? Or does this suggest that God—or holiness, or divinity of some sort—is somehow present in these fallen sparks even when they are trapped in the husks? Is debased love (*ahavah*) or fear (*yirah*) still connected to divine love and fear? How do you understand this and experience it?

2. Levi Yitzhak plays on words here, not only in connecting the quality of the sparks to the place-names, but also in "starting points" and "travels." The root of the Hebrew word for "starting point" also has the meaning of "origin" as well as "finding." Do you think that Levi Yitzhak means that finding our origins provides the ground from which we set out on our journeys? Does he mean that when we set out on our life journey, we are also returning to our origins? What, indeed, are we to find on our journey—where we really start from or where we're going?

3. What are "debased" fears, loves, beauty, etc.? How do they come to be debased, and how does our attention, or intention, redeem them? How

aware are you of generating "debased" sparks? How might you become more aware? Is this concept useful at all today?

Taking It into Your Life

In the last paragraph Levi Yitzhak slips in a new thought: "'Their travels as directed by *YHVH*': this teaches us that their endeavors were directed by God through their travels." That is, the raising of the sparks actually was accomplished by God by means of the work of the Israelites in their travels.

This echoes a teaching of the Baal Shem Tov: "The steps of a man are established by *YHVH*, then he delights in his way" (Ps. 37:23). All of our steps are established by God to accomplish some end that God desires we fulfill. That is the path we follow. We delight in our way, thinking that we are on our way to do our own business, but in truth everything is God's way. God made it turn out that we would go in this way, to accomplish God's goal: raising the sparks that we will find in that place.

This lesson reflects a key element of Hasidic theology and spirituality, and it is quite challenging. Wherever we go, whether we think that we have set our own course or find ourselves on a detour, it has come about by the Holy One so that we can raise a spark that only we have the power to lift up. Would knowing this lead you to take less responsibility for deciding where to go, how to get there, and what to do in any moment, since it is all directed by God? Would it lead you to take your daily travels more seriously? Would you pay more attention to everything around you, looking to find the spark waiting for you in every place, in every moment?

How would you enact this practice? How would you identify the quality (*middah*) that needs repair in any given moment, at any particular place? How would you energize that *middah* in yourself in response? How can you transform all existence into the realm of the holy through your attention and intention?

The Book of
Deuteronomy

Devarim

"These are the words that Moses addressed
[to all Israel on the other side of the Jordan,]
in the wilderness, in the Aravah, toward
Suph, between Paran and between Tophel,
[Laban, Hazeroth, and Di-zahab]" (Deut. 1:1).

We can start off by connecting the word *aravah* with the word *erev* (evening). We know—as it is taught at the opening of the tractate Berakhot (2a)—that at Creation evening preceded morning. In the same vein, the early days of our lives are like the "evening."

So now we can now interpret the phrase "**in the Aravah, toward Suph.**" At the start of our lives, we should immediately direct our deeds toward the *Shekhinah*, who is also known as "The End" (*soph*). "**Between Paran**": this signifies that place from which the forces of procreation emerge (cf. Shabbat 89a: *sheparu veravu aleha*). "**And between Tophel**"—understand this as did Rashi, who interpreted it to be a synonym for "speech" (as in *tiphlut*, "frivolous or slanderous speech").

Thus, these two place-names signify the covenant of sexuality and the covenant of speech. Thus, "**between**" sexuality and speech all should be directed "**toward Soph,**" with holiness and with careful attention.

FOR FURTHER THOUGHT

This is a classical Hasidic *derashah*. It relies on puns, on mystical references, and on creative rereading of the original biblical text. More, its focus on guarding speech and sexual practice—tied as they are in the twin covenants—directs us to two areas of traditional Jewish teaching, here presented in a new and creative form.

The concept of the covenants of the mouth and of the sexual organ has its roots in *Sefer Yetzirah* 1:3: "Ten *Sephirot* of Nothingness, in the number of ten fingers, five opposite five, with a singular covenant precisely in the middle, in the circumcision of the tongue and in the circumcision of the *membrum*" (translation from Aryeh Kaplan, *Sefer Yetzirah: The Book of Creation*, Revised Edition [York Beach, ME: Weiser Books, 1997], p. 32). This teaching draws a connection between the covenant of circumcision—which signifies sexual awareness and direction of sexual forces in proper ways—and the circumcision of the lips (cf. Exod. 6:12), which signifies the proper use of speech. We are bound to serve God through awareness. Our most profound methods of connecting with other people (and so with God) are through speech and through the intimacy of sexual relations. Each of these is bound by covenantal obligations, making them paths to holiness. There is a general correlation between the emergence of physical maturity and the capacity to be morally self-regulating (and so more in charge of our speech and sexual energies). Therefore, the age at which religious obligations fall on us is when we are also expected to devote our maturing bodies and consciousness to being holy.

In Levi Yitzhak's terms, this means devotion to raising up, delighting, and not further alienating the *Shekhinah*. He brings her into this lesson through the pun on the word *suph*, which has its origins in the Zohar:

> Come and see: Pharaoh imbibed from this judgment (*din*), until he and his people perished. As soon as this judgment aroused against him, the prince appointed to rule over them was removed and eliminated; then all those below perished, as it is written: *He removed the wheel of his chariots* (Ex. 14:25). Who is *the wheel of his chariots*? *His chariots*—Pharaoh's. And, who is their *wheel*? That prince ruling over them. So, they all died in the sea. Why in the sea? Well, the Supernal Sea aroused against them, and they were obliterated out by Her hand. Consequently it is written *they were drowned in the Red Sea* (ibid. 15:4). R. Yose said: Certainly so! Therefore it is written *be-yam suf*, in the Red Sea—*sofa*, end, of rungs. [*Be-yam suf … sofa …* *Shekhinah* is symbolized by *yam suf*, the Red Sea, because She is *sofa*, "end," of rungs, consummation of the ten *sephirot*.] (Zohar II 50a; Daniel C. Matt, trans., *The Zohar*, Pritzker ed., vol. 4 [Stanford, CA: Stanford University Press, 2007], p. 245ff.)

Thus, starting in the evening (*erev/aravah*) of our lives—the emergence from childhood—we are to direct our attention to the *Shekhinah* (*soph/suph*), in particular guarding our sexual behavior (*paran/*

paru veravu) and our speech (*tophel/tiphlut*). Levi Yitzhak thus presents Moses speaking to us, in our lives, in this moment. Rather than denying sexuality and speech, Moses (and Levi Yitzhak) invites us to employ them in serving God, in striving for holiness.

Questions for Reflection

1. How do you experience—if at all—the connection between guarding your speech and your sexuality?

2. Part of the symbolism of the *Sefer Yetzirah* has to do with the position of the mouth and the sexual organs along the centerline of the body (as opposed to hands and feet, which are on either side). How do you sense your own core? How do you find your balance and center yourself? What throws you off-balance, and how do you regain it? How might this be tied to your reaction to speech or sexual forces?

3. How do you experience speech and sexuality as the basis of serving the *Shekhinah* (if at all)? How might these behaviors serve to raise up the *Shekhinah* or extend her exile?

Taking It into Your Life

We tell stories and we recognize that a story has a beginning, a middle, and an end. We apply the frame of narrative to our lives and so come to "tell our story" in the same manner. But whenever we relate that narrative, we have still not come to its end. At best we have concluded a chapter, but even then we do not know the true direction of the rest of our "story" nor how it will conclude—except as all lived narratives end.

The lesson of *Mase'ei*, the preceding parashah concluding Numbers, still echoes here: the narrative of the Israelites wandering in the wilderness actually foreshadows and parallels the work of each of us in our lives—to move from point to point, from experience to experience, from stage to stage, identifying and raising up the sparks to be found in each moment. Levi Yitzhak uses the opening words of our parashah to identify how we should engage in spiritual practice in our youth, but he clearly also means to suggest that we should sustain this practice throughout our lives.

Of course, as we move through the stages of our lives, the interrelation of speech and sexuality shifts and changes. Hormonal levels fluctuate, the nature of our work shifts, family and work relationships grow and develop, our perspective on our life's course deepens and changes. Now may be a time to reflect on your own life's through the lens of the two covenants: speech and sexuality. Where do you sense greater energy, productivity, creativity, and wisdom? How do your spiritual practice and sensibilities affect your expression in these areas? Do your words speak to your sexual expression?

Levi Yitzhak's interpretation of these verses from the start of Deuteronomy leads us to think of the verse "I place *YHVH* before me always" (Ps. 16:8). He is asking us to bring these powerful inner forces into line with this verse, so that they are always devoted to discovering God's presence in our lives. Whether we are speaking or expressing our love through sexual relations, we are to remember that we are always "before the *Shekhinah*" (*mul soph*).

Reflect.

"[It was in the fortieth year, on the first day of the eleventh month, that] Moses addressed the Israelites in accordance with the instructions that *YHVH* had given him for them" (Deut. 1:3).

We will consider this verse in light of the teaching of the Zohar (III 149a–149b) regarding the Rabbinic teaching: "Any aspect included in a general proposition that later goes out from that general proposition to teach (something specific), does not go out to teach only about that specific instance, but its intent is to teach something about the general proposition" (*Sifra* 1:1).

The holy Torah has an interiority of hidden mysteries. That which is reported in the Torah as stories of events—as in the deeds of the Patriarchs Abraham and Isaac, the events surrounding Jacob and Laban, the tales of the Matriarchs, the narrative of Balaam and his ass— truly contain hidden spiritual mysteries. Still, even from the body of the Torah, that which is depicted in the story, it is possible to learn good qualities. So, for example, the story of Abraham—we can learn from Abraham to act lovingly; the story of Jacob depicts the righteousness of Jacob; the story of the Matriarchs depicts and teaches us about the righteous ways of the Matriarchs. Consider the righteousness of Rachel, who brought her rival into her home (Gen. R. 73:4) and whose merit continues for us. In this regard Scripture says, "[Thus said *YHVH*:] A cry is heard in Ramah [—wailing, bitter weeping—] Rachel weeping for her children. [She refuses to be comforted for her children, who are gone]" (Jer. 31:15).

From this we see that the stories were written to teach each of their particular qualities (*middot*). So the story of Balaam and his ass were written to demonstrate the obnoxious of that wicked man so that we can keep away from his deeds. This is reflected in the teaching "What is the difference between the disciples of our Father Abraham and the followers of the wicked Balaam?" (Avot 5:19): recognizing this, we will draw near to the qualities of Abraham and keep away from those of Balaam. The Torah was written in stories so that even from the narrative itself we might learn some good quality. Still, the story also contains infinite hidden mysteries, as does even the rest of the Torah that teaches specific mitzvot.

This is how we should understand our original teaching: "Everything included in a general proposition [*bekelal*]"—this refers to the Torah, which is the totality containing all worlds (i.e., "general proposition"; *kelal*)—"that goes out from that general proposition"—to appear as a story or narrative—"to teach"—so that we can learn something from the story itself, the quality that is inherent in it. "It does not go out to teach only about that specific instance, but its intent is to teach something about the general proposition"—not only are there mysteries in the stories of the Torah, but there are also mysteries in the portions that explicitly teach the mitzvot. This is the meaning of the phrase "but its intent is to teach something about the general proposition," as is explained somewhat in the Zohar.

Now Deuteronomy was not written as a narrative, only the clarification through the mitzvot of God's *middot* and godly ways, and reproof of Israel that they should turn away from evil ways and cleave to the good path, the way of God. Why is this? The generation that came out of Egypt had been immersed in the impurities of Egypt and thereby angered God (cf. *Sifrei Devarim* 1 and Rashi on Deut. 1:1). That is why the Torah to this point was garbed in stories and narratives, as we said above. But here in Deuteronomy, Moses was addressing a more upright generation, those who entered the Holy Land. They had not been immersed in the impurity of Egypt, and therefore they received the Torah without any garment, as above.

This, then, is how we should understand "These are the words" (*eileh hadevarim*) (Deut. 1:1): "R. Abbahu said: Wherever the word 'these are' (*eileh*) is written, it negates the preceding; 'and these are' (*ve'eileh*) adds to the preceding" (Gen. R. 12:3). The Torah—which had been garbed in stories—was told to the previous generation because of its various sins and mistakes "in the wilderness in the Aravah" (per Rashi). But "after he had defeated [Sihon king of the Amorites, who dwelt in Heshbon, and King Og of Bashan, who dwelt at Ashtaroth Edrei, on the other side of the Jordan, in the land of Moab,] Moses undertook to expound this Torah" (Deut. 4:3–5). **Moses addressed the Israelites in accordance with the instructions that *YHVH* had given him for them**" (Deut. 1:3), directly, as above.

FOR FURTHER THOUGHT

We enter the book of Deuteronomy at a critical time of the Jewish year. The Shabbat on which we read the opening chapters of the book always falls in the week preceding Tisha B'Av, the anniversary of the destruction of the Temples. In a sense, this is the lowest point in the year. Yet, immediately following this Shabbat and Tisha B'Av begins the period of seven weeks leading up to Rosh Hashanah and Yom Kippur. However flawed we may have become—even to the extent of meriting the destruction of the Temple and the continuation of our exile—we sense God's welcoming love and desire for our self-transformation and renewal. Levi Yitzhak senses this and perceives in the opening verses of Deuteronomy a shift in intensity, a directness that calls for our deeper attention to what God desires of us and our greater capacity to respond with love and devotion.

Deuteronomy—*mishneh torah*, "a second law, a repetition of the Torah"—presents a problem. What is really new here? While some new laws are enumerated, the Rabbis assume that they, too, were given at Sinai. Nothing really new happens in the book, there is only one story: Moses's slow movement toward death. Thus, Moses's words here must mean to communicate something different, in a different mode and method. This difference allows Levi Yitzhak to point his students to the inner and outer qualities of Torah, to acknowledge the importance of the narratives for teaching *middot* (moral qualities). Yet, at this time of year, it is even more important to access the hidden, supernal mysteries of Torah. It is in the nature of this book to communicate them.

What follows is the passage in the Zohar (III 149a,149b) on which Levi Yitzhak based his lesson, hewing closely to its message:

> R. Eleazar opened and said: "How beloved are the words of the Torah. In each and every word are supernal mysteries, and the Torah itself is called the sublime general rule. Now, one of the thirteen exegetical principles of the Torah is: 'Any aspect included in a general proposition that later goes out from that general proposition to teach (something specific), does not go out to teach only about that specific instance, but its intent is to teach something about the general proposition.' So it is with the Torah itself, which is the supernal all-comprehensive rule. Yet even when one story goes out from it the story does not come to show about itself, but to show supernal matters, mysterious matters. 'It does not go out to teach only about that specific instance, but its intent is to teach something about the general proposition.' That story in the Torah, or that deed, even though it went out from the whole of the Torah, it was not to show about itself alone, [but] to reflect on the general rule of the Torah as a whole."

Questions for Reflection

1. How do you balance your knowledge of the historical background of the Torah, and literary, historical, and philological analysis, with reading Torah for spiritual meaning?

2. How do you see the distinction that Levi Yitzhak makes between the obvious, surface lessons of the biblical narratives and the more mystical ones he points to? Are the moral lessons, those that point to improving our qualities (*middot*), of greater or lesser significance to you than the mystical teachings? How or how not?

3. Even the uninitiated reader will recognize that Deuteronomy is different from the other books of the Torah. How do you experience that difference? What do you find most moving, and what do you find least engaging about this book versus the rest of the Torah?

Taking It into Your Life

I met with a woman who had been very active in her life until quite recently, when she went through major back surgery. Following the surgery, she engaged in physical therapy and sought to go back to as much of her "normal life" as possible—until she fell and cracked a vertebra (C2) high in the spine, in a place that could have been and could still be fatal. She is in a brace, moving more slowly and carefully, still trying to engage in her life. But she feels as if she is not doing enough; it is hard to be so weak and so dependent.

Yet as she spoke about how she is managing her life, she explained, "I can't do much physically now, since I get so tired. But I spend my time sitting on my patio, surrounded by the big trees, making calls to friends who are not feeling well, and writing 'thank you' notes." On reflection, I suggested to her that the world would be a very much better place if all of us could remember to reach out to people in need and to say 'thank you' for kindnesses. We tell a story about our lives, yet we do not always recognize its hidden meaning. Often there is more than we realize, both simple moral instruction and sometimes even mystical secrets.

Pay attention to how you tell your story, how you narrate the events of your life. When do you sense that the story is simply "what it is," just the stuff of your life, the sequence of events, the words that were spoken? When do you mean your story to be a "lesson," communicating some moral or other teaching to the listeners? Are there ever times that you intend—or come to realize—that your story points to deeper, more significant dynamics on the spiritual plane?

> "On the other side of the Jordan,
> in the land of Moab, Moses undertook
> to expound this Torah, [saying:]"
> (Deut. 1:5).

Check out Rashi's comment on this verse: "He explained it to them in seventy languages." Why did Moses explain the Torah to them in seventy languages at this particular time? We can explain this with reference to the verse "*YHVH* will inscribe in the script of nations that this one was born there. Selah" (Ps. 87:6). Now sometimes we find Aramaic words in the Torah, such as *yegar sahaduta* (the mound of witness) (Gen. 31:47). So, too, words in other languages appear, such as "*totaphot: tat* in Coptic means 'two' and *pat* in African means 'two'" (Zevachim 37b); likewise we read, "*Hen* in Greek means 'one'" (Shabbat 31b). Similarly the languages of all the other nations appear in the Torah.

There is one reason for all of this. The language of any nation is its root vitality, but *leshon hakodesh* (lit., the holy tongue; Hebrew) is only for the Jews. Now in truth, Israel heard the Torah at Sinai only in Hebrew. But the blessed Holy One sees both beginning and end at the same time and saw that Israel would someday wind up in exile. Therefore, God included the language of all the other nations in the Torah. In this manner, the Jews would gain access to their vital forces, through their language as it appears in the holy Torah, and thus they would be able to survive in exile.

This is hinted at in our verse (Ps. 87:6) "*YHVH* will inscribe in the script of nations": the blessed Holy One wrote in the Torah the script of the nations, of all the other peoples "this one [*zeh*] was born there, selah." God did this so that the tzaddik will be able to survive there. The tzaddik is called "this one" (*zeh*), as the Sages taught (Berakhot 6b), "The whole universe was created only in order to connect with this one [*zeh*]." That is the import of "this one was born there, selah": so that the tzaddik will be able to survive in exile. That is why this was taught **in the land of Moab**, since in the Land of Israel there was only *leshon hakodesh*. But in the land of Moab, a land of the nations outside of the Land of Israel, Moses needed to **expound this Torah** in all of the languages, so that Israel would be able to survive in exile.

FOR FURTHER THOUGHT

That Levi Yitzhak finds such significance in the Hebrew language is not a surprise. Further, it is not surprising that he would consider the experience of exile so difficult, so distancing from the divine source that we might have to get our vital force from the language of our neighbors. It is through their language, which we know and in some sense has been sanctified through the Torah, that we are able to draw strength even in exile. And yet, there is something worth noting in that move—a sort of redemption, not only for Israel, but also for their neighbors. As debased as the language of the nations might be (and let us not ignore the ethnocentrism—and possibly outright racism—in some of Levi Yitzhak's comments), it still has the power to help sustain and even ultimately redeem Israel. The spark in foreign languages derives from Torah, too. Nothing is so cut off that it cannot ultimately be lifted back to its source.

There is a problematic phrase in the text, obscured by the translation. We read above, "The language of any nation is its root vitality." A more literal translation would be "The language of all nations is the vital force of that nation." This way of reading the text makes a deep connection between language and identity. Not only is it a determining factor in national consciousness, but also language itself is generative. It calls a people into being (and separates them off from others, in turn). The very form of the language shapes consciousness, forms the world, and gives energy for national purposes. It might be possible, on the other hand, to translate this phrase as "The language of any nation derives its vitality from the people." In this sense, it is the use of the language, how it is expressed and employed by its speakers, that gives it force and purpose. In a sense, this sounds like a Hasidic/mystical concept: the letters are the building blocks of creation. Their use in language vivifies all things (in that things have names made up of letters; in that words of speech employ letters), and the intentional speech of the Jewish people transforms the world (for good and ill).

 ## Questions for Reflection

1. The thrust of this lesson is that when Jews employ the language of the nations, it sustains them in exile. But could Levi Yitzhak also mean to suggest that when Israel derives vitality through the language of host nations, this also helps support the nations? How do you understand this dynamic? How do you conceive of the relationship between "Jewish" language and "other" language?

2. Let's say that the answer to the question above is that indeed Levi Yitzhak meant that Israel's use of the host nation's language is to provide support for the hosts. Is this an argument for a vital Diaspora? Does this reflect an understanding of the contributions of Jews to global culture? Is there something Kaplanian in this—suggesting the importance of the American expression of the Jewish civilization and its place in American democracy? Or is this idea still too ethnocentric—all blessing ultimately is through Israel? How do you read this?

3. Think of the language in which you pray. Which prayers are in English, which in Hebrew or some other language? In what language do you experience divine energy (*chayyut*)? Through which words does God's vital force flow for you?

Taking It into Your Life

A clear-eyed reading of Jewish history reveals that the Jewish people have adapted and adopted practices and beliefs from their host cultures. We have dressed like them; we have shaped our cuisine to be like theirs; we have spoken their languages and brought their words and concepts into our speech. It may be unique in our time, however, that Hebrew as a language of the Jews has fallen so far from popular awareness. True, many of our ancestors may only have had prayer-book knowledge of Hebrew, but it was a language toward which they had positive attitudes. It is only a small minority of American Jews today who can read or speak Hebrew, let alone write it.

What does this lesson suggest about the role of language in shaping a people? What might it mean as we consider what it will take to sustain the Jewish people in America? Which language should we struggle to teach (if we have to select only one): Hebrew or the symbolic/ideational language of traditional texts (perhaps in translation)? How easy have you found it to teach the latter without some sensitivity to the former?

Pay attention to how you express yourself, how you formulate your thoughts. How easily can you map Hebrew terms onto your primary concerns? When do you find that some concept in English (and more: when the English word is an import from another spiritual system, from another culture altogether) expresses your deepest truth and awareness better than does Hebrew? How has living in the American culture enlivened you? How has the American language helped sustain you as an individual and as a Jew? When do you sense that your Jewish language is what preserves you in the American "exile"?

Reflect.

Va'etchanan

Another explanation of "I pleaded with *YHVH*
at that time to say" (Deut. 3:23).

The word "**to say**" (*leimor*) is superfluous in this verse. We can understand
its place in light of the discussion in the Talmud (Berakhot 9b) regarding
the insertion of the verse "*Adonai*, open my lips so that my mouth may
tell Your praise" (Ps. 51:17) between the conclusion of the prayer for
redemption (*ga'al yisrael*) and the beginning of the *Amidah*. There, the
Sages concluded that this verse is not to be considered an interruption
(otherwise not permitted) even in the morning prayers, but rather "since
the Sages instituted this practice, it is all to be considered like one long
prayer." This may be true. Nevertheless, this verse was not part of the
prayer first established by the Men of the Great Assembly, and so the
later practice was only "like" an extended *Amidah*.

The reason that it could be added onto the original form is because
the verse "*Adonai*, open my lips" is itself a prayer that we be able to
pray. Surely in the time of the *Tannaim* and their predecessors, there
was no need for this sort of prayer, for surely their prayers were clear.
But as over time the quality of hearts diminished, it became necessary
to establish a prayer to pray with such purity. So we now have two
aspects to prayer: the prayer itself; the prayer to be able to pray.

Surely, Moses's prayer was always at the highest level of prayer;
his prayer was always fluent in his mouth and accepted. But here we
see that his prayer was not accepted, and so it follows that his prayer
was not fluent in his mouth, and he had to pray to be able to petition
God to offer his prayer to enter the Land of Israel. Therefore, he
asked of God the capacity to speak, as Scripture says: Moses "**pleaded
with YHVH**" precisely "**at that time**" (for the ability) "**to say**"; that
he be able to recite words of prayer properly. This had never been the
case previously, since the font of prayer had never been stopped up at
its source. Indeed, the *Shekhinah* herself spoke from Moses's mouth,
and the divine word had never departed from him....

FOR FURTHER THOUGHT

This is part of a longer exposition on prayer, on how the *Shekhinah* spoke through Moses and related matters. The key point, however, appears in this selection. When we are fully connected to God, the flow of spirit through us emerges in natural, spontaneous prayer. We have only a few instances of Moses's petitionary prayer. Other than that, we would not think of Moses praying liturgical prayer. What this suggests is that all of Moses's speech constituted prayer.

This is worth considering for our own lives. We often think of prayer in terms of familiar categories and frameworks: praise, petition, thanksgiving; dirge, celebration; formulaic recitations. But prayer is more than that. It is the natural turning of the heart in attention to the Divine, and it may or may not emerge in speech. When it does, it may be directed to God alone, or it may address God only indirectly, disguised as communication with others. This sort of prayer requires the training of the heart, deep attention, and clarity of mind and intention.

Most of us have not attained these qualities, and none of us can compare to Moses in this regard. Therefore, we have to pray to be able to pray in such a manner. We may never attain it. But Levi Yitzhak offers a consolation: in praying to be able to pray, we turn our hearts toward God, and in that very movement we may attain what at times seems so elusive or far away: the true prayer of the heart.

Questions for Reflection

1. What do you need to do to prepare to pray? Does it make sense to you to pray to be able to pray? When, how, why, or why not?

2. What have you always wanted to be able to say but have not? What would help you do so? How might you pray for that help?

3. Levi Yitzhak suggests that Moses's common speech was actually a constant prayer to God. Can you imagine your common speech being a form of prayer? Would you want it to be? When, how, why, or why not?

Taking It into Your Life

This selection invites us to engage in the practice of *hitbodedut*. This is a form of prayer, an active kind of meditation, taught by R. Nahman of

Breslov. Rebbe Nahman recommended engaging in this practice an hour each day. It is a verbal practice, and so he recommends that we find a place where we will not be overheard, where nothing will inhibit our free expression (such as out of doors, away from habitations). Still, that is not always possible, and we can be alone under a tallit, behind our hand, or simply speaking internally with our eyes closed.

The practice: Set the intention to speak directly to God without self-censor. Leave aside all questions of who or what God is, whether God hears, what difference it would make to God, etc. Simply prepare to speak out loud all that comes out of your heart/mind. When ready, simply begin speaking. It may be helpful to begin with a single word or phrase (e.g., *ribbono shel olam* / Master of the Universe; please; God). Repeat it over and over until you sense a new thought or feeling arising. Note it out loud; speak what is happening; tell yourself what is going on. Allow words to flow without directing them, without "thinking" about what you are saying—and keep on talking. If the flow of ideas reaches an end, return to your single word or phrase and see what comes up next. Continue until the end of the time that you have allotted.

Allow emotions to accompany your words. Speak the feeling of the words, and feel it in your body. This will help prompt whatever needs to come next in the flow of words. Do not stop to evaluate, to inquire from the outside. If your heart leads you to ask about what you are saying, do so as part of your unbroken flow of words.

If you can, do this practice while walking. This makes it possible for the body to enact some of the sense and intention of the words. Your movement may also prompt the emergence of new thoughts, words, and feelings. Allow yourself to move in accordance with your feelings.

When you are done, reflect on what you heard your heart tell your mind, your soul speak to God. You will have prayed, and you may be more able to pray following this practice.

Another explanation of "You, who hold fast to the Lord your God, are all alive today" (Deut. 4:4).

There is a principle (Eruvin 22a):

R. Yehoshua ben Levi stated: What is the implication of the verse "Therefore, observe faithfully the Instruction—the laws and the rules—which I command you today to do them" (Deut. 7:11)? It means: "today you are to do them," not "tomorrow to do them"; "today to do them", but "tomorrow is reserved for receiving reward for doing them."

Surely the reward is only to be experienced "tomorrow," but when we perform a mitzvah or learn Torah, we also receive an infusion of vital energy (*chayyut*) from this mitzvah or Torah study. So this reward is "today," and this vital energy is the awe we sense in the moment of performing the mitzvah or studying Torah. From this awe, we merit wisdom, as it says, "Indeed, fear of *YHVH* is wisdom" (Job 28:28), and "Wisdom enlivens [*mechayeh*] the one who possesses it" (Eccles. 7:12).

This, then, is how we should understand our verse: "**You, who hold fast to the Lord your God**"—when we cleave to the blessed Holy One, the key part of reward is indeed "tomorrow"; but, the vital energy that comes to us from doing the mitzvot is experienced "**today**." That means: "**you ... are all alive**" (*chayyim*): the vital energy we receive from doing mitzvot and studying Torah comes to us "**today**."

FOR FURTHER THOUGHT

Levi Yitzhak constantly seeks to enliven the quality of traditional Jewish practice. Prayer, mitzvot, and Torah study that are performed by rote have no life and accomplish no meaningful spiritual end. The Torah and her teachers are sensitive to the forces of the human heart and recognize a fundamental characteristic of "capitalist" energy: people apply themselves to what brings them reward. The degree of energy often is proportional to the proximity of the reward. That which will come sooner calls forth greater effort than that which may not be seen or will only be enjoyed in the more distant future. While it may be more mature to be able to delay gratification—and may indeed bring greater reward—our first impulse is to seek immediate response and satisfaction.

This presents a problem for Levi Yitzhak, who knows from tradition that there is no reward in this world for the fulfillment of the mitzvot. Yet he also knows from experience (shaped by the teachings of the Maggid of Mezritch, his teacher, and of the Baal Shem Tov) that there is a divine response to engaging in Jewish practices. The performance of the mitzvot with intention facilitates the flow of divine energy that sustains and enlivens us. That, too, is a boon from the Holy One, a reward experienced in this world. Yet it also cycles back on itself: *mitzvah goreret mitzvah*, the performance of one mitzvah brings another in train. God delights in our loving devotions and responds by providing us with the energy and commitment to do more.

Note that Levi Yitzhak does not directly say that the mitzvot and Torah study that bring this reward emerge from deep spiritual awareness. He simply says, "When we perform a mitzvah or learn Torah, we also receive an infusion of vital energy [*chayyut*]." He does not say that we have to be spiritual adepts fully able to cleave to God in *devekut*. He allows the verse to bring that quality into his discussion, so that we sense the quality of cleaving to God, *devekut*, as a moment-to-moment experience. It arises in the moment in which we perform a mitzvah or study Torah and turn our attention to God. It is in that turn that we connect with God, and it is that turn that opens the channel by which we receive the divine vitality, *chayyut*. In this manner, we truly come alive.

Questions for Reflection

1. The verse on which this lesson turns is recited before reading Torah during worship services. How is our liturgical reading from Torah a means of "cleaving" to God? How does this reading make us more alive?

2. Do you expect a reward for performing mitzvot? Do you experience a reward for performing mitzvot? Discuss.

3. How do you experience *chayyut*, divine vital force, in your life? Do you sense it in your body, your feelings, your mind, your soul? All? None?

Taking It into Your Life

Many of us have the sense that "if I do good, I should get good." We want God to reward us with life, ease, and happiness for being good people, for living Jewish lives. And often we are disappointed: the world does not work that way. Levi Yitzhak reminds us that we cannot calculate compensation for our goodness in any meaningful way; it is beyond our ken. But we can more easily—and powerfully—notice God's "reward" in each moment: vital energy, the force of life in our bodies.

This suggests the moment-to-moment awareness that we aim to develop in mindfulness practice, through which we may connect more directly to our experience in the moment, making clearer to us the quality of our experience. We will be more able to sense how, where, and in what manner we feel the movement of energy and aliveness in each moment (and if we sense it at all). When we are more able to perceive this aliveness, we will also be able to connect that awareness to the acts from which it emerges, in that manner experiencing the "reward" of which Levi Yitzhak speaks.

As you move through your day, make it a habit to bring your awareness to sensation in the body. Notice: What are the sensations in your hands, feet, stomach, back, shoulders, eyes, etc.? What is the movement of emotion in your heart/mind/body in this moment? Do you sense constriction of any sort—tense muscles, limited vision, hardened heart, shallow breath, confusion? In response to your experience, you may sense greater or lesser awareness of aliveness. This may help you notice when and how you connect with, cleave to God.

And inversely, when you do mitzvot, study Torah, engage in your life with intention, you may sense your body and heart more clearly alive.

Reflect.

"Hear O Israel! *YHVH* is our God, *YHVH* is one" (Deut. 6:4).

When we pray and say in the *Amidah*, "the great God," God clothes Himself with greatness. When we say, "the Mighty," God clothes Himself with might. When we say, "the Powerful," God clothes Himself with power. That God clothes Himself through our prayers is called "Mother" (*eim*), signifying measurement, as in a measuring stick (*amah moddedet*).

But we, however, must bind ourselves to the One who clothes Himself, to the root from which concealment in garments emerges. This is the concept of "touching and yet not touching." In this manner, there is no separation, heaven forbid.

This is the unification we accomplish when we recite: "**Hear O Israel!** *YHVH* **is our God,** *YHVH* **is one.**" "**Hear O Israel,** *YHVH*": this refers to the state in which God has not yet been clothed through our perception. When we say "**our God**" we mean that God constricts Himself in order to be clothed through our prayers. Still, we must cleave ultimately to the root. The second mention of God's name

"*YHVH*" signifies our return to that original root, through which we then unify God as "**one**," and all is then united.

Another interpretation of "**Hear O Israel**" can be brought out in light of the teaching (Zohar II 5a): "Every day a *bat kol* [heavenly voice; divine echo] comes forth from Mount Horeb, saying, 'Woe to those who forsake the service of their Master; woe to those for the disgrace of the Torah.'" Yet, the righteous merit hearing that call each day. That is the sense of our verse: "**Hear O Israel**": you, Israel, listen each moment and each minute to that voice that comes forth saying, "***YHVH* is our God, *YHVH* is one**."

Another interpretation of "Hear O Israel! YHVH is our God, YHVH is one" (Deut. 6:4).

It is possible for us to connect ourselves in all of our actions to the fear of God, just as we say, "Know Him in all your ways" (Prov. 3:6). We can perceive God's unity and oneness in all of our actions, when we act in accordance with the Torah.

In this light we can understand why we say, "**Hear O Israel**": we might wonder that if Moses said this to the Israelites, are we to respond "***YHVH* is our God, *YHVH* is one** "? But, instead we realize that "**Hear O Israel**" is directed to us personally; that we are able to hear and so perceive the unity of the Creator. In all of our actions we are able to perceive that "***YHVH* is our God, *YHVH* is one**"—the unity and oneness of the blessed Creator.

Another interpretation of "Hear, O Israel, YHVH our God, YHVH is one" (Deut. 6:4).

God is absolute oneness, yet the truth is that there are varieties of ways to serve God. There are those who serve God with the quality (*middah*) of love, others through the *middah* of fear, yet others through the *middah* of beauty, and so on with all of the other *middot*—and none are the same as the others.

We can understand this in the following manner: the name *YHVH* refers to God's own being, while the name *elohim* points to the ways in which we serve the blessed One. This is the meaning of Rashi's comment on Gen. 35:7, where he says that there are many places where the name *elohim* is actually treated as a plural noun—and, indeed, there are many ways of serving God, as we said above. Still, in whatever manner, with whatever *middah* we might come to serve the blessed Creator, we must nevertheless attach ourselves to the name *YHVH*, which signifies the *middah* of absolute unity.

Further, this is the intent of the verse "and you who cleave to *YHVH* your God [*eloheikhem*]" (Deut. 4:4)—that is, you have to attach yourselves to "*YHVH* your God," each and every one according to his manner of service has to cleave to *YHVH*: absolute oneness. And even though there are different paths of service, each one of them in the end must be connected to *YHVH*, as above.

This, then, is also the meaning in our verse "**YHVH** … **our God** [*eloheinu*]." That is, "**YHVH**" points to God's own being, which is absolute oneness; "**our God**" reflects the many diverse ways through which we serve God. And while there may be many different aspects to our service, we must all ultimately attach our service to God. This is the meaning of "**YHVH is one**"—that we have to cleave to *YHVH*, the ultimate, absolute unity.

FOR FURTHER THOUGHT

The *Shema* is too central to our worship and to our spiritual lives not to have included several of Levi Yitzhak's brilliant teachings on the verse. Through them all he grapples with the challenge of perception: how are we to connect with this God to whom we swear fidelity in this declaration?

One of the problems is that we say here that "God is one," yet we experience diversity in the world, and we speak of this God with a variety of names. There are many ways that the Hasidic and mystical traditions have dealt with this seeming problem. In all, the movement is away from the understanding of more modern biblical scholarship, which would suggest that the *Shema* is a declaration of fidelity to one particular God, *YHVH*: "*YHVH* is our God, *YHVH* alone." It may indeed have been that our ancestors were not absolute monotheists, rather monolatrists, worshipping one unique god above all others. But in the end, what emerged as Judaism was monotheism, with a clear sense that there is (was and will always be) only one God. Nevertheless, the suggestion of a plurality of gods, of divine forces, did not die away over the millennia. The Zohar and the mystical tradition, down to Levi Yitzhak here, struggle with the question of "the One and the many." Do not be deceived, they say: there is, in the end, only one One, and whatever diversity we may see or experience is only a way of getting back to that simple, absolute unity of all Being.

It is not only the multiplicity of names of God that may be confusing, but the many ways in which God appears in the world, the many ways we seek God, worship God. And there are many ways we can be distracted from God, turn away from God. This verse calls to us each day, in every moment, to remind us that in every act, in everything that we do or witness, we can recognize God's existence and God's unity, the unity behind all multiplicity.

Questions for Reflection

1. The *middot* can serve as paths of divine service. That is, one can worship God through the experience of love, or of fear, or through an awareness of the glory or beauty of Creation and God's work, etc. Are these paths exclusive of one another, or are they alternatives to be used at different times? In your own spiritual work, do you find that you employ the *middot* as different modes of approach, or do you devote yourself to one particular path? What is to be gained from becoming an *ahavah* (love) or a *yirah* (fear) devotee? What is gained by using the *middot* according to the need or experience of the moment?

2. Following up on the previous question—do you think that Levi Yitzhak was concerned that people following different devotional paths might mistake their experience of God, through their particular experiential lens, with the essence of God? Is the danger one of schism or of competition or of polytheism? Do we face a similar problem today—different approaches to Judaism based on different God concepts creating a seeming division in God's very self? How are we to deal with our commitment to pluralism, while still pushing to get beyond separateness to one simple unity?

3. In the last selection, Levi Yitzhak does not comment on the end of Deut. 4:4: "are all alive today." Is there a connection between being fully alive and moving beyond the multiple experiences of the Divine to the simple, absolute oneness? Is there a connection between realizing or experiencing the simple, absolute oneness of God and being alive, or present "today," in this moment? How does the first selection reflect on your answer here?

Taking It into Your Life

Of course, we have a practice for this already: to recite the *Shema*! But Levi Yitzhak is asking for more. In reciting the *Shema*, or in some other way, we learn to experience the oneness that stands behind and enlivens the multiplicity of life. That oneness, the One, is always present, yet it is hidden. It is easy to miss when we get caught up in the push and pull of our hearts and minds. We need a practice that can either settle the heart/mind or help us see through it.

This would be meditation. Sit comfortably: feet on the floor, pelvis slightly tilted forward, spine upright, shoulders at ease. You might close your eyes or allow them to rest in a broad focus on the floor. Feel the sensations of sitting: the pressure of the floor on your feet, the chair on your bottom holding you up. Feel the air against your skin. Notice the sensations of your body. Bring your attention to the feeling of the body breathing: the movement of breath at the nostrils or in the chest or belly. Return your attention to the breath over and over again, connecting to the sensation in the body.

Thoughts may arise, but you allow them to pass by, letting go and bringing your attention back to the breath. Memories or plans may come to mind, but you choose not to engage with them, instead bringing your attention back to the sensation of the breath. Over and over you connect your attention to your intention: to hold your attention in the sensation of the breath.

Over time you may notice the thoughts, feelings, ideas, and images that flow through the mind. They pass without distracting you from your breath; they are present as part of your experience without being the focus of your attention. At this point you become aware of the quality of awareness: the spacious aspect of consciousness that can hold all that is happening without being caught up in it. Awareness does not change. We may be more or less attentive to it, but it is bright, open, welcoming, balanced. Everything can be present in it. Awareness is unperturbed and at ease.

Practice. Notice your experience of awareness. Consider: how is it that all can be present, that multiplicity can exist, within awareness without being divided in itself? Consider: how is it possible that all that is transient, impermanent, or empty is fully alive in the context of awareness? *YHVH*, awareness, is surely filled with multiple and complex processes and beings. Yet *YHVH*, awareness, is still infinite, undifferentiated, complete, and one.

Eikev

Another interpretation of "And as a consequence [*eikev*] of your listening [to these rules and observing them carefully, *YHVH* your God will maintain faithfully for you the covenant that He made on oath with your fathers]" (Deut. 7:12).

This is how it works. There are those who serve the blessed Creator, perceiving God's unity through intellectual investigation. They inquire into the oneness of the Creator and perceive with their intelligence God's divinity and oneness—and then serve God. But there are others who serve the blessed Creator, perceiving God's unity through faith. They believe that there is a God who created all existence—without any intellectual inquiry at all.

People have heads, heels (feet; *eikev*), and hands. In the same way, divine service has a beginning, a middle, and an end. The first quality above—serving God and perceiving the Creator's unity through intellectual investigation, discerning that there is a God and knowing God's oneness—is called "beginning" (head; *rosh*). The second quality—serving God through faith, trusting in God's divinity and oneness and then serving God—is called "heel," as this is the end point. "Hands" signify the love of the blessed Creator. So sometimes the hands are raised, near to the head. This signifies that we have love of the blessed Creator because we perceive God's divinity and oneness through our intellect. This is how we come to love God, and this is represented by raised hands. But sometimes our hands are down. This signifies our love of the blessed Creator based on our faith, knowing through faith God's oneness and divinity.

This is the sense of our verse, "**And as a consequence [*eikev*] of your listening**." Rashi interprets this phrase: "If you will listen to those simple mitzvot that people trample underfoot [*dash b'akeivav*]." This suggests that the essence of our service of God and the way to perceive the oneness of the blessed Creator is through faith, which is the end point. Any of us can serve God through faith, believing with a perfect faith that there is a God in the world. This is signified in the phrase "**as a consequence**" (*vehayah eikev*): the word *vehayah* is an anagram of the divine name *YHVH*. The letters *Y"H* signify the first quality above, serving God and perceiving God's oneness through intellectual inquiry. The letters *V"H* signify the second quality, serving God through faith. So this phrase teaches that the key to divine service is through faith (as signified in the word *eikev*), as in the word *vehayah* the letters *V"H* precede *Y"H*.

FOR FURTHER THOUGHT

A key to this lesson is the identification of *eikev*/heel with the "end." In some instances, this signifies the lower, lesser dimension of spiritual life. So for instance, Jacob—*ya'akov*—is identified as the lower, less developed spiritual person. In our case, as elsewhere, the "end" applies to the lowest of the *sephirot*, *Malkhut* (the *Shekhinah*), and by association, Faith/*Emunah*. In this light, Levi Yitzhak can read our verse, "Faith is what supports listening to and obeying the commandments."

But if there is an "end," there must also be a "beginning"; if there is a heel, there must be a head. If the "heel" is faith, then the head is intellect, thought. In the system of the *sephirot*, "thought," or wisdom, is associated with the two supernal dimensions of *Chokhmah* and *Binah*. While it may be difficult (if not impossible) to fully conceive of these *sephirot*, employing our intellect to contemplate God helps connect us to them.

Further, in the mystical tradition, each of the four letters of the divine name *YHVH* is associated with some aspect of the *sephirot*. *Y* is *Chokhmah*, and the first/upper *H* is *Binah*; *V* represents *Tiferet* and the five other *sephirot* surrounding it, extending from below *Binah* through to *Yesod*; the second/lower *H* signifies *Shekhinah*. Thus, *Y"H* represents the upper *sephirot* of wisdom. While they are exalted, it is easier and more effective to perceive God through faith. Connecting directly to the world around us, sensing God's presence in all things, we put ourselves into relation with the *Shekhinah*. Sensing, in turn, that all is enlivened, supported, and sustained by God, we acknowledge God's sovereignty, *Malkhut*. In this manner, we come to connect with God, to know and acknowledge God, through the lower *sephirot* identified as *V"H* first, only later arriving at the higher stage of *Y"H*.

Questions for Reflection

1. In your experience, what aspects of God have you come to know through the intellectual investigations? How inspiring has this been to your spiritual life? What do you feel is missing for you in this mode of knowing, and what are its advantages over faith?

2. In your experience, what aspects of God have you come to know through faith? How inspiring has this been to your spiritual life? What do you feel is missing for you in this mode of knowing, and what are its advantages over intellectual investigation?

3. How do you understand the connection (implicit in this lesson) between knowing and serving God out of faith and the rewards that flow from listening to and obeying the commandments? How might faith serve you to recognize these blessings in your life?

Taking It into Your Life

The image of the raised and lowered hands is suggestive; the former feels active, the latter passive. So perhaps this lesson is as much about "intellect" and "faith" as it is about loving and knowing God through engagement in the world and loving and knowing God through quiet contemplation.

Consider two different practices. Pay attention to how you serve God based on what you "know." You may have developed a philosophical rationale for engaging in Jewish ritual, for pursuing justice, for honoring the infinite value of every person, for healing the planet. How do your values become manifest in action? How do your ideas prompt you to act? When you are engaged in doing something Jewish (whether ritual or values based), do you feel your ideas or philosophical conceptions in your body, your heart, your mind? What nurtures your ideas, what deepens your commitment to action?

Pay attention to how you serve God based on "faith." You may have a sense of knowing something about God, about your connection to God that is beyond explanation. You may feel God in your life, in the world. Where did that feeling come from? What nurtures it? What is the impact in your life of having this faith? Does it move you to act? Does it console your heart? Does it clarify your mind? How do you nurture this faith, and what sustains it? How does your faith impact the world?

> "Should you say to yourselves, 'These nations are more numerous than we; how can we dispossess them?' Have no fear of them" (Deut. 7:17–18).

Rashi focuses on the meaning of the word *ki* (here translated "should"):

> You must agree that the meaning of *ki* is "lest/perhaps," so that we would read this verse in the following manner: "Perhaps you will say in your heart that because they are more numerous I will not be able to dispossess them. But do not say that. Do not fear them." It would not be possible to interpret this word in any of its other meanings and still make sense when followed by "do not fear them."

In truth, if any obstacle should arise for you (heaven forbid) in your service of the blessed Creator, then the most important thing to do is not to respond in terror or fear. Surely, then, with the help of the blessed Creator, nothing will afflict you. This is implied in the verse **"Should you say to yourselves, 'These nations are more numerous than we'"**—you are permitted to think this, but the Torah adds a piece of advice. You may ask, **"How can we dispossess them?"** and the Torah gives advice about how we can dispossess the impediments to our service: **"Have no fear of them."** Then, certainly, you will be able to dispossess them.

FOR FURTHER THOUGHT

Here, again, is a mindfulness teaching. What prevents us from moving ahead in our lives, from being able to function effectively, to respond with compassion and justice? Our projections and our fears, anxieties, judgments, and imaginings in response to the moment-to-moment events of our lives, as well as the desires and passions that fill our hearts, distract and deflect us from our true selves. When we are able to see clearly, to respond out of a place of balance and openness, these impediments fall away, and we are able to move ahead. The road may still be difficult, we may have to work hard and do things we don't like or that we don't feel competent to do, we may even feel fear, but we will be able to do what we can unencumbered by the stories of our fears. Thank you, Levi Yitzhak, for reminding us to open our eyes and see the truth clearly.

Questions for Reflection

1. The plain meaning of the Torah in these verses is that fear in the face of the nations would be a failure of faith in God, who wrought wonders and punishments in Egypt and who will do so here again. Levi Yitzhak could have used this argument as a way to negate spiritual impediments as well. Why do you think he did not choose to do this? Which argument works better for you: Do you draw strength from faith built on previous experiences? Do you draw strength from faith in God's former acts for our ancestors (and us)? Does mindfulness practice, which does not rely on faith in God's previous deeds but on our own experience of witnessing the truth, work better for you? When, how, why?

2. Notice how smoothly and unself-consciously Levi Yitzhak moves from the verse in the Torah to his interest—how to engage in spiritual work. Is that how you like to read the Torah, as a guide to spiritual work? Do you read the sections of commandments in that manner, as the Torah giving you advice as to how to deepen your spiritual experience? Does this sort of approach reinforce your commitment to observance (of whatever mitzvot you do observe), or is the spiritual work more important than the specific observance?

3. We can restate this teaching as follows: spiritual work (divine service) is like making our way into the Promised Land. The numerous nations are spiritual impediments, possibly preventing us from entering the Promised Land and serving God in truth. Do you experience your spiritual work as overcoming impediments, of working to hold some faith so that you might see clearly, face life without debilitating fear? When, how, why?

Taking It into Your Life

This is the second week leading from the ninth of Av to Rosh Hashanah. This is the time for *teshuvah*, self-transformation and self-correction. That is not easy work, yet the consequences of failing to engage in it are serious. There are many reasons that we might not wish to look hard at our lives: awareness of our many mistakes and the pain of acknowledging them forthrightly to ourselves and to those whom we have harmed; fear that we will find something in our hearts of which we are not aware, that might challenge our self-image, our sense of self-worth; resistance to undertaking self-assessment when we sense that it is possible that others may not do so, particularly those from whom we may wish an apology. These are all obstacles to doing what is good and right—and necessary. The power of these obstacles is as great as the "nations" whom the Israelites might have feared. Levi Yitzhak knows these obstacles well, and tells us simply, "Do not fear them."

How can we not fear? We need to slow down, to allow the obstacles—these hard feelings—to come to mind. We need to sit quietly, to create the inner space in which they might arise in heart and mind. And then, paradoxically, we must allow the feelings to arise in their full force in our bodies, our hearts, and our minds. The practice, though, is not to allow these feelings to bring their associated stories along with them. Rather, focus on the feelings. See where they sit in the body. Notice their characteristics. See how they change: where they arise, where they go. In meeting our feelings this way, we will learn that they need not take over our hearts and minds. They can arise and pass away without our having to engage in them.

In the end, the instruction is: do not fear your fear of your feelings. The feelings will come and go. Adding fear to them will make them stronger, prolonging your pain, raising the likelihood of inner resistance and failure to change. We do not control our feelings—they arise of their own accord. We cannot simply tell ourselves, "Do not fear." But we can choose not to add to our fear or to fear our feelings and the obstacles they raise. In this choice we may truly dispossess them and enter the land, redeemed.

> "And now, O Israel, what does *YHVH* your
> God demand of you? Only this: to fear
> [*YHVH* your God, to walk only in His paths,
> to love Him, and to serve *YHVH* your God
> with all your heart and soul]" (Deut. 10:12).

This is how it is. We must be humble in all of our dealings and doings. But you may think then that we are to be humble in serving God as well. Heaven forbid saying so! Rather, we should say, "That which I do, performing God's mitzvot, is important to the blessed Creator. God delights in my mitzvot, the things that I do." For, if we were humble in performing God's commandments, saying, "What significance do my deeds have before God?" we would deny God! Instead, with regard to performing God's commandments we must say, "That which I do to fulfill God's desires are significant in God's eyes, and God delights in my deeds, the mitzvot I perform."

The Sages taught that a student of the wise (a scholar) must have some small quantum of pride, even if it is an eighth of an eighth (cf. Sotah 5a), because the world of delight is the eighth *middah* (*sephirah*). This means that the blessed Creator delights in the mitzvot that we perform, and we must derive delight that we bring ease of spirit to the blessed Creator. We must cleave to that eighth *middah*, the world of delight. This is actually what "an eighth of an eighth" signifies: we derive delight from the fact that the blessed Creator derives delight from the mitzvot that we perform before God. This is as the Sages taught: "Israel provides sustenance for their Heavenly Parent." "Sustenance" signifies delight, and so we see that God delights in the mitzvot that we perform.

So, our verse: **"And now, O Israel, what does *YHVH* your God demand of you? Only this: to fear."** The word **"what"** (*mah*) signifies the quality of humility, as the Sages taught: Abraham expressed his humility, saying, "I am but dust and ashes" (Gen. 18:27); Moses's humility was even greater, as he said "We are nothing" (*venachnu mah*) (Exod. 16:7). So, **"what"** signifies humility. But, **"What does *YHVH* your God demand of you? Only this: to fear,** etc.": to the extent that you develop fear of God, you are not to match it with the humility that leads you to say, "What, are my deeds significant before God, that I could be someone who would fear God and perform God's commandments?" This is unacceptable!

FOR FURTHER THOUGHT

In general, we would think that humility is a central spiritual quality. And that is where Levi Yitzhak begins. But he, as many Hasidic teachers, recognizes that humility can also be debilitating, and false humility can be used as an excuse not to do anything. This is the key to our lesson. Levi Yitzhak depicts (false or excessive) humility as an impediment to dedicating ourselves to serving God. We might think that we have no standing before God, that our prayers or devotions are too insignificant to be worthy of God's notice. But that is hardly the case. We were created to serve God, and our dedicated devotions bring God delight and ease of spirit! Refraining from serving God would actually be debilitating to God and a failure to fulfill our highest purpose.

But Levi Yitzhak is also careful. He wants us to know that we are not to swing to the opposite pole, of haughtiness. Rather, like all scholars (*talmidei chakhamim*), we are permitted—even required—to have an eighth-of-an-eighth portion of pride, enough to inspire us with the audacity to serve God. Some haughtiness is necessary to overcome the humility that we would otherwise feel standing before God, to claim our rightful place before the blessed Creator.

In this teaching, Levi Yitzhak displays an aspect of the "humanist" side of Hasidism. Hasidic teachers recognize the full humanity of their students and see them in a balanced way. Because they know—deeply—the oneness of all existence, its inseparability from the essence of God, they shy away from sharp dichotomies, either-or propositions. So, they do not ask that we always and only be humble, nor do they allow us to be too prideful. Instead, as Levi Yitzhak does here, they seek balance, the utilization of both qualities to more fully and perfectly serve God.

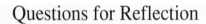

Questions for Reflection

1. What tools or inner measures do you have to assess your humility? Is it possible to know whether you are humble at all—isn't thinking that one is humble a sign of pride? What keeps your ego in check?

2. Do you feel any pride—self-esteem, self-affirmation—in your religious life? Do you feel that you are required to assert yourself to serve God? What gives you the strength, the audacity, to stand before God?

3. Whose voice do you hear in your head/heart that tells you that you are not good enough? Whose voice do you hear in your head/heart that tells you that you are good just the way you are? Which of these voices do you tend to listen to? When, why?

Taking It into Your Life

This lesson is an earlier and slightly different formulation of R. Simha Bunim's teaching of "two pockets": one that contains the verse "I am but dust and ashes," and the other holding the Rabbinic teaching "The world was created for my sake." It is not meant just as a nice idea. This is a practice: we are to access each of these sayings regularly, to apply them as needed to keep us balanced, clear, and honest.

As you make your way through the day, pay attention to the times when you sense an inner voice crying out: "Look at me!" "What about me?" "Where's mine?" Notice when you feel left out or when you feel that you have not received your due. Notice as well resentment of others' success, anger at others' well-being.

As you make your way through the day, pay attention to the times when you sense an inner voice cooing, "I'm really good," "I just nailed it," "He's such a loser." Notice when you feel at the center of attention or when you feel that you deserve all that is coming to you and more. Notice as well your resentment of others' success, fear of others' well-being.

Feel into your heart. What is it telling you? Do you feel too small and unimportant because that is true or because you are afraid that it is true? Do you feel accomplished and successful because it is true or because you are afraid it is not true? Is your impulse toward self-promotion to claim what is your rightful place, or is it your attempt to keep others from having any success at your expense? When do you need to bolster your self-esteem by remembering "for my sake was the world created" and that your dedicated efforts—no matter how seemingly small, no matter how "successful" in others' eyes—are desired by God? When you sense that your self-promotion is inaccurate and comes at the expense of others, recall that you are "but dust and ashes," barely a blip in the cosmic landscape.

But, in the end, have compassion for yourself, for your bruised ego, your needy heart. Remember that you are God's beloved.

Re'eih

Another interpretation of "See, this day I
set before you blessing and curse; blessing
when you obey ..." (Deut. 11:26–27).

The commentators focused on the words "**when [*asher*] you obey**." To
have been parallel it should have said, "if you obey," as in what follows, "if
[*im*] you do not obey" (Deut. 11:28). The teaching of the Sages is familiar:
"There is no reward for obeying the mitzvot in this lifetime" (Kiddushin
39b). But, there is one reward we can indeed receive in this lifetime: the
reward for fulfilling a mitzvah is a mitzvah (cf. Avot 4:2). That is, the
reward of a mitzvah is in doing the mitzvah itself, and no one needs
more than that. Merely the fact that one merits to fulfill a mitzvah, and
so bring delight to the Creator—there is no reward greater than that.

This is the intent of our verse when it says, "**See, this day I set before
you blessing**": that is, even now in your lifetimes, when you fulfill the
commandments of the Creator, you will receive a blessing in this world.
It then goes on to say what that blessing is, as the verse continues: "**when
you obey**." This very fact, that you obey Me and do My mitzvot, this
itself will be a blessing, since there is no greater delight than this. Thus,
the reward for a mitzvah is the mitzvah itself, as above. One cannot say
the same regarding the curse (heaven forbid). The curse will come about
specifically "if" you do not obey, and therefore the Torah had to say "if"
(Deut. 11:28).

FOR FURTHER THOUGHT

This is such difficult material. For many people, particularly after the
Shoah, the idea of reward and punishment has no meaning and is
even offensive. At times, it feels as if we have made a bargain with
God: "Don't bother with rewards, and we won't bother with expectations. But please, God, stay out of the punishment business, too. We'll
deal with the consequences ourselves." The downside: God and we

are polite with each other, but not too intimate; we don't have expectations of each other. As strange an idea as it might be—so anthropomorphic, so infantile—could we reclaim a sense of intimacy by seeking to bring delight to God? Is that a role and a relationship that is meaningful and inspiring? Can doing the mitzvot be not only for our sake but also for God's; not for ulterior or material blessing, but for spiritual edification and inner growth?

 ## Questions for Reflection

1. In the JPS translation of the verse ("blessing, if you obey … curse, if you do not obey"), there is no distinction made between the blessing and the curse, between "when/*asher*" and "if/*im.*" Is there no semantic difference between these words? In most other instances, *im* indicates some doubt, something conditional, while *asher* is concrete, evident. Even without accepting Levi Yitzhak's teaching, do you prefer the system implicit in the JPS translation, or something more subtle, where the punishment is conditional and the blessing more concrete?

2. Even though Levi Yitzhak acknowledges that there will be reward for fulfilling the mitzvot in the world-to-come, he generally points beyond that expectation, wishing to avoid "serving the Master in order to receive a reward." In the end, he comes back to the same place: serving God to bring God delight. This is sound spiritual advice. Anything else would be creating expectations, telling ourselves a story about our actions, setting ourselves up for disappointment, conflict, grief. Have you had experiences that confirm Levi Yitzhak's instructions? That contradict them? Does this make sense psychologically—do, or can, people actually live this way, where the reward for an act is doing the act itself?

3. Ibn Ezra comments on our verse: "'Blessing'—an increase in goodness. 'Curse'—lack." This suggests that a "curse" is the absence of the good. On the other hand, Levi Yitzhak argues that the reward of a mitzvah (i.e., blessing) is the act itself, bringing delight to God. That "reward" is immaterial and intangible. To enjoy that sort of reward, one would have to work hard to diminish the ego. An ego that is too much engaged in itself would not so easily offer delight to another and might actually experience offering to another as taking something away from itself. Wouldn't that then be experienced as lack, absence, curse? Can we thin out our protective shields enough to not sense "lack," and so be open to "blessing" just in what is?

Taking It into Your Life

There is a relation between experiencing the blessing of fulfilling a mitzvah in the act itself and the way this verse opens: "See, this day I set before you." That is, we can come closer to experiencing this sort of blessing if we live more in "today," in the fullness of each and every moment. When we allow our thoughts to lead us into an unknown future with expectations of a particular outcome, we create our own suffering. Our expectations are a fantasy—perhaps with some grounding in cause and effect, but still subject to forces beyond our control—and may never be fulfilled. The blessing that we hope for will always be beyond our reach, always tomorrow, next week, next year. We will never find peace in this moment with what is because we will always be looking forward to what is yet to come.

As you make your way through the day, meet each event with "thank you." Found a parking space? Thank you. Missed a parking space? Thank you. Met a deadline? Thank you. Went overtime? Thank you. When you notice yourself looking ahead and anticipating one outcome or another, take a breath and connect with this moment: what is here for which you can say "thank you"?

Receive each moment, each event, with welcome. Greet it as a friend. Recognize it as a blessing. So long as you remain connected to this moment, here and now, with intention and integrity, there is nothing more for you to do than to welcome whatever is with gratitude, as a blessing.

"[Rather, to the place that YHVH your God chooses from among all your tribes to put His name there,] His dwelling place [*leshikhno*] you are to seek out and are to come there" (Deut. 12:5).

"**There**" (*shammah*) has the same letters as *Mosheh* (Moses). The *Tikkunei Zohar*, in a similar vein, teaches that the initial letters of the words *M"immekhon Sh"ivto H"ishgi'ach* ("From His dwelling place He gazes"; Ps. 33:14) also spell *Mosheh*. The Sages teach that "Moses is equal to the whole of Israel" (Song R. 1:65), and so each Jew must also have some quality of Moses in him or her.

Thus we read the verse from Ps. 33:14: "From His dwelling place He gazes on all the inhabitants of the earth": through Moses the blessed Holy One oversees "all the inhabitants of the earth," that is, Israel. That, then, is why our verse says we "**are to come there**" (*uvata shammah*): through the quality of Moses we can draw the *Shekhinah* to dwell on us. This is the sense of "**His** *Shekhinah* [*leshikhno*] **you are to seek out and are to come there.**"

FOR FURTHER THOUGHT

While the verse in context has to do with the centralization of the cult in one sanctuary, Levi Yitzhak interprets it to teach about our contemporary spiritual practice. It is not that there is only one place for us to go to worship. Rather, this verse teaches that in connecting with the quality of Moses in each of us, we can draw the *Shekhinah* to dwell upon us. We are to seek out and connect with the *Shekhinah* by coming into our own dimension of Moses.

Here is the passage from Song R. 1:65:

> Rabbi (Yehudah HaNasi) was once preaching, and the congregation began to fall asleep. He sought to rouse them. He said, "One woman in Egypt gave birth to six hundred thousand from one womb." There was a student there named R. Yishmael ben R. Yose, who said to him, "Who was that?" He replied, "Yocheved who bore Moses, who was counted as equal to six hundred thousand of Israel." This is as Scripture says, "Then Moses sang, and the Children of Israel" (Exod. 15:1); "The Children of Israel did according to all that *YHVH* commanded Moses" (Num. 1:54); "Never again did there arise in Israel a prophet like Moses" (Deut. 34:10).

The implication of Rabbi's teaching is that Moses contained and represented all of Israel. When he sang, all of Israel sang; when the Israelites followed his instructions, it was as if he fulfilled them himself; Moses was unique but is present in every prophet, in each generation.

The *Tikkunei Zohar* loves to play with words and letters. In the following passage we see how Moses is present all over Scripture, and so both available to us and involved in our lives (*Tikkunei Zohar*, *tikkun* 69, p. 111b ff.):

> R. Shimon said: Friends, surely the blessed Holy One has agreed with us for the upper and lower domains to be bound together. Happy is the generation in which this has been revealed. In the future all of this

is to be renewed by Moses, at the end of the last generation, to fulfill the verse "That which happened is what will happen [*M"ah Sh"ehayah H"u sheyiheyeh*]" (Eccles. 1:9). At that time [p. 112a] is also "From His dwelling place He gazes [*M"immekhon Sh"ivto H"ishgi'ach*]" (Ps. 33:14). "Happy is the people for whom it is thus [*shekakhah*]" (Ps. 144:15)—*shekakhah* is numerically equivalent to *Mosheh*—"happy is the people for whom *YHVH* is their God." Regarding Moses is it written, "A generation goes and a generation comes" (Eccles. 1:4), and there is no generation less than six hundred thousand. Regarding this it is written, "the matter that He commanded to a thousand generations" (Ps. 105:8)—and Moses extends through each and every generation, each tzaddik and scholar who engages in Torah, even to six hundred thousand, to make them all complete from their blemish. The mystery of the matter? "He is wounded because of our sins" (Isa. 53:5), for he is equal to them all. This is as the masters of the Mishnah established: one woman gave birth to six hundred thousand—and who is that? Moses, who is equal to all six hundred thousand. That is why Scripture says, "A generation goes and a generation comes" to that world: before that generation comes he will come first.

The person of Moses and the quality of Moses are present to anyone who engages in Torah throughout the generations. God's concern for us is expressed through Moses's presence through to the end of time. What he did in the past—to free us and to give us Torah—he continues to do even now.

Levi Yitzhak employs these two teachings to make his point: God's providential oversight (*hashgachah*) extends to us through Moses, who is present in us, revealing Torah each day. When we "come to Moses" (*uvata shammah*), we connect with the root of Torah. In seeking Torah, we are seeking the presence of the *Shekhinah*, through whom God's divine grace flows to us as blessing.

 ## Questions for Reflection

1. Is your spiritual practice aimed at seeking out the *Shekhinah*? When, how, why, or why not?

2. What might it mean to you to sense that Moses is in you, actively teaching you Torah, present when you gain some new insight? Where would you sense Moses in you? How might you nurture your Moses quality?

3. If Moses is equal to the whole of the Jewish people, could it be that the collective consciousness of the Jewish people is equal to Moses? What would that mean to you about what brings about liberation or revelation? What would be your role in creating the whole of the Moses-force in the world?

Taking It into Your Life

We can work at developing a "Moses consciousness" by reflecting on the phrase *M"immekhon Sh"ivto H"ishgi'ach*, "From His dwelling place He gazes" (Ps. 33:14). Moses observes all that happens to us, observes all existence. His awareness does not imply action. Rather, through his observation he gains awareness, which in turn provides us with an ongoing connection with revelation.

This suggests mindfulness practice. As you make your way through the day, pause periodically to observe your own mind. What are the thoughts passing through? What stories are being told about your current experience—how you feel about it, how you feel about others and their behavior, the associations that you make between this situation and others in your life? What is the state of your body: tense, relaxed, tired, energized? How are you reacting to how your body feels?

Nothing need be done—just observe. Allow what is to be as it is. Notice how feelings, sensations, and thoughts arise and pass away. Inquire: What remains? What is truly present, what dwells within each moment? It is possible to engage fully in your life while also observing, noticing so as not to get caught up in reactive feelings and behavior. Observing arising and passing away, noticing how things are from moment to moment, you may witness awareness arising—your sense of "this is how it is, and I can be OK in it." Perhaps this is revelation; perhaps this is Moses at work in you.

Shofetim

"You shall appoint magistrates and officials for you in all of your gates [that *YHVH* your God is giving you,] and they shall judge the people with due justice" (Deut. 16:18).

The blessed Holy One judges the Jewish people (*knesset yisrael*) on the Day of Judgment with the greatness of His compassion and love. But this requires arousal from below, to arouse the quality of compassion above. What is it that arouses this quality of love? When we below behave with love and judge others favorably, for merit. In this manner, that very quality of love is also aroused above, and so our fellows and all Israel are judged favorably and held with love as well. Thus we, through our actions below, arouse the highest gate, to open the gates of love, that blessing may rain down on all of Israel (cf. Malachi 3:10).

This is the meaning of our verse, **"You shall appoint magistrates and officials for you in all of your gates"**: that is, you, yourself, must establish and determine the divine judgment through your **"gates,"** the gates that you create and arouse through your actions. Thus we **"shall judge the people with due justice"**: that is, each one of us must train ourselves to learn to judge others with "due justice," to offer positive testimony (*tzedakah*) and innocence for all others. In this manner, we can arouse the gates above and also come out innocent in judgment: "The way a person measures (others) so is he measured" (Megillah 12b).

FOR FURTHER THOUGHT

Here we hear an echo of the metaphor of the "shadow" that we've met in previous texts—what we do here below effectuates response above. Although God's intention is to do good for us, to bless us, to judge us with compassion and love, it is easier, and the blessing fuller, when our behavior "inspires" God to act. There is a wonderful circle of effects here: I do for another, directing my attention toward another with love, for his or her benefit. God witnesses my action on behalf of another and blesses them. But while blessing the person to whom I attend, God also blesses me and everyone else as well. On the other hand, if I were to pray only for my own good, that I might be acquitted in judgment, those heavenly gates would not open so wide, and innocence and blessing might not spread so far.

It is worth considering the echo of the verse from Malachi. Here is the verse in its context (3:7–12):

> From the very days of your fathers you have turned away from My laws and have not observed them. Turn back to Me, and I will turn back to you—said *YHVH* of Hosts. But you ask, "How shall we turn back?" Ought man to defraud God? Yet you are defrauding Me. And you ask, "How have we been defrauding You?" In tithe and contribution. You are suffering under a curse, yet you go on defrauding Me—the whole nation of you. Bring the full tithe into the storehouse, and let there be food in My House, and thus put Me to the test—said *YHVH* of Hosts. I will surely open the flood-gates of the sky for you and pour down blessings on you; and I will banish the locusts from you, so that they will not destroy the yield of your soil; and your vines in the field shall no longer miscarry—said *YHVH* of Hosts. And all the nations shall account you happy, for you shall be the most desired of lands—said *YHVH* of Hosts.

The emphasis here is on bringing the tithes to the Temple, in response to which God will pour out blessings on the people from the heavens. Levi Yitzhak transforms this quite powerfully. That is, not only do we have to find the good (*tzedakah*) in others, finding them righteous, but Levi Yitzhak also wants us to understand that our doing *tzedakah*, giving charity to others, is the equivalent of bringing in the tithes, the result of which will be unending blessing for us and for all creation.

And do please note how Levi Yitzhak reads the second half of the verse. If we establish the proper sorts of judges and magistrates—that is, those who will act lovingly and assess others for good—then "they will judge" (*veshaphtu*) with due justice—that is, the forces above will judge accordingly. Our actions here do determine how things work out. What we do has consequences.

Questions for Reflection

1. In reading this lesson, let us not pass over the wordplay on the word *sha'ar*. It routinely means "gate," but it can also mean "rate" (as in rate of exchange, the cost of something) and "measurement" (as in *shi'ur*). How would this lesson sound if in the second paragraph we were to substitute "measurement" (or "assessment") for the word "gate"? How might this reading impact the verbal echo of Mal. 3:10 that appears at the end of the first paragraph? How might this help us understand the practice of finding righteousness (*lelammeid tzedakah*) in others?

2. When you read the second half of the verse Deut. 16:18, "and they shall judge the people with due justice" (*mishpat tzedek*), do you think of *tzedakah*? Is due justice always *tzedakah*? Can due justice always be compassionate and loving? How? Is this what we call today "tough love"? Or is Levi Yitzhak suggesting that in our relationships with others we must always and only respond with love and compassion? How would you bring this teaching into practice?

3. It is not by chance that Levi Yitzhak opens his teaching with reference to "the Day of Judgment" (*yom hamishpat*). How would you use this lesson in your personal work of *teshuvah*, of preparing to stand before the Holy One in judgment during the High Holy Days?

Taking It into Your Life

R. Israel of Koznitz (his book is *Sefer Avodat Yisrael*, based on *Sefer Yetzirah*, ch. 4) taught that the "gates" at which we have to set judges and magistrates are the seven gates of the head (eyes, ears, nose, mouth) and particularly those of the senses. We have to be very careful about what goes in and what goes out of our mouths, what we see and how we interpret it, what we do with our hands and what we feel or touch, etc.

This lesson invites us to integrate it into mindfulness practice. That is, to be fully aware of what is true in the moment, we need to become attentive to all the ways that we experience the world and how we tend to react. Our reactions are assessments, as well, and these too are gates (*she'arim*). We receive messages through all of our sense gates, not only through our minds, and we are as likely to react—in judgment, in assessment—to scent and sight as we are to thought.

Make a practice of focusing on one sense experience each day. Notice all the ways that you experience sensation, all the places on your body that you register the sense of touch, heat or cold, pressure, movement, etc. Pay attention to your response to sound: What do you experience as intrusive "noise," and what do you experience as appealing resonance? Which smells attract your attention, and which do you find repulsive? Which tastes do you find pleasant, and which are unpleasant? Where do you allow your gaze to linger, and from what do you turn away immediately? How do you respond to each of these sense experiences? What is the nature of your inner judgment in response to each of them?

What do we have to know about our experiences—how we take in the world, how we relate to it—to be able to judge all others as innocent?

"You shall prepare for yourself the way, and divide into three the boundaries of your land [that *YHVH* your God has allotted to you, so that any manslayer may have a place to flee to]" (Deut. 19:3).

No mind can fully conceive of the Holy One. But God contracted God's self in the quality of Abraham to do loving-kindness; in the quality of Isaac, so that we might revere God; and so also in the quality of Jacob to be compassionate. In this manner (as if it could be so), a boundary or limit was set for God, and this is how it is possible for us to consider the land ours.

This, then, is how we should understand our verse. "**You shall prepare for yourself the way**"—this is how we can prepare a way to perceive God: through God's qualities. In this manner, we can "**divide into three the boundaries**," and so also experience God in the land, in "**your land**."

For Further Thought

In only the second of God's qualities (Isaac) is it clear that this *middah* is relational between God and Israel. That is, God has the quality of "fear" (*pachad yitzchak*) so that we might experience the true fear of God, awestruck by God's exaltedness and greatness. With regard to the two others—love and compassion—Levi Yitzhak simply says that the *middah* is so that love and compassion might be done. It is tempting to suggest that Levi Yitzhak did not want to speak in terms of God causing fear, or even to speak of the quality of limitation and rigor in God, perhaps not to tempt the evil eye. But since God acts lovingly and with compassion, and since we are to love and have compassion for others, he could be more ambiguous with his language, leaving it unclear who enacts the love and compassion.

In speaking of "your land," the verse is clearly speaking of the Land of Israel. In our reading above, he seems to suggest that we merit calling the Land (and perhaps, by extension, the whole of the earth) "ours" when we recognize the boundaries, the garments, by which God is known in the world. We tend to see the material world as ours, mundane, separate from God. Our haughtiness in claiming the earth as "ours" leads to exile, suffering, and alienation. Recognizing God's presence intimately woven into the material world gives us permission to use the world and call it ours. Yet, Levi Yitzhak also hears this as pointing to "earthiness," our human, physical experience. When we embody the *middot*, we bring them into our bodies. But as these are divine qualities, we also gain intimacy with God. This is how God becomes perceptible to us, in our embodied experience.

Thus, the way to come to know God is to cleave to God's qualities, *middot*. By following that path, particularly as we enact the *middot* in the world, being loving and compassionate toward others while maintaining a clear sense of fear of and reverence for God, we also come to experience God's presence in the world. God then becomes ours in the sense that the *middot* are also ours, when we recognize that "the whole of creation is filled with God's glory" (Isa. 6:3), including us.

In all, then, this lesson is a brief statement of the dynamic tension between *yesh* and *ayin*, between the physical manifestation of creation and its true emptiness except as a garment, hiding yet also revealing God. We cannot know God except through the *middot*, and through them we may gain deeper awareness of the truth of God's existence. The more we know in that regard, the more we realize that there is nothing but God and that the world is insubstantial. Yet, in recognizing that there is nothing but God, but that God reveals God's self through the *middot*, we come to see that it is in the world—our bodies—that God is to be found, for there is no place devoid of God.

Questions for Reflection

1. How do you understand the nature of God's self-contraction? Is it that God withdrew from the world to make room for existence (and human endeavor) or that God contracted into physical existence in order to become present in manifest creation? What do you sense might be the difference in outcome of holding one or the other position? How does it seem to you that Levi Yitzhak understands it, at least in this lesson?

2. How would you explain the relationship between fear of God and the capacity (and intention) to express love and compassion toward others?

3. A significant element of Hasidic practice is *avodah shebegashmiyut*, serving God through corporeal life. The physical world can be a realm for divine service, but it can also be a snare. We can get trapped in our need to make a living, in the physical pleasures this world affords us. This experience is often referred to as *artzi'ut*, being bound up in the mundane, caught in the grip of materiality. Levi Yitzhak is at pains to demonstrate how, by recognizing God's self-limitation in the *middot*, the land (*eretz*) can become ours. What do you think he is saying about *artzi'ut*? Is this an invitation to serve God through the physical?

Taking It into Your Life

Generally we read this parashah during the first week of the Hebrew month of Elul. A classical play on its character uses each of the letters that spell the month as the initial letter of four words from Song of Songs (6:3): *A"ni L"edodi V"edodi L"i* (I am my beloved's and my beloved is mine). This month is one of the high points of the year. We turn to God in love, seeking to know ourselves better, to acknowledge the truth of our mistakes and failings, and lovingly to turn to do better. We are able to do this freely, and with grace, because we trust that God loves us as well.

This relational character lies behind Levi Yitzhak's teaching regarding the *middot* and invites us to practice today. Levi Yitzhak suggests that God's self-contraction in the quality of love and compassion is so that we might act lovingly and with compassion. Quite naturally this leads to the following awareness: God is in my loving act, in my compassionate act. When I wish to perceive God in the world, I need only look for love and compassion.

Set an intention that this month be one in which you nurture your capacity for love and compassion. You may ground it in loving-kindness practice: in meditation, bring to mind the image of the people in your life—both near and far, beloved and difficult—and sense the wish in your heart that they feel safe, that they feel content in life, that their bodies be well, that their lives unfold with ease. Wish them the blessings of loving-kindness, compassion, joy, and peace. Make the focus of the exercise the experience of the feeling in your heart—not an intellectual idea, that this might somehow come about, but truly wishing it for the other by sensing it in yourself (and so, you might begin this practice with yourself).

In a more concrete sense, you might also devote this month to doing acts of loving-kindness and compassion. Attune your eyes to seeing where your help might be needed. Pay attention to the subtle messages that invite a response of compassion. This is not a contest; you need not fill in a calendar of "successes." Rather, this is a practice, a dedication of heart, mind, body, and soul aiming to act in a certain manner. When you miss a chance, remember to have compassion on yourself, so that you remain free and open, available to do the next act that comes your way. (And note when you sense the awesomeness of this practice, how endless is the need for love and compassion, and what is called for from you to respond. This may be a way of experiencing the fear of God, completing the threefold path Levi Yitzhak lays out.)

Bring this quality of heart and soul into your High Holy Day preparation.

Ki Teitzei

"When you chance upon a bird's nest [along the road, or in any tree or on the ground, with fledglings or eggs and the mother is sitting over the fledglings or on the eggs, do not take the mother together with her young. Do send away the mother, and take only the young, in order that you may fare well and have a long life]" (Deut. 22:6–7).

We know that there are two forms of arousal: arousal from above and arousal from below. We must not allow ourselves to rely on arousal from above, but rather benefit from the work of our own hands, arousing ourselves. In response, the spirit of God will rest on us, aroused from above. The blessed Holy One "gives the wisdom to the wise" (Dan. 2:21): when we arouse ourselves, and so demonstrate that we have attained that quality of "wise," God gives us wisdom, sending us supernal arousal.

Consider: When a child is small, the mother has to incline herself toward him so that he can nurse. And that is how God works, too. When we have no awareness to prompt us to arouse ourselves, we are sent arousal from above. Nevertheless, remember that the *Turei Zahav*, commenting on *Shulchan Arukh* (*Orach Chayyim* 1:2) urges us "to arouse the dawn, and not to wait to allow the dawn to arouse us." That is to say, we should seek to arouse "the dawn"—that is, supernal arousal—through our own efforts, and not rely on "the dawn" to arouse us.

That is the meaning of our verse: "**When you chance upon a bird's** [*tzipor*] **nest**"—bird/*tzipor* suggests "morning" (Aramaic: *tzaphra*), which signifies clarity. Thus, when you attain some measure of clarity, and arousal from above enlightens you "**along the road**"—that is, in the ways of God, the pathways of the world-to-come (i.e., good deeds)—"**or in any tree**"—that is, the Tree of Life (i.e., the Torah), still "**the mother is sitting over the fledglings**"—because you are still a "fledgling," still too young to arouse yourself, therefore the mother (the "Supernal Mother") has to sit over you first. And even though it is God's manner to give wisdom to the wise, you still have not attained sufficient awareness to be able to arouse yourself from below. Nevertheless, "**do not take the mother together with her young**"—do not rely on arousal from above, the Supernal Mother sitting over you (*al*). Rather, read this as "it is on the young (*al habbanim* or *alekha*)" to act "**in order that you may fare well**": that is, through your own efforts at arousal the Creator derives even greater delight, as the Sages taught: "Israel provide sustenance for their Divine Parent." The delight that we bring to the Creator is called "sustenance." Thus, through your own arousal God gets even more delight, and the more delight, the greater your reward and you will fare well.

This is carried even further in the next phrase, "**and** [you may] **have a long life**": a further boon will accrue to you through your own self-arousal in the ways of holiness, through your good deeds. Your efforts will create the conditions that the supernal arousal may remain with you for an extended time, which is not the case when the supernal arousal comes first. Then you lack everything, and the conditions are not present for arousal to remain with you for a long time. That is the sense of the phrase "**and** [you may] **have a long life**" (*veha'arakhta yamim*): *yamim* suggests clarity. The clarity that was given to you from above will allow you to extend it, so it will remain with you for a longer period. "**Do send away the mother**": the sense of the verb "send away" (*shalei'ach*) is stripping away, in the sense of stripping off your awareness of physicality. This is what you must do when you desire the "the Mother"—supernal arousal. This is what you must do so that you can serve as a resting place for her to dwell.

FOR FURTHER THOUGHT

This lesson is like others that outline a process of spiritual awakening. While there is an aspect of this text that seems to challenge those who have not attained higher spiritual levels—that is, those who are like children or "eggs" and are unable to arouse themselves—it is also an invitation and encouragement to all of us to attain to greater spiritual awareness through practice. And it also promises that our efforts are not wasted. Every stirring of the soul in awareness brings down greater divine light and ultimately helps us wake up more fully to God in our lives.

The flow of the argument in this lesson might seem a little confusing. In the third paragraph, where Levi Yitzhak begins his direct interpretation of the verse, he sets the circumstances at the point where we "attain some measure of clarity, and arousal from above enlightens" us. The question here is whether this "clarity" constitutes arousal from below; from the unfolding of the argument it appears not. We have started on the path, but we are still "fledglings." When we engage in good deeds and Torah study, we set the stage for our own arousal, and that does indeed invite God's attention, so that God sends some degree of clarity, a sort of arousal, but not its fullest experience. Rather, it is offered (in the sense of the "mother sitting over the fledglings") so that we might arouse ourselves further, no longer to rely on the "mother." When we no longer rely on the mother— "do not take the mother together with her young"—we create the conditions by which God receives "sustenance," the Supernal Mother finds a place to rest, and the potential is created for arousal to last for a long(er) time. Indeed, it is through shedding our connection with and concern for our physicality that we most fully create that last condition.

The Zohar is the source of the image of the mother bird as the *Shekhinah*. Isaiah Tishby (*The Wisdom of the Zohar*, vol. 3, trans. and ed. David Goldstein [Oxford: Oxford University Press, 1989], p. 1095) cites *Tikkunei HaZohar* 6 (21a–21b), asserting that the *Shekhinah* never leaves those "'young' (i.e., chicks) who are the exponents of kabbalah, it is said of them 'you shall not take the mother upon the young,' for the mother never leaves them." That is, the *Shekhinah* remains with those who devote themselves to the study of Torah and its esoteric meaning, what Levi Yitzhak and the Hasidic tradition turn into experience. The study of Torah has as its goal gaining a bit of clarity, of awareness, to inspire arousal and connection with the Divine.

 ## Questions for Reflection

1. What is your experience of being inspired—or spiritually aroused—independently of your own actions? How did it feel? What were the conditions in which it occurred?

2. How do you prepare yourself for inspiration? What do you do to arouse yourself spiritually? Have you found that your efforts invite any response that deepens or extends your experience?

3. In your experience, what leads to spiritual laziness? How can we keep from remaining in the state of "the mother sitting on the fledglings"?

Taking It into Your Life

While the laudable goal of this lesson is arousal from below, initiative on our part in stirring our souls to love and serve God, Levi Yitzhak recognizes that this is not common or spontaneous in most people. But he hints how we might find our way there: "When you attain some measure of clarity, and arousal from above enlightens you." That is, we might engage in some practice—good deeds, Torah study, prayer, meditation, ritual celebration—and, through that, experience some small degree of clarity. That initial experience is offered from above in response to our "fledgling" efforts, our practice that as yet may not have sufficient clarity or energy to serve fully as "arousal from below." Still, if we can recognize just that moment of clarity, it can serve us. First we acknowledge its existence; we become aware of our capacity to wake up. Then, we can bring the full experience of that clarity into our minds and bodies; we can feel the opening of waking up. This prepares us to shift our sense of our activity (good deeds, Torah study, prayer, meditation, ritual celebration) from the mundane to the divine. We no longer are "just doing" these activities as mundane activities; they are an opening into true devotion. We can pour more energy of mind, heart, body, and spirit into our actions. Through this we engage in arousal from below.

While Levi Yitzhak does affirm that God's delight in our actions will bring response in arousal from above, that is not our concern. Rather, it is to make sure that we connect with the initial moment of clarity, that first breaking of the dawn in our hearts, minds, and bodies, awakening us to God in the world.

As you engage in your daily activities, bring attention to each act, to every moment, to attend its unique quality. Take nothing for granted, and allow no act to be simply "what I'm doing." Everything can become devotion; all acts can initiate arousal.

Reflect.

"When you build a new house, you shall make a parapet for your roof, [so that you do not bring bloodguilt on your house if anyone should fall from it]" (Deut. 22:8).

Here's the practice: when we experience some joy from the blessed Creator, we should make a point of putting it into words. Bring this joy into expression through the letters of words of Torah, prayer, songs, or praise, in order to connect this joy above in the blessed Creator.

This is the intention in the verse: "**when you build a new house**"— when you experience some new joy—"**you shall make a parapet**"—you should raise this joy higher and higher through the letters, as above. This is the significance of "**parapet**" (*ma'akeh*), since we build the parapet on the highest part of the house.

But this also is the significance of the word "**your roof**" (*legagekha*): to bring the joy into the letters. As we know (Zohar II 126b), the power that animates the letters is the name *YHVH*, the power that is in the very letters of the name *YHVH*. And the numerical value of *gagekha* is, like *YHVH*, twenty-six.

FOR FURTHER THOUGHT

This is such a wonderful "wake me up." It is certainly possible to read this verse and concentrate on the obligation to *do* something— build a parapet—and miss the beginning. That is: *wow, a new house!* How often do we move right by something new and miss the opportunity to see in it a moment of "new joy"? This lesson is such a reminder of what we might experience when we say *Shehecheyanu*. First, there is the experience. Then, there is the directing of heart, mind, and intention back to the Source. Even if it is "just" new underwear for the coming New Year on which to say the blessing, isn't it amazing that something new has come into our lives, that we get to be renewed?

Note that the experience of "some joy" comes from God. It is not a matter of our separate, subjective, independent experience, in which we determine that we have joy—it is a gift. As such, it is not something that we are to "enjoy" and keep to ourselves. It is not a possession so much as an inspiration. When we experience joy, it is an invitation to express ourselves in words of praise, thanksgiving, or prayer. Rather than hoarding joy, we are to bring it into the larger cycle of experience—return the energy through our words of Torah or prayer.

Again, note the very Hasidic emphasis on the letters of language. The letters are the building blocks of all words, and therefore of all expression. They are the foundation of creation, and are the packets of energy that enliven and sustain all existence. Bringing our inner energy and attention to our speech, we acknowledge and identify that energy, and thereby connect with the Divine in the letters. Our experience of joy has the potential to be a moment of experience of the Divine in our lives.

Questions for Reflection

1. Levi Yitzhak starts out by describing the situation in which we "experience some joy from the blessed Creator"—a moment without reference, without orientation in time or space. Have you ever found yourself suddenly, "inexplicably" filled with a divine joy? When was that? How did you respond? Are there any conditions that might make this more or less likely to happen (intellectual, emotional, physical, spiritual)?

2. Levi Yitzhak suggests a connection between getting/having something new and experiencing joy. Is that your experience? Do you experience having things as a joy or as a burden? What brings you joy? How long does it last? When is joy not present, and how do you respond?

3. Most of our homes don't have or need parapets. We don't spend time on our roofs, and (except for expert roofers) we don't expect anyone else to be up there either. So get a picture in your mind of what a "parapet" would look like around the flat roof of an ancient biblical home. In your imagination, make an association between the "parapet" and the place where Levi Yitzhak wants you to bring your joy. Could the "parapet" be a crown and thus hint at raising everything up to *Keter*, to the *Ein Sof*? What is the relationship between experiencing joy from the Holy One and experiencing spiritual nothingness (*ayin*)? But if the goal is to experience *ayin*, who would be the "I" who is experiencing the joy? Does the experience of joy help or hinder in the spiritual process of self-effacement, of letting go of physical permanence to step beyond the limits of "I" to enter the "One"?

Taking It into Your Life

Is this a Jewish teaching or what! Whatever happens to you—talk about it! Yet, from contemplative practice, we also learn that silence is a great teacher. Is there anything in what Levi Yitzhak teaches, in how he approaches "putting things into words," that might redeem this practice from our overly verbal, noisy culture?

Consider: Is Torah study different from conversation? Is sacred conversation different from normal chatting? Do you have a form of prayer that is not so wordy, that helps focus your joy? What about singing—would that work for you as a way to raise the joy back up to its source?

Practicing silence is not censorship, nor does it deny the value of speech. Rather, it is an invitation to notice, deeply, clearly, personally, how we wish to speak, what words truly need to be said. Out of silence, it is possible to turn even mundane conversation into sacred speech. It is possible, as the Baal Shem Tov taught, to be connected to the Divine even when engaged in telling stories or carrying on a conversation. Rather than being distracted, having two things going on in one's mind at once, this practice is supported by being clearly focused on and connected to God, so that the words of conversation and even entertainment carry the message: God is here, too.

Pay attention to your speech. Reflect.

Ki Tavo

"You have affirmed this day [that *YHVH*
is your God, that you will walk in His
ways, that you will observe His laws and
commandments and rules, and that you will
obey Him]" (Deut. 26:17).

We hold that the effulgence that flows from the blessed Creator can
be called "speech" (*dibbur*), as Scripture states: "By the speech [*bidevar*]
of *YHVH* were the heavens made" (Ps. 33:6). When we are at a high
spiritual rung, then (as it were) we generate "speech" in the blessed
Holy One so that blessing flows forth onto us. If we do not bring this
about, then the situation would be as the Sages taught (Gittin 56b) on
the verse "Who is like You among the mighty" (Exod. 15:11):

> "In the school of R. Yishmael it was taught: 'Who is like You
> among the mighty [*ba'eilim*]?' (Exod. 15:11)—Who is like You
> among the dumb (i.e., speechless) (*illemim*)?"

This is the significance of our verse: "**You have affirmed** [*he'emarta*
this day"—you are the active force that today generates speech in the
blessed Holy One, to pour out blessed effulgence. This comes about
when we are on a high spiritual rung of experiencing "**today**"—such
that each and every day is experienced as new.

For Further Thought

This is another formulation of the interconnection between arousal
from below and arousal from above; between our capacity to affect
the cosmos through speech (e.g., prayer, study) and the divine
response in the outflow of blessing. What is unique here is the
claim that the flow of blessing (*shefa*) is analogous to, or perhaps
even equal to, divine speech. God's direct communication with us
is through the quality, quantity, and directness of the flow of goodness. Our devotions have the capacity to instigate this divine speech.

And (as it were) our failure to do so may have the consequence of God's silence, dumbfounded even in the face of our suffering.

This lesson is based on the odd word that appears in this passage in the Torah: *he'emarta* (affirmed; vouchsafed). The JPS notes that the meaning of this word is uncertain. Clearly its root is *aleph-mem-resh*, related to "speech." That it is in the *hiphil* suggests that it has to do with causing some sort of speech. So while the translation we have treats this verb as "affirmed," Levi Yitzhak reads it more literally: "You have caused *YHVH* to speak." Further, we have done so through our experience of "today"—today, the day in which we experience ourselves, the world, and our relationship to God through the Torah as completely new.

Questions for Reflection

1. How do you understand the connection between "being on a high spiritual rung" and the experience of being new every day?

2. How do you feel about being made responsible for bringing God into speech? Do you feel that God's silence is only in response to our spiritual dullness? When? Why or why not?

3. Consider: the flow of God's goodness is God's speech. Does this change how you might seek to hear God speaking today? How?

Taking It into Your Life

Levi Yitzhak focuses on the first part of the passage in the Torah: our capacity to bring God into speech. But the Torah goes on (Deut. 26:18–19):

> And *YHVH* has affirmed this day that you are, as He promised you,
> His treasured people who shall observe all His commandments,
> and that He will set you, in fame and renown and glory, high
> above all the nations that He has made; and that you shall be,
> as He promised, a holy people to *YHVH* your God.

If we allow ourselves to extend the parallel that the Torah invites, we might suggest that God, in some manner, brings us into speech. What is the "high rung" that God attains relative to us that brings us into speech? What would it mean for us to be "dumb" relative to God?

Think of it this way: if the product of our attention to God is the flow of goodness and blessing—that is, God's speech—then perhaps the experience of God's blessings can induce speech in us. This requires precise attention. This cannot be conditional. That is, we cannot sit around waiting to see what goodies will fall into our laps. We cannot be picky in what we consider to be a "blessing." Rather, with precision from moment to moment, seeing each moment as new, we can develop our perception of what each moment brings. We thereby might learn to sense the blessing in what is, whatever it is. Even with this attention, we may find that we are appreciative in a quiet, inner manner. What this lesson asks is that we seek to make a connection between our experience of blessing and our capacity to bring our thanks, our happiness, our awareness (even of difficult blessings) into speech. Bringing joy into song is a trope we have met before. Bringing awareness into "prayer, songs, and praises" is another (as in the previous lesson in *Ki Teitzei*).

Experiment with the two steps of this practice. Pay attention with precision from moment to moment. What are the goodnesses and blessings that you come to notice? Pay attention to the inner movement of awareness, and seek to connect that to some verbal expression.

Reflect.

"Moses and the levitical priests spoke [to all Israel, saying: Silence! Hear, O Israel!] Today you have become the people [of *YHVH* your God: Listen to the voice of *YHVH* your God and observe His commandments and His laws, which I enjoin upon you this day]" (Deut. 27:9–10).

Rashi comments on this verse: "Every day they should be in your eyes as if they were new." How can we experience each day as if it were new? Through our belief that with each and every breath we receive renewed vital force (from God). Thus, with each breath we are made a new creation. Through this faith we can merit to hear each and every day (the sound of the giving of Torah at) Sinai.

Now, if we can hear Sinai, then it makes sense for Moses to say in the next verse, "**Listen to the voice of *YHVH* your God.**" That is, without the experience of being renewed each day (and so, standing at Sinai) we will not actually be hearing God's voice, only words of Torah. But, if we merit hearing Sinai in each moment, then we will also merit hearing the very "**voice of *YHVH* your God.**"

FOR FURTHER THOUGHT

At the conclusion of the first teaching in this parashah, Levi Yitzhak simply asserts that a "high spiritual rung" is to experience each day as if it were new. There, it is quite possible that Levi Yitzhak meant that each day should appear new, because that newness could stimulate spiritual awareness. Here, the experience of the newness of each day helps us sense that we, too, are new and so able to hear the voice of Sinai. And in this instance, to support his argument, Levi Yitzhak quotes Rashi on the Torah, but in a manner that is not quite precise.

Rashi on Deut. 26:16 seems to be the source for his words here:

> "*YHVH* your God commands you this day": every day they (the mitzvot) should be in your eyes as if that very day you were commanded to do them.

However, this is slightly different from Rashi on our verse:

> "This day you have become the people [of *YHVH* your God]": every day should appear in your eyes as if on this day you enter the covenant with Him.

In both instances, Rashi takes the idiomatic speech of the verse—"this day"—and argues that Scripture meant to address not only those who heard Moses's words but also all who would read (and hear) them in the future. "This day" means today, right now, even as we read these words. We should not allow the commandments to become old hat, routine, dull. We should strive to experience them as if they were brand-new, given today. The fact of the covenant between us and God should not become a given, concluded and an artifact of the past. We should seek to experience our relationship with God as renewed each day.

That Levi Yitzhak reads one Rashi into the other supports his larger purpose in this lesson. That is, "becoming a people" is to enter the covenant; this echoes Sinai. But receiving the commandments directly from God is the experience of Sinai. Levi Yitzhak needs both of these to make the point in this lesson: it is possible to hear God's voice—the voice of Sinai—beyond merely the voice of Torah or of the commandments. But we have to experience the newness of both the covenant and the commandments to do so.

Questions for Reflection

1. What is the difference between hearing the "words of Torah" and hearing the "voice of *YHVH* your God"? Would you have made this distinction before seeing it in this commentary? Do you think that it is indeed possible to hear God's voice? How? When?

2. Levi Yitzhak characterizes the experience of hearing God's voice directly today as hearing God's voice at Sinai. How do you understand the relationship between the capacity to truly be present in the moment, to sense oneself new each day, each breath, and receiving a direct revelation of God's will, knowing what Torah applies in this moment (as opposed to relying on what is contained in Torah as we have it)?

3. Remember also that the encounter at Sinai took place before the Golden Calf. At Sinai, Israel was at the apex of enlightenment and awareness of God, expansive consciousness of the highest order. Could it be that Levi Yitzhak is suggesting that it is possible for us, in this moment, on any day, every day, to become present to God without distractions, without self-interest, without any intervening conceptions, only God awareness? Have you a sense of what that might feel like? Have you had any moments in your life in which you sensed your "self" effaced, present only to the Self of All? What are the implications of that sort of experience for *teshuvah*, for self-transformation?

Taking It into Your Life

Consider using this image, this experience, as practice in these last weeks before Rosh Hashanah, as a means of cleansing, clarifying, and preparing to present yourself before God. In this practice, we would bring together the two ways in which Levi Yitzhak has used the trope of "with each and every breath": as a new creation we can more easily do *teshuvah*; as a new creation we are more able to hear God's voice.

Think of this in light of a story that has been told about Levi Yitzhak:

> There is no final conquest of the self. The ego is too elusive, subtle and deceiving. It is an eternal struggle demanding eternal vigilance.
>
> Each evening before he went to sleep it was the custom of Rabbi Levi Yitzhak to take a *Heshbon ha-Nefesh*—that is, to examine his thoughts and deeds for that day. If he found a

blemish, he would say to himself, "Levi Yitzhak will not do that again."

Then he would chide himself, "Levi Yitzhak, you said the same thing yesterday."

Then he would reply, "Yesterday Levi Yitzhak did not speak the truth. Today he speaks the truth." (Samuel H. Dresner, *The World of a Hasidic Master: Levi Yitzhak of Berditchev* [New York: Shapolsky Publishers, 1986], p. 163)

In this story, Levi Yitzhak listens deeply to his own heart and pays close attention to both his intention and his actions. He may be critical of his failures, but he does not become mired in them. He recovers quickly enough to recognize that the moment of failure has passed, and that in this moment—as a new being—he has the power to hear his own intention ("the voice of God"?), to speak the truth and move toward *teshuvah*.

How can you bring this into your own life?

Nitzavim

"You stand this day, all of you, before *YHVH*
your God [—your tribal heads, your elders
and your officials, all the men of Israel]"
(Deut. 29:9).

In this lesson we will come to understand the passage in the Talmud
(Rosh Hashanah 34b):

> Our Rabbis taught: "On most fast days the omission of one blast
> (of the shofar) is no bar to another, and the omission of one
> blessing is no bar to another, but on Rosh Hashanah and Yom
> Kippur the omission of one blast or one blessing is a bar to the
> others." What is the reason? Rabbah said, "God proclaimed:
> 'Recite before Me on New Year kingship, remembrance, and
> shofar verses; kingship verses to declare Me king over you;
> remembrance verses, that the remembrance of you may come
> before Me for good; and through what? Through the shofar.'"

This is the principle: the way of the blessed Creator is to do good,
particularly to Israel. This is God's desire: to pour out goodness and
blessings on His people Israel. But if (heaven forbid) we are not worthy
that God pour out goodness on us, this is not according to the desire of
the blessed Creator. Rather, God's will and delight is to bless us with
goodnes when we are worthy of this goodness and blessing (and heaven
forbid if the opposite is true, for that is not God's will).

Now, understand this principle: that which the divine will desires is
called "face" (*panim*); that which the divine will does not desire is called
"back" (*achor*). We can see this in the Talmud passage above: "Recite
before Me kingship"—when you declare Me king over you, may it be
in a relationship of "facing" (*panim*); "recite *before* Me remembrance
verses"—the remembrance should come in a relationship of "facing"
(*panim*) and not turned away ("back/*achor*"). Do this so that your
remembrances will rise "before Me [*lephanai*] for good." When I pour
out goodness for you, My desire in doing so is so that you will "face"

Me, because that is how your remembrances rise up before Me—facing Me (*panim*)—for the good, since it is My will to pour out goodness.

This is the sense of our verse: "**You stand this day, all of you, before YHVH**"—today you appear before *YHVH* with the quality of "facing" (*panim*). This is the significance of what follows: "**your God**"—the aspect of God that pours out blessings to Israel is called "your God" (*eloheikhem*). So, because you are standing today before *YHVH* with the quality of "facing" (*panim*), goodness will be poured out for you, which is signified by the word "your God" (*eloheikhem*). Understand this: the word "face" (*panim*) is related to the word "turning" (*poneh*), which signifies God's goodness. That is, God wishes to turn to His people Israel for the good; but, God does not desire the bad (which is called "back/*achor*"), for God does not turn (*poneh*) toward that.

FOR FURTHER THOUGHT

We might read the Rabbinic dictum from tractate Rosh Hashanah as a magical teaching. That is, everything must be done "just so" for the desired effect to come about. Reciting the verses of *Malkhuyot*, *Zikhronot*, and *Shofarot* on Rosh Hashanah are the means by which we induce God to favor us in the New Year. It is as if by reciting the prescribed verses we remind God of God's intention to remain in relationship with us.

Levi Yitzhak transforms this completely. God doesn't want the verses per se. Rather, the verses are the means by which we demonstrate our continuing, devoted relationship with God. We are not asking for anything. Instead, we turn to God, declaring our commitment by acknowledging God as sovereign; we affirm our awareness of God's continuing interest and involvement in our lives. While what we say is important, more significant is how we recite these words: they must come without self-interest. We have to turn toward God for God's sake, reaching out to touch the inner core of the divine will, to acknowledge our deep need one for the other, and to present ourselves wholeheartedly to God. God does not turn "His back" from us (as it were) but cannot effectuate the flow of goodness to us if we turn our back to God. Should we approach God solely petitioning for our own good, solely interested in what God can do for us, it will be as if we turn our back to God's true self, closing ourselves off from our own deepest desires. Approaching God "face-to-face," where our will is to do God's will, God's deepest desire and will respond in kind.

The conclusion of this lesson is built on the Zohar's identification of the combined name *YHVH elohim* as true completion. The two parts of that name are identified respectively as *Tiferet* and *Shekhinah*. It may be the former toward whom we turn in our prayers, but it is through the latter that all goodness flows from above into our realm. Thus, when we stand before—that is, facing—*YHVH* (*Tiferet*), we energize the divine will, and goodness pours out to us through *elohim* (*eloheikhem*)—that is, through *Shekhinah*.

Questions for Reflection

1. *Parashat Nitzavim* always falls the week before Rosh Hashanah, so we can read this as preparation for the holiday. How might this lesson affect your experience of the special readings on the holiday?

2. When, if ever, do you experience God's face turned toward you? When, if ever, do you experience God's face turned away from you? What is the effect on your life in each instance?

3. In your interpersonal relationships, when do you feel that love, harmony, goodness, and blessing flow most fully and freely? What supports that, and what hinders it? What is the role of "face/*panim*" and "back/*achor*" in your experience?

Taking It into Your Life

Levi Yitzhak surely would not discourage anyone from praying to God for help, support, sustenance, or health. Indeed, those are key motivations for prayer, and God is dependable to respond. Yet, we could learn from this lesson that turning to God with our personal needs in mind might actually be like turning our backs on God. The classical term for self-interest in Hasidic literature is *peniyah*—also a form of turning. It is expressed as the slight shift of the eyes away from direct contact, dissembling, shaving the truth, or seeking honor or personal advantage. It might also be experienced as turning away from God (or others) in looking after only our own needs.

Let us attend to the latter. That is, the divine will desires to flow forth with goodness and blessing. Yet, its free flow is dependent on direct access to its beneficiaries. We have to turn fully to God to effectuate that clear channel. In a sense, our turning to God—declaring God sovereign, acknowledging

God's capacity and desire to remember us for good—is acting for God's sake. Still, we bring these declarations and remembrances before God so that God will indeed bless us in the coming year. So we need to be able to present our needs before God with the knowledge that our needs are not exclusive of all others; that God's need for us, indeed all of creation's need for us and our attention, exist along with our personal, selfish needs.

Our practice, then, is to pay attention to our own needs and concerns and then use that awareness to turn to others in need. When we honestly and clearly express our own needs, we can let go of our worry that our needs won't be known or that they won't be met. Freed of this inner fear—this *peniyah*—we can turn toward others, more fully recognizing their needs as well. And, perhaps, facing them fully in this way—secure that our needs are known and will be addressed—we can attempt to fulfill their needs. This is the movement of mindfulness practice: noting our own suffering, bringing compassion to our own pained hearts, in order to become free to notice the suffering of others and respond with compassion to them. This is the nexus of *teshuvah* (self-awareness), *tephillah* (prayer), and *tzedakah* (acts of righteousness and charity) by which the negative valence of our circumstances is eased. Doing *tzedakah* at this time of year is not prophylactic (at least it should not be). Rather, it is an expression of our awareness of our own low estate, out of which we then turn to others to offer them succor. And that goes for God as well.

Practice. Reflect.

"And *YHVH* your God will grant you abounding prosperity in all your undertakings, in the issue of your womb, the offspring of your cattle, and the produce of your soil. For *YHVH* will again delight in your well-being, as He did in that of your fathers" (Deut. 30:9).

So this is how we can understand what is written in *Sefer Raziel*: God is called a "lowly king" (*melekh aluv*), which has the sense of shame. How can we understand this? Consider: A wise person may ask advice of others—to do something or not—and they advise not to do so. Should this wise person not follow their advice, and does so, if the matter does not unfold appropriately (heaven forbid), and the end result is as the advisors had predicted (heaven forbid), then (heaven forbid) the wise person will feel shame. And so it is with God. When it arose in God's mind to create human beings, God said, "Let us make man" (Gen. 1:26). But the angels said, "What is man [that You have been mindful of him, mortal man that You have taken note of him]" (Ps. 8:5; cf. Gen. R. 8:5). Still God, in mercy, did not pay attention to their advice and created humankind. Now, when (heaven forbid) they behave against God's will, and it would have been better had they not been created (cf. Eruvin 13b), it is as if God can be called "a lowly (ashamed) king" (*melekh aluv*).

This is how we should understand the verse, "It is a law for Israel, a judgment of the God of Jacob" (Ps. 81:5; cf. Rosh Hashanah 8a–b). Now, by all rights this verse should have said, "The judgment of the God of Jacob is the law for Israel." But in light of the above, we can understand this verse as follows: "It is a law [*chok*] for Israel"— without a doubt there will be *chok* for Israel, God's holy people, where *chok* means "sustenance" (as in "How do we know that the term *chok* refers to food?"; Beitzah 16a). Now how do we know that Israel will certainly receive sustenance? The verse continues to explain, "It is a judgment of the God of Jacob": while there may be those who wish to judge Israel (on Rosh Hashanah), whether to provide them with sustenance or not, the locus of judgment is not in Israel! The judgment is only of the God of Jacob, as it were ("the judgment is of God"; cf. Deut. 1:17 and Rashi there).

This echoes the Zohar (II 32b, mentioned earlier in the lesson): it cites the verse "I saw *YHVH* seated upon His throne, with all the host of heaven standing in attendance [*alav*] to the right and to the left of Him" (1 Kings 22:19) and comments, "*Alav*: this means 'against Him.'" The forces of opposition and accusation may have come to accuse Israel on Rosh Hashanah, but they were silenced before God's people. Judgment is not against them; it is against the blessed Creator. Therefore, those hosts are seized with fear and trembling to even open their mouths, because then God's anger would surely blaze, and God would then judge them. Even though they are holy angels, they would not emerge innocent in God's eyes, as it says, "[He puts no trust in His holy ones;] / The heavens are not guiltless in His sight" (Job 15:15; cf. the *Unetaneh Tokef* prayer)....

This is the meaning of the *Tanna* when he taught (Avot 3:15), "The world is judged [*nidon*] with goodness." That is, when God wishes to pour out blessing for the world, it is as if He, too, is judged with the world: should they receive this good or not, and will God then receive delight and ease from this? We know that this must be so, since the word "judged" (*nidon*) is third-person masculine singular and so therefore refers to God. The judgment refers to Him. Therefore, when God desires to pour out abundant good and blessings for us, He does not examine us to see if we are worthy or not (heaven forbid!)—it is, after all, His will and desire to bless us, and there is no reasoning about God's will. (This is not the case, however, with the other nations, since He looks to see if they are worthy of His blessing.)

This is the intention of the phrase "**And YHVH your God will grant you abounding prosperity**" (*vehotirkha YHVH elohekha ... letovah*): that is, when God pours out goodness and blessing, God will leave (*yotir*) you and your deeds aside, since He will not look at you at all to see your deeds and merits. Rather, He will pour out His blessing as an expression of the goodness of His will. This is the meaning of *hotirkha*. This helps us to understand, as well, the end of this verse. Why is it that God deals thus with you? "**For YHVH will again delight in your well-being, as He did in that of your fathers**"— that is, so that He will be able to receive joy and delight from our receiving such goodness from Him. Amen.

FOR FURTHER THOUGHT

One of the fruits of mindfulness practice is that we more readily, and willingly, recognize our reaction to another person or situation as our personal perspective, our inner experience, and not all of reality. Indeed, what is happening now is the product of infinite interactions, creating the conditions that brought about this precise situation. We learn to see that what disturbs us in others is a reflection of something we find embarrassing or difficult in our own self. This prompts a response of compassion—for ourselves, and for the other. The Baal Shem Tov taught the same lesson: when you are disturbed in prayer or study by another, consider it for your good, to make you aware of some aspect of your own being that needs to be raised up. And apparently this applies to the Holy One as well! God's desire to bless us will not be impeded by our "sinful" actions (not that this lets us off the hook). God recognizes God's own degree of responsibility for the fact of our failures (sins) as well and thus learns to respond with compassion. When combined with our sincere acts of *teshuvah*, judgment will be changed to blessing.

The source that Levi Yitzhak cites that identifies God as a "lowly (shamed) king" (*melekh aluv*) is actually *Pirke Heikhalot Rabbati* (24:4; found in the collection *Battei Midrashot* I), a fairly early text of *Heikhalot* mysticism. This appellation appears in an alphabetical acrostic in praise of God, each letter having three terms (the other two in this instance are "a helping king," *melekh ozeir*, and "a humble king," *melekh anav*). There are other, later texts that make this connection as well. Consider this (*Tanna deBei Eliyahu Zutra* 4):

> The Sages taught: One must be lowly and humble (*aluv ve'anav*) before all people, and one's household more than anyone. How do we know this? Learn it from the blessed Holy One, who was lowly and humble before His people in all instances, and did not deal with them according to their ways, and did not judge them according to their sins. Rather, He dealt with them in His humility. How do we know this? Consider the 120 days—from the day the Torah was given until Yom Kippur—if the blessed Holy One had not dealt with Israel with humility, the Torah would not have been given to Israel (again, on Yom Kippur).

The ultimate meaning of lowly (*aluv*) in this instance is not developed in the same way as Levi Yitzhak did, but the connection to Yom Kippur and to judgment is suggestive. If God holds back from judging Israel according to its deeds, it may be because God takes some responsibility for their failures.

Here is the source from the Zohar:

> R. Eleazar opened, "*One day the sons of Elohim came to stand against YHVH, and Satan also came among them* (Job 1:6). *One day*—the day of Rosh Hashanah, when the blessed Holy One stands to judge the world. Similarly, *One day he came there* (2 Kings 4:11)—that day was the holiday of Rosh Hashanah. *The sons of Elohim came*—those appointed princes, sent to the world to examine the actions of humanity. *To stand al, before, YHVH*—as is said: *I saw YHVH sitting upon his throne, with all the host of heaven standing by Him, on His right and on His left* (1 Kings 22:19). However, *to stand before YHVH*—in this verse I have discovered the love of the blessed Holy One for Israel. For these messengers—commissioned to examine the deeds of humanity—go roaming and snatch all those deeds, and on

the day that Judgment rises to judge the world, they become accusers, standing over human beings. Come and see: Of all the nations of the world, they stand to examine only the actions of Israel, because they are the children of the blessed Holy One. When the actions of Israel are found to be unseemly, those appointed messengers—seeking to stand over those actions of Israel—stand, as it were *al*, *against YHVH*, surely. For when the deeds of Israel are improper, they weaken, as it were, the power of the blessed Holy One; when deeds are proper, they provide power and might to the blessed Holy One. Of this is written *Give strength to God* (Ps. 68:35). How? By proper actions. So, on that day all those appointed princes gathered *al YHVH—against YHVH*, surely! For since they gathered against Israel, they gathered against Him. (Zohar II 32b; Daniel C. Matt, trans., *The Zohar*, Pritzker ed., vol. 4 [Stanford, CA: Stanford University Press, 2007], p. 137ff.)

Questions for Reflection

1. God's primary desire is to do good for the world. Does that mean that it doesn't matter what we do? How shall we hold ourselves accountable for our behavior if God is going to bless us anyway?

2. God shares in responsibility for our behavior, as the Creator is responsible for His creation. Does this mean that we are not responsible? How shall we hold ourselves accountable for our behavior if God made us this way?

3. This passage does not suggest that people are fundamentally good. Yet, its message is that during the Days of Awe, at this time of judgment, fear is not a helpful response. What spiritual and emotional positions do you think Levi Yitzhak suggests we might adopt at this time? Is this how you generally have approached the High Holy Days? Why or why not? What is your spiritual orientation as you come into this season of Awe?

Taking It into Your Life

In this lesson, Levi Yitzhak suggests that the process of judgment is reversed, that God is judged for our actions. We might think that gives us a "pass" and that we have nothing more to do than stand by and let God let us off the hook. But that would be a mistake. When we think that God will judge us, we pray for God's compassion and mercy. If God is being judged, then perhaps our response should be compassion and love for God. How might we display this compassion? Through our actions toward others. Levi Yitzhak has taught us before that how we behave below causes a similar, parallel action above. Rather than imagine that by doing *tzedakah* (in all of its forms) we will direct God to do so for us, we might imagine that by being compassionate here below, we energize compassion—for God!—above.

Make this time before the New Year one in which you offer compassion to God, who is judged for our misdeeds, by being compassionate to others and to yourself. May this be a source of energy for your personal transformation through *teshuvah* and of redemption for all.

Vayeilekh

"Moses went and spoke these things to all Israel" (Deut. 31:1).

We can interpret this verse in light of the Sages' two idioms for leading prayers: "going down before the ark [*hateivah*]" and "passing before the ark [*hateivah*]" (e.g., Shabbat 24b; Ta'anit 16b; Berakhot 34a).

When a righteous person prays before God, he must attach himself to the words (*teivot*) that he is praying. Those holy words, in turn, direct him in prayer. But there are those who are at a higher spiritual degree, and they direct the words of prayer. This is the level of Moses, who is master (husband; *ba'al*) of the Matronita, as it says in the Zohar.

So one who "goes down before the ark" is led by the words, and he is below the words (*teivah*). But there is a righteous one who "goes before the ark," and she leads the words (*teivah*), she stands above them. Here we are at the end of Moses's life when the wellsprings of wisdom were stopped up from him (cf. Sotah 13b), and so, instead, the first quality applied to him and the words lead him. That is the sense of our verse: "**Moses went and spoke**"—he went toward Speech, and the word was above him.

From this we understand something quite wondrous, why Moses's prophecy is quite obscure in the poem *Ha'azinu*, unlike anything else in the Torah. This is why: Moses's prophecy had been through a clear glass (a speculum that shines), but the rest of the prophets through an unclear glass (a speculum that does not shine) (Yebamot 49b). Because Moses prophesied through a clear glass, he had the capacity to speak the words precisely as he had heard them from God, without any garment, by way of parable or riddles. This was not the case with the rest of the prophets, who did not have Moses's capacity and had to dress their prophecies with parables and enigmas (like the prophecies of Zechariah and the other prophets that are quite obscure). That is the meaning of "an unclear glass." But, before Moses's death, the transmission of wisdom was taken from him and given to Joshua. That is why the poem *Ha'azinu* is obscure: it is covered in garments.

FOR FURTHER THOUGHT

Of course, we moderns reading the Torah would have a different explanation for the difference between the language of *Ha'azinu* and other passages in the Torah. But Levi Yitzhak is always looking to connect Torah to lived experience, to help us apply it to our own lives. Although none of us may ever experience biblical prophecy, we can surely understand what it is like to see things clearly and be able to explain them clearly, and what it is like to see things but without clarity, or to see things but lack language to explain them. This is the difference between Moses and the other prophets, and between Moses in the midst of his mission and at the end of his life.

Further, Levi Yitzhak frames that experience in terms of prayer. The experience of (Moses's) "prophecy" is likened to the experience of one who prays with such concentration that authentic words of prayer issue forth with clarity and intention. We can assume that this sort of prayer is grounded in the siddur but extends beyond it. The words of the prayer book may be the start of prayer but no longer lead the person in his or her devotion. This is, in Levi Yitzhak's eyes, a higher form of prayer. The lower form—"going down before the ark [word; *teivah*]," being led by the words of the siddur—is still that of a righteous person (a tzaddik), and so laudable. The challenge to us, perhaps, is to investigate how we pray, how we pray the words of the siddur, and how we express ourselves through those words and beyond in our prayers.

Here is the passage from the Zohar in which Moses is identified as the master/husband of the Matronita (i.e., the *Shekhinah*):

> Come and see what is written: This is the blessing that Moses *ish ha-elohim*, the man of God, bestowed (Deut. 33:1)—master of the house, master of the Matronita—as it is written: *ishah*, her husband may let it stand or *ishah*, her husband may annul it (Num. 30:14). For look, it is written *kalat Moshe*, the bride of Moses (ibid. 7:1)! [The written form actually says *kalot Moshe, plene.*] So Moses blessed whomever he wished and did not fear....

Surely, *ish ha-elohim*, husband of God! He did as he wished with the house, as has been established: her husband may let it stand or her husband may annul it. Her husband may let it stand—as it is written: Moses said: Arise, O *YHVH*! (ibid. 10:35). Or her husband may annul it—as it is written: And when it came to rest, he would say: Return, O *YHVH*! (ibid., 36). The master of the house surely did as he wished, with no one hindering him. (Zohar I 236b; Daniel C. Matt, trans., *The Zohar*, Pritzker ed., vol. 3 [Stanford, CA: Stanford University Press, 2007], p. 434)

Here we must note the various ways in which the Zohar identifies the *Shekhinah*: she is *kalat Moshe*, Moses's bride; as we have seen, she is identified with the divine name *elohim*, and so Moses is her husband, *ish ha'elohim*; she is called "house" (*bayit*). In every case, we see that Moses is connected to her as her master, the one who was able to direct her to bless Israel. And, finally, we should note that "Speech" (*dibbur*) is also a name for the *Shekhinah*.

Would that we were able to pray like Moses, and so more perfectly direct the flow of blessing to the world.

Questions for Reflection

1. Our synagogues are arranged so differently from those of antiquity. There is no way that one can physically "go down" to lead the prayers. Indeed, generally one can only go "up." What is your experience of the change of placement of the leader of prayers and how it affects you and the practice of communal prayer? Would changing the physical setting of the synagogue change your experience of prayer?

2. How do you relate to the words of the prayer book? Do they lead you, or do you fill them with your intention and meaning? Does this change over time? When, how?

3. Have you had an experience in which you were particularly aware of your capacity to speak clearly, forcefully, with a sense of connection to God's word and will? When? What was that like?

Taking It into Your Life

When you next sit to pray with the siddur, prepare in this manner: Sit quietly, and allow your mind to settle. You may notice that your thoughts run to and fro, but as you bring your attention to your breath or some other single point, you may be able to remain more balanced from moment to moment. When you sense a degree of inner balance, even if your thoughts still wander, pose this question to yourself: "What is my deepest prayer?" Allow images, words, and thoughts to arise. Notice them all, and repeat your question: "What is my deepest prayer?" Over time, you may notice that one item, one concern, recurs and holds your attention.

Having identified your primary concern, your deepest prayer, you might now turn to the siddur. Hold this concern in your heart and mind as you begin to recite the words of the prayer book. Bring your primary concern into your prayer, allowing it to play into the words that you are reciting. Notice how the words of the siddur and your primary concern, your deepest prayer, interplay—how one shapes, illuminates, deepens, and challenges the other. As your deepest prayer unfolds through the words of the siddur, notice how the words of the prayer book speak differently (if at all) from your previous experience.

Consider: Could this be how we might "lead the words" of prayer? Is this how the words of the siddur can be awakened? Could this lead us to a new awareness, one that shares an element of prophecy?

Reflect.

Ha'azinu

"Who is a God like You, forgiving iniquity
and remitting transgression; who has not
maintained His wrath forever against the
remnant of His own people, because He
loves graciousness! He will take us back in
love; He will overcome our iniquities, He will
hurl all their sins into the depths of the sea"
(Micah 7:18–19).

The Sages taught (Rosh Hashanah 17a):

The House of Hillel say: God "abounds in kindness" (*verav
chesed*)—He inclines toward loving-kindness and grace.

How is that done? R. Eliezer says: He presses down the scale of
merit, as it says, "**He will take us back in love; He will overcome
[*yikhbosh*] our iniquities.**" R. Yose bar Hanina says: He raises
the scale of iniquities, as it says, "**forgiving** [lit., raising up, *nosei*]
iniquity and remitting transgression."

What this means is that God raises up the scale-pan in which our
sins rest, and then the blessed Holy One, out of great compassion
and love, inclines toward loving-kindness and grace. In this manner,
then, God raises up the scale-pan with our sins, and so automatically
our merits weigh down the scale. Alternatively, God overcomes our
sins: God covers up and so wipes away the sins from that pan, and
automatically the pan of mitzvot sinks, determining for our merit. In
this way God inclines toward loving-kindness and grace. Thus, there is
no real disagreement in our verse: first it says, "**Who is a God like You,
forgiving iniquity**"—raising the sins up—and then the verse says, "**He
will overcome our iniquities**"—so that ultimately it is our mitzvot that
are lifted up before Him.

In this light we can interpret the lesson in the Gemara (actually,
midrash *Tanchuma*, *Emor* 22):

"You shall take for yourself on the first day ..." (Lev. 23:40)—
now, is this day truly the first day? Does not Sukkot actually fall
on the fifteenth of the month? Rather, it is the first day for the
calculation of sins.

Now this midrash actually does not make sense, as is evidenced in
the lengthy attempts at explanation among the early commentators.
Still, there is something to this lesson. At this season, between Rosh
Hashanah and Yom Kippur, each and every person certainly has his
or her eyes open to examine all their ways to return to God, each one
according to their insight and their spiritual development, fearing God
and the glory of His exaltedness when He rises to judge the earth, for
the "day of *YHVH* is near." And who can stand justified in judgment?
And who would not fear? And which soul is it that will not afflict itself
in response? For when they come to be judged before the Judge of
the earth for all their deeds, will not they who tremble at God's word
employ the heights of their awareness to put right that which they have
perverted? This sort of *teshuvah* is called "*teshuvah* from fear."

But after Yom Kippur, when they turn to the mitzvot of sukkah
and *lulav* and the four species and *tzedakah* with generosity and love,
according to God's goodness, seeking to serve God, worshipping with
joy and a full heart, they engage in what is called "*teshuvah* from love."

Now, the Sages taught: By means of *teshuvah* from fear, intentional
sins are considered as if they were errors, and by means of *teshuvah*
from love, intentional sins are treated as if they were positive acts (cf.
Yoma 86b). Now, the blessed Holy One—out of great compassion and
love—desires the restoration of those who seek truly to do *teshuvah*
from love and does not desire the death of the sinner, rather that they
repent of their sin and live. Therefore, on this festival we come to
shelter in the shade of *shaddai*, through the mitzvot and good deeds
that we do out of love of the blessed Holy One. Then God counts up
our sins to know how many mitzvot it will take to balance them out.
This is not the case before Sukkot, since till then the *teshuvah* has come
about from fear, and God does not count the sins up at all, since they
still only have the status of errors. But, on Sukkot, when the *teshuvah*
is from love of God, then God counts and numbers our sins, in order
that they might be transformed to positive acts, which will then argue
for the good of all Israel.

This is the meaning of the original question, "Is this truly the first
day?" Indeed, this festival is called "the first," and it has the right to be

called so, since on it the number of sins is raised up (and turned into merits). Then God pours out goodness and blessing on us, according to His blessed will (which is to bless us always), for more than the calf wishes to suck, the mother desires to suckle (Pesachim 112a).

Now, in this light, we can understand our opening verse. Surely, every Jew wants to dwell under the wings of the *Shekhinah* at all times. Further, as the poet taught, "all desire to fear God's name," but what prevents this? "The yeast in the dough" (cf. Berakhot 16b–17a). So, if God were to have compassion on the remnant of His people and remove the evil inclination (*yetzer hara*) from them, their desire at all times would be to fear God because He is master and ruler, the root-source of all worlds. Further, the Sages taught (Sukkah 52b):

> R. Hana bar Acha stated: It was said at the schoolhouse, "There are four things that the blessed Holy One regrets having created, and they are: Exile, the Chaldeans, the Ishmaelites, and the *yetzer hara*.

We then come before God with this claim: "How are we guilty for our betrayals and our offenses? Did You not bring this about? How have we transgressed and how have we sinned before You? Just remove the *yetzer hara* from us and we will surely serve you with fear and trembling at all times." When the Compassionate One hears the arguments of His children, God's compassion is aroused and God raises up our sins from us, and our mitzvot remain with us to argue on our behalf, so that God might pour out from that goodness stored up for us.

This is the sense of our verse: "**Who is a God like You, forgiving** [raising up] **iniquity**"—that is, Who is as great a God as *YHVH* the God of Israel, who conducts Himself according to his qualities always, with uprightness and goodness! That is, He raises up our sins from us to the heights so that our merits remain with us to argue on our behalf before God. That is the sense of "**He will take us back in love**" (lit., He will return to be compassionate toward us)—the *teshuvah* that we perform out of love brings it about that "**He will overcome our iniquities**," covering them over, casting our "**sins into the depths of the sea.**"

For Further Thought

This sermon would have been delivered on Shabbat Shuvah, between Rosh Hashanah and Yom Kippur. It has two elements: the quality of Sukkot, following Yom Kippur, energizes God's compassion and leads to forgiveness; we can bring our true desire to serve God, despite our failures and our sins, to move God to forgiveness. An aspect of the latter is a theme that we've met: our failures are really God's fault, since God made us who we are and is (in the end) responsible for the *yetzer hara* and its activities. Together these elements explain why God raises up and removes our sins from us, allowing our merit to prevail, and how God covers over our sins, again allowing our merits to rise up before Him.

The dramatic shift is from the quality of Yom Kippur—"*teshuvah* from fear"—to that of Sukkot—"*teshuvah* from love." The latter, in the eyes of the Rabbis, can transform intentional sins into meritorious acts. Or perhaps it is not the acts that are meritorious, but when we transform them into the energy that leads to *teshuvah*, those acts now gain a degree of merit. This is a higher form of *teshuvah*, one toward which Levi Yitzhak would have us strive. And from that stance we can approach God quite differently, engaging with God in a more loving relationship, more confident of forgiveness.

 ## Questions for Reflection

1. Levi Yitzhak spends a great deal of time describing the process of inner awareness, of spiritual alertness, that leads to *teshuvah* at this time of year. What do you think might have moved him to such full-throated preaching? Is he carried away with his own experience? Describing what he sees among his followers? Exhorting those whose hearts are still closed and unable to respond to the truth of the moment with open hearts and the desire to change? How do you hear this sermon?

2. Do you recognize the difference between "*teshuvah* from fear" and "*teshuvah* from love"? On which one does Levi Yitzhak lavish his attention? Why? Which do you prefer? Which is your characteristic mode of response as you move toward and through the High Holy Days?

3. Levi Yitzhak starts his sermon with the passage from Micah, the conclusion of the haftarah for Shabbat Shuvah, and *parashat Ha'azinu* is generally read on that Shabbat. Yet, the thrust of the sermon is toward Sukkot, and not so much Yom Kippur. What does this suggest to you about how Levi Yitzhak values "*teshuvah* from fear" relative to "*teshuvah* from

love"? Where does he want us to be pointing our attention? How might we experience Yom Kippur if we were to enter into it seeking to do "*teshuvah* from love"?

 ## Taking It into Your Life

Consider the two versions of "raising" the sins in this selection. In one, we have the familiar image of the scales, weighing out our merits and demerits. God lifts the pan of the sins to bring us greater merit, brushes off our sins from the pan so that our merits prevail. In the other, the lifting of the sins comes about as God transforms the quality of our sins such that intentional sins are made into positive acts to our merit. The first is certainly more familiar, and it grounds our *teshuvah* in our behavior. What we do, even the least motion toward righteousness, can tip the scales in our favor and in favor of the world. The second demands a more inner experience: *teshuvah* from love. The joy and devotion that we bring to preparing for Sukkot (and giving *tzedakah* to help others celebrate the festival) make the felt sense of love more possible.

In this we see two aspects of practice: effort and acceptance. In the first—dependent on our efforts—we might work on our capacity for love, generosity, and joy. And because we cannot guarantee outcomes, because the effect of our love and generosity may not bring about the ends we desire, we have to step back, allowing God to raise our deeds to wholeness and fulfillment.

There are three steps to the first:

1. Condition your heart to love. In a time of ease and attentiveness, bring your awareness to your spontaneous capacity to love. Feel it in your heart, your body. Know that it is present, that it is your natural desire. Over time, bring to mind the faces of people toward whom you feel that love. Extend to them that love, wishing them well, desiring only the best for them. Do this as well with the image of people you recognize but do not know—toward whom your feelings are more neutral. Extend love to them, as well. Know that you desire only the best for them. Then bring to mind the image of people with whom you have a difficult relationship. You do not have to love them now. But hold them in your mind's eye in that field of love in your heart. Realize that despite your conflict with or distaste for this person, you truly do not wish them ill, rather only the best.

2. Notice, when wishing others well, when you sense a reservation in the heart, the worry that perhaps you are giving too much away. Perhaps you are worried that your love will not be reciprocated. Perhaps you fear you will not be able to sustain this love. Relax—it is not your love. Just like the money in your pocket, it is on trust from God, the infinite source of love, waiting to be distributed. And besides, wishing others well, holding them with love, does not cost you. It only makes your heart larger, your capacity to care for others greater.

3. In holding others in your inner field of love, perhaps you then notice an opening, a sense of expansiveness. That is your heart opening larger, the expansion of your capacity to do for others. It feels good; in fact, it is a delight. Nurture that feeling—it is joy.

There is nothing more to do except, of course, act from your love and joy. Who knows what the right response is in any situation? Who knows what amount of *tzedakah*, how much time, will make a difference? The most important aspect of this practice is to nurture the love, generosity, and joy in your heart so that you can more freely act for the sake of others. In the end, our acts will be raised, and the world will be made whole.

Vezot Haberakhah

"Happy are you, O Israel! Who is like you, a
people delivered [by *YHVH*, your protecting
Shield, your Sword triumphant! Your
enemies shall come cringing before you, and
you shall tread on their backs]" (Deut. 33:29).

It is prohibited to be haughty. On the other hand, it is permissible for
pride to help you not to fear anything [other than God]; you can be
proud that you have a patron, your Heavenly Parent. This may be
what the Sages meant when they taught (Sotah 5a):

> R. Hiyya bar Ashi said in the name of Rab: A *talmid chakham*
> should possess an eighth part of an eighth of pride.

With this pride we are to defeat the power of the husks (*kelippot*).

That is the thrust of our verse. "**Happy are you, O Israel! Who
is like you, a people delivered [by *YHVH*, your protecting Shield,]**
your sword is your pride" (*va'asher cherev ga'avatekha*): that is, your
pride (*ga'avatekha*) knowing that God is **your protecting Shield** serves
as your sword, by which you dispatch the *kelippot*. Further: "**and you
shall tread on their backs**" (*bamoteimo*; lit., their high places)—that is,
by means of your inner pride (*ga'avah*) you will tread on those husks
known as *bamah* (i.e., high place), that is, haughtiness. You will destroy
them through their own haughtiness. They take pride in themselves,
and not in God.

FOR FURTHER THOUGHT

This is one of only two brief lessons on this parashah. Both can be
seen as "closing words" for a year of Torah study, capping the Holy
Day season of Tishrei. As deeply and profoundly as we are to turn
in contrition to God for forgiveness, we also trust that God, in love,
will accept our repentance. We must apply ourselves to a full and
complete self-scrutiny and moral inventory and commit to making

the changes demanded in its light. But we must not let that exercise lead us to deny our true worthiness, our true capacity to live in light of the truth of each moment, to live as God would have us do.

The tension between true self-criticism and legitimate self-esteem is reflected in our lesson. Levi Yitzhak knows that pridefulness is a negative quality; haughtiness precludes us from standing in God's presence. Yet pride is also an inner awareness of self-worth by which we recognize God's desire that we stand in God's presence, God's wish that we always do so. Levi Yitzhak reminds us, as did the Baal Shem Tov, that too much self-criticism risks tipping us over the edge into passivity, the denial of our capacity for change. But we are endowed by God with that agency and are expected to act with it to overcome our negative traits, to be strong in living up to our true potential. And in so doing, in making the attempt, we overcome the husks that separate us from God, once again drawing near, to begin a year of devotion and love of God.

Questions for Reflection

1. How do you understand the role of "pride" (*ga'avah*) in preventing us from fearing anything other than God? How do you see the danger of even a little pride preventing us from fearing even God?

2. The passage from the Talmud that Levi Yitzhak cites allows a little bit of pride to a *talmid chakham*. Who do you think he would have included in that term? Who would you? What do you sense is the relationship between being connected with Torah study and the capacity to exercise pride in a legitimate manner?

3. How do you understand the dynamic by which we employ the prideful energy of the husks to their own destruction? Is the small pride that we feel derived from the dimension of the husks? How can we keep from being sucked in or seduced by the pridefulness of the husks?

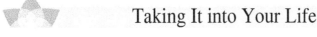

Taking It into Your Life

The reading of *Vezot Haberakhah* takes place on Simchat Torah, a day or two after we conclude our recitation of Psalm 27, which begins, "*YHVH* is my light and my help; whom should I fear? *YHVH* is the stronghold of my life, whom should I dread?" In our lesson, Levi Yitzhak teaches that having a small bit of pride will aid us in fearing nothing (but God). This psalm is suggestive of practices that we might take with us into the New Year. We will want to investigate the relationship between light, help, and stronghold and that small degree of pride.

As the sun wanes in the fall, we may sense a change in our inner balance. Lengthening darkness, for many people, may bring on a sense of lethargy, possibly depression. Yet even now, it is possible to take a moment to sit or stand with our face in the sun. Take some moments to do so each day (weather permitting). Notice what the sunlight feels like on your skin. Sense the light filtered through your eyelids. Register how even now, as the seasons change, there is still light. God continues to illumine the world and embrace you and all creation with radiance. In those moments in the sunlight, check your inner state. How do you feel? What is your sense of energy, of possibility, of ease or unease? How might this offering of light support your inner sense of balance, energy, and purpose?

As the season changes, temperatures tend to drop. We add layers of clothing to help us stay warm. We might say that we do so to "fight off the cold." In that light, we could look upon our garments in a negative way—something we have to do to keep from getting cold. Alternatively, we may see our coats and hats and gloves as our "stronghold," what we wear to contain and sustain our inner warmth. In that light, we would see our garments in a positive way—that which embrace us, energizing us even in the face of the cold. When you venture outdoors and you sense the cold of the air, stop for a moment and feel your own inner warmth. Sense how your clothing helps keep you warm. How do you feel knowing you will stay warm? What is your sense of energy, of possibility, of ease or unease? How might this moment of being held in strength support you in your inner sense of balance, energy and purpose?

Reflect.

Acknowledgments

This book would not exist were it not for my connection with—and employment by—the Institute for Jewish Spirituality. The Institute was created in 1998 to bring the rich, challenging, and inviting teachings of classical Hasidic spirituality and Jewish mysticism to the mainstream. More than a post-graduate program of study for rabbis and cantors, the Institute aimed to connect these teachings experientially, in the lives of the participants. Toward this end, the clergy (and educator, and later lay leader) program was based in four five-day retreats of spiritual practice: mindfulness meditation, prayer, Torah study, intentional conversation, and embodied practice (yoga) in a safe and supportive community. Moreover, between the four retreats the participants would continue to practice mindfulness meditation and sustain their study of Hasidic and other texts. Without having fully articulated it at that time, the Institute had the goal of nurturing mindful leaders in order to transform contemporary Jewish life.

There were two sets of founders of the Institute. Rabbi Rachel Cowan was the director of the Jewish Life and Values program at the Nathan Cummings Foundation. She had been tasked with "doing something" to facilitate bringing Hasidic teachings and mindfulness practice into the mainstream. It was the Cummings Foundation that provided the initial fundamental (and long sustained) funding to establish the Institute. Rachel turned to her classmate, Rabbi Nancy Flam, to whom she had provided funding to begin the Jewish Healing Center in the Bay Area, and with whom she worked to develop that project. Nancy was, once again, tasked with developing and directing this new program. Together, Rachel and Nancy talked with leading scholars and practitioners, and began to shape the program to come. They were the institutional founders.

Among the people involved in these early conversations, three went on to become the founding teachers in the program. One was Sylvia Boorstein, who was also my congregant and friend in California. Sylvia is a nationally recognized and beloved teacher of mindfulness and Buddhism. The mindfulness meditation that she would teach in the program was to ground the spiritual lessons in practice. Rabbi Jonathan Omer-Man has a well-deserved reputation as a teacher of Jewish mysticism and practice. The community he founded in Los Angeles, Metivta, was a gateway for young—and older—Jews who had gone looking for personally meaningful spiritual teachings and practice outside of Judaism to come back into the Jewish community. But rather than forcing them to give up what they had learned and the practices that they knew supported their spirits, Jonathan was able to help them connect their experiences to Jewish teachings and practices, and he brought this expertise to the Institute. Dr. Arthur Green is one of the leading scholars of Jewish mysticism of our generation. His interests, though, extend beyond the academy to the lived experience of the texts he teaches. He was one of the founding members of Havurat Shalom in Somerville, Massachusetts, in the early 1960s. He has served as a professor at the University of Pennsylvania and Brandeis University, and as president of the Reconstructionist Rabbinical College, and the rector at the Rabbinical School at the Hebrew College in Boston. Art's influence as master teacher and practitioner was central to the development of the Institute.

I was in the first rabbinic cohort of the Institute, from 2000–2001. I had already completed a program in Jewish mindfulness meditation with Sylvia, but had a very limited sense of the scope and significance of Jewish mysticism in general and Hasidism in particular. Yet I had an inkling that there was a connection to mindfulness practice. It was only when I studied Hasidic texts in a more systematic way with Art, while also spending significant parts of the day in meditation and contemplative silence, that these connections became more evident to me. My experience was that there was a direct confluence between the two, as if the Hasidic teachers were practicing mindfulness, their lessons couched in Jewish language and practice.

During the course of the program the need arose for translations of the texts we were studying. Most of them had never been translated, both because mainstream Western Judaism had disdained Hasidism as retrograde and unimportant and because the Hebrew in which they were written was uniquely Hasidic and difficult to follow. Yet I found that I had facility with the texts—they spoke directly to me. I, along with a few other folks, offered to provide some translations. I knew then that Hasidic text study was going to be a central interest of mine following the program, and so I made a point to deepen my connection with Art.

I recall one afternoon of the last retreat of the program. I had signed up for a meeting with Art. I had a question to ask him about a text I was studying, but I also wanted to speak with him about what was next for me. I knew that I would be leaving my congregation to resolve a long-term, bi-coastal relationship (more on this later). I was not planning to seek a new pulpit, but I thought I might try to create some sort of spirituality center where I could teach mindfulness meditation and Hasidic texts. I also had an idea for a major translation project that I wanted to talk about with Art. He listened appreciatively, but responded: "Your job is to figure out what you are meant to do. For the time being, sit with that. If this project is the right thing, it will happen—but the most important thing is for you to do what is meant for you." I didn't know what to make of his advice, but left the meeting with a new question: What do I have to offer in sharing and promoting the study of Hasidic texts and spirituality?

I moved from California in the summer of 2001 back to Westchester County where I'd grown up. There I finally had one home with my now wife, Barbara. Although I had truly enjoyed my congregational work, she encouraged me to take advantage of this geographical change to consider something new, something that would challenge and nurture me. Taking her advice opened the opportunity of working for the Institute, which has, indeed, been so rewarding. Barbara's support and faith in me over these years have been fundamental to getting me to this moment. I am forever grateful.

Not long after I arrived in New York, Nancy Flam asked if I would consider developing and directing a program for cantors similar to the one I had just completed. And so began my work with the Institute. Over the years my role has shifted and changed, grown and developed. Through this work I have maintained a connection with Art and the other teachers of the Institute. One of those people is Rabbi Sheila Peltz Weinberg. Sheila was also Sylvia's student, and became *the* mindfulness meditation teacher of the Institute in 2002. I have worked with her since then, and have learned a great deal from her. She has supported me and encouraged me along the way—including bringing this collection of translations and teachings to publication.

In 2002 the rabbinic alumni of the first cohort contacted Nancy to ask her to help them continue studying Hasidic texts. She knew that I'd done some translations during the first cohort, and even afterward. She asked if I would provide some study materials. That first year I studied *Kedushat Levi* and shared what I learned and what little I knew with my colleagues. My work was well received. The second cohort came to an end and they, too, wanted to continue their studies. I was asked to offer translations and commentary once again. I have continued doing so since then. These volumes are a product of that Institute program.

It should not be taken for granted that the Institute could have supported this project. While we have asked our participants to pay to receive the teachings, to support the Institute, the income has never matched the time I've expended on the preparation. I am grateful to Nancy Flam for having the faith in me to get this project going. I am indebted to Rachel Cowan who succeeded Nancy as executive director of the Institute for keeping that faith, and raising the money to support the project. And I am thankful to Rabbi Lisa Goldstein, our current executive director, for encouraging me to take the next step, to bring these volumes to publication.

I appreciate the vision of Stuart M. Matlins, publisher of Jewish Lights Publishing. He has come to see the importance of these texts in the broader Jewish conversation on spirituality and meaning. He took a big leap and published *Speaking Torah: Spiritual Teachings from around the Maggid's Table*, an anthology of Hasidic teachings translated with commentary by Art Green and his students Ebn Leader, Ariel Evan Mayse, and Or N. Rose. Having jumped with that project, he was prepared to take the next step with these volumes. Emily Wichland, vice president of Editorial and Production, and the rest of the staff at Jewish Lights have been a delight to work with: responsive, courteous, and supportive. I am thankful to my copyeditor, Debra Hirsch Corman, for helping me gain greater clarity in my writing and consistency in my voice.

I have written about Art's role in my entrance into and involvement with Hasidic texts. What I've said above is incomplete. Art's influence in the Institute runs deep. His reading of Hasidic spirituality informs everything that we do. His writings are regular touchstones in our programs. His vision for the future of the Jewish people has inspired us in our work. I have been struck, reading through these pages once again, how often an observation, reflection, spiritual insight, or theological musing jumped off the page as something I had learned from Art. I have learned it, however, in my own way. Outside of the Institute programs, I have been Art's student at a distance. I have read his works and struggled with them on my own. I have argued with him in my head, and then heard his voice as I came to agree with him in the end. I have recognized my own imperfect spiritual understandings reflected in his clearly articulated prose and deeply felt writings. I am Art's student, and I am grateful to have him as my teacher. I am honored that he has embraced my work, including me in the grand project that he has undertaken of reviving Hasidic spiritual teachings in a new form, with a new voice, for this century. (Of course, any flaws in translation or teaching in these volumes are solely mine!) I am grateful for his friendship, expressed in writing the foreword to this book.

Finally, I am grateful to have been kept alive, supported, and brought to this moment by the blessed Creator whose life force flows through all things, enlivening, inspiring all. All blessing, honor, and glory to the blessed Holy One, for this work is the product of God's own awareness coursing through all being, emerging in Levi Yitzhak and flowing through me. Praise God.

Suggestions for Further Reading

Boorstein, Sylvia. *It's Easier Than You Think: The Buddhist Way to Happiness*. New York: HarperCollins, 1995.

———. *That's Funny, You Don't Look Buddhist*. New York: Harper Collins, 1997.

Dresner, Samuel H. *The World of a Hasidic Master: Levi Yitzhak of Berdichev*. New York: Shapolsky Publishers, 1986.

Fine, Lawrence, and Eitan Fishbane and Or N. Rose. *Jewish Mysticism and the Spiritual Life: Classical Texts, Contemporary Reflections*. Woodstock, VT: Jewish Lights Publishing, 2011.

Green, Arthur. *Ehyeh: A Kabbalah for Tomorrow*. Woodstock, VT: Jewish Lights Publishing, 2004.

———. *Radical Judaism: Rethinking God and Tradition*. New Haven, CT: Yale University Press, 2010.

———. *Seek My Face: A Jewish Mystical Theology*. Woodstock, VT: Jewish Lights Publishing, 2003.

Green, Arthur, with Ariel Evan Mayse and Or N. Rose. *Speaking Torah: Spiritual Teachings from around the Maggid's Table*. Woodstock, VT: Jewish Lights Publishing, 2013.

Lew, Alan. *Be Still and Get Going: A Jewish Meditation Practice for Real Life*. New York: Little Brown, 2005.

Matt, Daniel C. *The Essential Kabbalah: The Heart of Jewish Mysticism*. New York: HarperOne, 2009.

Michaelson, Jay. *Everything Is God: The Radical Path of Nondual Judaism*. Boston: Trumpeter Books, 2009.

Roth, Jeff. *Jewish Meditation Practices for Everyday Life: Awakening Your Heart, Connecting with God*. Woodstock, VT: Jewish Lights Publishing, 2009.

Slater, Jonathan P. *Mindful Jewish Living: Compassionate Practice*. New York: Aviv Press, 2004.

Printed in the USA
CPSIA information can be obtained
at www.ICGtesting.com
JSHW022217140824
68134JS00018B/1115